Dane S. Claussen

Anti-Intellectualism in American Media

Magazines & Higher Education

PETER LANG
New York • Washington, D.C./Baltimore • Boston • Bern
Frankfurt am Main • Berlin • Brussels • Vienna • Oxford

Library of Congress Cataloging-in-Publication Data

Claussen, Dane S.
Anti-intellectualism in American media: magazines & higher education /
Dane S. Claussen.
p. cm. — (Higher ed; v. 11)
Includes bibliographical references and index.
1. Mass media and culture—United States. 2. Education, Higher—United States.
3. United States—Intellectual life—20th century. I. Title. II. Series.
P94.65.U6C58 302.23'0973—dc21 2001050656
ISBN 0-8204-5721-3
ISSN 1523-9551

Die Deutsche Bibliothek-CIP-Einheitsaufnahme

Claussen, Dane S.:
Anti-intellectualism in American media: magazines & higher education /
Dane S. Claussen.
–New York; Washington, D.C./Baltimore; Boston; Bern;
Frankfurt am Main; Berlin; Brussels; Vienna; Oxford: Lang.
(Higher ed; Vol. 11)
ISBN 0-8204-5721-3

Cover design by Lisa Barfield

© 2004 Peter Lang Publishing, Inc., New York

Printed in the United States of America

To Elizabeth P. "Elli" Lester Roushanzamir,
of course

Table of Contents

Acknowledgments

For their help in researching this book, I thank Dr. Elizabeth P. "Elli" Lester Roushanzamir, Associate Professor of Advertising and Public Relations; Dr. Anandam P. "Andy" Kavoori, Associate Professor of Telecommunications; Dr. Karen S. Miller Russell, Associate Professor of Advertising and Public Relations; and Dr. Leonard N. Reid, Associate Dean for Graduate Studies and Research and Professor of Advertising and Public Relations; all in the Henry W. Grady College of Journalism and Mass Communication; and Dr. Ronald M. Cervero, Professor of Leadership and Lifelong Learning, College of Education, all at The University of Georgia.

For their various types of help as I rewrote and edited the manuscript of this book, clearly the most credit goes to Elizabeth A.R. Boleman-Herring, who—as always—was a superb line editor. She also was infinitely supportive of, and enthusiastic about, this research from the very beginning, as well as all of my other research and publishing projects. Thank you, "Literate Chigger."

I believe that all direct quotations in the book fall within the parameters of the "fair use" provisions of U.S. copyright law, but I also should thank Steve Zuckerman at AOL Time Warner for giving me permission to quote material from *Time* and *Life* magazines. All quoted material from those magazines were copyrighted, by Time Inc., as of the date of publication cited.

Thanks also must go to my former graduate assistant, Corrine Rushkowski, and my former work-study student, Katie Krause, both at Point Park College, and Dr. Peggy M. Kreshel, Associate Professor of Advertising and Public Relations, Henry W. Grady College of Journalism and Mass Communication, The University of Georgia, for their special assistance.

Other individuals who should be recognized and thanked include Dr. Glen T. Cameron, now The Maxine Wilson Gregory Chair in Journalism Research at the University of Missouri School of Journalism, who was enthusiastic about this project from the beginning; my parents, Jerry and Earlene Claussen, as always; my fellow doctoral students in the Henry W. Grady College, particularly Carolina Acosta-Alzuru and Lisa Lyon; my faculty colleagues at Point Park College; my students at Point Park College and The University of Georgia; and my friends who have been neglected during the hours, days, and months that I researched, wrote, and edited this book.

Introduction

To begin providing the necessary historical and theoretical context for this textual analysis of popular magazine coverage of higher education, an overview of the history of U.S. higher education is helpful. This approach contextualizes the questions to be asked such as whether popular magazines have overemphasized or underemphasized news of particular aspects of higher education, whether the amount of coverage was consistent with the growth of higher education, and so on. Likewise, although this book adopts Richard Hofstadter's definition of U.S. anti-intellectualism and Daniel Rigney's theory of U.S. anti-intellectualism —each of which is detailed in the first chapter and elsewhere—Hofstadter and Rigney's work cannot be considered in a vacuum. It is helpful, of course, to understand what scholars other than Hofstadter and Rigney have written about anti-intellectualism in American higher education and about intellectuals, although this book is not about intellectuals. This is because American anti-intellectual attitudes, practices, and even policies are rarely targeted only at intellectuals, who—unless one defines that term to include all well-educated persons—make up a small percentage of any population group. Rather, American anti-intellectual-ism often biases many types of interactions with a large, diverse group of people.

History of U.S. Higher Education Since the G.I. Bill

Colleges and universities play a major role in the economy, science and technology, politics, culture (including sports), and much else in the United States, in addition to their purely educational function. College athletic events are widely covered in news media. More than 50 percent of high school graduates are starting college and more than half of them finish, up from 4 percent and 2 percent, respectively, in 1900. The more than 3,000 colleges and universities are located in every corner of the nation. University presidents and professors are regularly appointed to government posts, and the news media cite results of academic studies as authoritative sources in fields from economics to medicine. Ironically, though, higher education's role grows only precisely because it becomes increasingly anti-intellectual in a country that, according to Hofstadter, has been anti-intellectual since the early nineteenth century. American universities tend to be known by the public for their football teams and perhaps their biochemists, but much more rarely for their libraries or philosophy professors.

Anti-intellectualism therefore is the usually unstated background to such perennial questions in the United States as, "What is higher educa-tion supposed to accomplish?" or "Why is going to college worth the time and money?" or "What should an average college graduate be like?"[1] The relationship between higher education and the mass media, and various cultural and critical theories of higher education, intellectuals and/or anti-intellectualism, are explicated in chapter three. This brief history highlights some of the key issues relevant to this book.

1940s: Ex-GIs Flood Higher Education

When the U.S. Congress passed what would be commonly known as the G.I. Bill (short for G.I. Bill of Rights) in 1944, it wasn't an expression of pure gratitude to returning servicemen.[2] Although largely forgotten now, the bill's primary rationale was that the more men who went to college, the fewer who would swamp the job market with deleterious economic effects. Support for the program was not unanimous. The University of Chicago's Robert Maynard Hutchins, a towering figure in U.S. higher education then chairing the press freedom task force known as the Hutchins Commission, complained that colleges would inevitably increase their vocational and professional training at the expense of traditional curricula. He also predicted that veterans would perform more poorly in college than students right out of high school. Hutchins, however, received little support for his views.[3]

The veterans were better prepared than the universities. State support dollars per college student had been decreasing since the early 1930s.[4] In 1946, college enrollment doubled, but contrary to Hutchins's fears, veterans performed better in class than non-veterans. Hutchins had been correct that the doubling enrollment would have major effects, however. The barrier between family life and college life was broken, as many more students were married (some with children), and this in turn led to the invention of "married student housing." Because of their students' schedules, shortages of teachers and/or classroom space, institutions became more flexible about when classes were offered, how many courses students were required to enroll in, and so on. Graduate students were increasingly pressed into teaching as class sizes continued to increase. (One of the more surprising results of dramatic increases in college attendance was that the percentage of women graduate students actually declined; in 1946, 19.1 percent of doctorates were awarded to women, but by 1970, the percentage had declined to 13.3 percent.[5])

The country experienced a wave of "too many" college graduates. By the late 1940s, the situation was even more complex: having a college degree was increasingly necessary for obtaining certain jobs, but the number of college graduates still outpaced the number of jobs requiring a college degree. Even though college degrees were increasingly required by employers, they held less status with the general public.[6]

In 1947 and 1948, the first of two major postwar presidential commissions on higher education was charged with answering the question, among others, of "[h]ow can higher education make society more democratic?" The question's real intent had less to do with public policy or participation in government, and more with how higher education could help enlarge the middle class. One commission—understanding that colleges were no longer to be "merely the instrument for producing an intellectual elite"—obliged.[7] Complaining that the talent of U.S. young people was being "wasted" because only 45.5 percent graduated from high school and only 16 percent started college, the commission optimistically concluded that 49 percent of the U.S. population was intellectually equipped to earn a two-year college degree and that 32 percent was competent enough to earn a four-year degree (more than fifty years later, the promise of these percentages still has not been realized, although the United States is finally approaching the latter figure only). *Commonweal* magazine asked in response if a college education was changing from an intellectual experience to a social one, but *Life* magazine went a step further than even the commission, supporting the idea of a college education as a right for all Americans. Harvard College Professor Barrett Wendell, responding to *Life*, acidly suggested that all U.S. citizens be given a college degree at birth so that only those who actually wanted to learn would take up space on campuses.

In 1949, a *Fortune* magazine survey demonstrated that parents' interest in, and support of, their children going to college was high, but at the same time, public knowledge of and opinions of higher education were confused. Specifically, 83 percent of respondents said they would send a son to college and 69 percent said they would send a daughter to college. Preparation for a better job and greater earning power was cited by a majority as the most important reason for attending college. College students were most often described by poll respondents (in rank order) as "intelligent," "ambitious," "well-informed," "well-mannered," "hardworking," "democratic," and "time-wasting." Respondents of the unscientific poll least often checked (in rank order) "snobbish," "radical," "conservative," "soft," "hard-drinking," "immoral," and "overworked."

1950s: Higher Education a Right?

Higher education, as in every decade this century, experienced tremendous successes and crises in the 1950s, but perhaps nothing was as traumatic as the McCarthy era's loyalty investigations. A wedge was driven for years between "free thought" scholars, such as Hutchins, Henry Steele Commager, and others, who believed that professors should be free to be communists, and mediating scholars who were both anti-communist and anti-McCarthy, such as Arthur Schlesinger, Norman Thomas, Sidney Hook, Roger Baldwin, and others. Still, Americans were supportive of higher education; in 1952, a national survey of college graduates showed that 98 percent would go to college again if they were to relive their lives, and 84 percent said they would attend the same college. Only about one-quarter said they would choose a different major, although 56 percent said they would complete a curriculum that was either more specific or more general than the one they had taken. Finally, 70 percent of graduates said that college had helped them in their current occupations; during the 1950s, students had begun realizing that being a "grind" in college was a better bet to get ahead in life than being a traditional "college man."[8]

The balance of enrollment between public and private institutions started shifting dramatically after World War II (public universities enrolled a majority of students for the first time in the mid-1950s, and three-quarters by the 1970s), and the public was ambivalent about what this trend meant. The majority believed that private institutions were better than public ones, but many respondents were unable to explain how or why they thought so.[9]

Because of desegregation, McCarthyism, the increase in parents with degrees, the expanding economy, and other reasons, the federal government continued to focus on higher education. In 1956, President Eisenhower formed the Committee for Education Beyond High School to examine two-year and four-year colleges and their alternatives. Federal tuition assistance received a major boost in 1958 with the Soviet Sputnik-inspired National Defense Education Act, which provided increased loans and grants to college students. The Higher Education Act of 1965, and the Higher Education Amendments of 1972 provided additional increases. Federal funding for research boomed after Sputnik, growing to $356 million in 1959 from only $169 million in 1955. (By 1968, federal funding of university research would be $2 billion.) State government support of higher education also zoomed up, an increase of more than 1,000 percent from 1950 to 1970.

As noted, the percentage of graduate degrees obtained by women actually decreased as the number of men in college skyrocketed. Societal norms largely encouraged the notion that women who went to college were not expected to launch careers, but to meet a highly educated young man to marry. This attitude finally changed in the late 1950s, almost solely due to Sputnik.[10]

In the meantime, in 1954, *Newsweek* reported that the GI Bill encouraged a "growing and debatable" conviction that "everyone—regardless of ability—ought *somehow* go to college" (emphasis added), at the same time that all of the World War II GIs had finished college, and campuses were becoming reoriented to young, single students.

1960s: From "Socializing an Army of Young People" to Demonstrations

Higher education in the 1960s is best known for curriculum reform, a one-third increase in the number of colleges and universities, a dramatic increase in the number of graduate students, and another doubling of total enrollment from 3.6 million in 1960 to 7.9 million in 1970 (much of it attributed to Congress's dramatic expansion of financial aid[11]), and student and faculty activism. One result was a sort of "trickle down" effect in enrollment as selective institutions that could have grown simply became more selective, while schools that lacked the resources necessary for judicious growth did so anyway.[12] Of course the 1960s also are remembered for the youth culture, anti-war protests, and the beginning of the end for the "*in loco parentis*" doctrine.[13] These latter trends started primarily in the mid-1960s and continued for the remainder of the decade and into the following one.

The early 1960s are most noted for "teenage anxiety over college admission"[14] and the release of University of California President Clark Kerr's controversial book, *The Uses of the University*. Wary of an academic-industrial complex in the same way that President Dwight Eisenhower had warned against a "military-industrial complex," Kerr pointed out that government and business had both come to rely on a "knowledge industry" of professors who worked as consultants, contract researchers, and so on. However, author David D. Henry claimed that this broader role of scholars in society was generally welcomed; in other words, the academy's relative isolation was no longer considered a virtue.[15]

Kerr also complained that, for all of the reforms that already had been made in higher education, undergraduate students had not benefited. Rather than being engaged as budding intellectuals, he complained, undergraduate students saw themselves as an oppressed class, perhaps as the *lumpenproletariat*. After all, in the 1960s, "[t]he university was still expected by society to provide a site for socializing an army of young people, most of whom were more familiar with the television screen than with the printed page and had been raised in utmost security by permissive parents."[16] Krista E. White has pointed out that even in the mid-1960s, when college enrollment was skyrocketing and women were finally being widely urged to attend college, old norms had not disappeared.[17] Her evidence for this is a 1965 article in *U.S. News & World Report* entitled "If Your Daughter Wants to go to College..." Written by an Eastern public university's president, the article suggests that admitting too many women to college would "deny careers to men in many fields where they are needed."

The public was interested in the education of its own children, but not knowledgeable about, or interested in, public policy questions about higher education. Training for a good job was named the top reason for sending boys (72 percent agreed) and girls (56 percent agreed) to college. Fewer than half of respondents pinpointed any negative aspects of going to college, and among those who did, they feared that college might create snobs, make kids think they were getting something for nothing, cause young people to adopt radical ideas, or break down their standards of morality.[18]

Scannell, in his 1966 study of city leaders' and "typical citizens'" knowledge and attitudes about higher education and media consumption habits, found that at least 90 percent of all respondents said a boy, and at least 85 percent said a girl, should attend some college rather than go to work immediately after high school. When asked why a boy should do this, 31.3 percent (citizens) to 62.5 percent (leaders) of respondents said he would still obtain "financial, career" benefits, 1.5 percent (citizens) to 9.8 percent (leaders) said some college would make the boy more mature, and 10 percent (leaders) to 20.2 percent (citizens) expressed confidence that the typical boy would be motivated to discover a way to finish his college degree while working. Percentages for girls were only slightly lower. When asked a more general question of what a boy should obtain from attending college, at least 94.5 percent specified training for a good job, at least 95.3 percent said "increase his understanding of the world and himself," at least 92 percent said "learn to be sociable and get along with people," at least 81.8 percent said "develop his interest in good books, music and art," at least 58.2 percent said "chance to meet a better class of friends," and at least 45 percent said "chance to take part in sports and athletics." Again, percentages for girls were similar, except much lower for "sports and athletics."[19]

By the mid- to late 1960s, of course, three of the four fears expressed in the 1964 surveys did come to fruition for many parents, as some students believed themselves to be revolutionaries and anything but snobs. However, higher-education historian Helen Lefkowitz Horowitz reported that only 28 percent of students in college in 1969 had ever taken part in any kind of demonstration. The major student protests occurred at only a small percentage of campuses, and almost never at small, Southern or religiously affiliated colleges.[20]

Education historian Diane Ravitch added that, "In order for radicalization to occur, students had to be convinced that change within the existing system was impossible." Student protests were not limited to campus policies; Ravitch complained, "Mainstream culture valued hard work, deferred gratification, achievement, and material possessions, the counterculture celebrated sensual experience, immediate gratification, and unrestrained naturalism." Appeasement simply brought bigger demands and 68 percent of the public believed campus demonstrations to be unjustified.[21]

The combination of more research funds, more Ph.D. programs, more new Ph.D.s and other factors in the 1960s resulted in higher requirements for professors, and the increasingly common charge that they were out of touch with the "real world." Independent and government commissions studying higher education also criticized curricula for being "too academic" and graduate education for overemphasizing research. At the same time, research was also being accused of being too closely associated with government policies and practical problem solving.[22]

Politicians, many educators, and other putative leaders in U.S. society were convinced by Sputnik that U.S. higher education needed to improve, but public opinion researchers and others were beginning to find that the general public, particularly in rural areas, was still parochial about higher education.[23] However, even the clearly anti-intellectual alumni agreed with non-alumni that of eight goals listed on a survey, the institution's top goal should be "to teach the skills of various occupations and professions so that students can step into active and productive jobs when they leave the campus"—the most anti-intellectual choice of the eight.

Scannell reviewed then-recent studies on public knowledge of, and attitudes about, higher education and found repeatedly that public knowledge about higher education was minimal. Interestingly, while most citizens were mostly supportive of higher education, consistently only about 5 percent were "active supporters," and 15 percent were in the "disaffected group. Most of these latter respondents had some college education, but this group tended to embody the most critical and negative attitudes toward higher education."[24]

1970s: Subdued Classes and Hedonistic Socializing

Campus protests in the United States collapsed almost overnight between the end of the 1969–1970 academic year and the beginning of the 1970–1971 academic year. But colleges did not revert to pre–mid-1960s environments. Horowitz pointed out that "hedonism continued unabated." The ranks of both "rebel" college students and traditional "college men" declined dramatically in the 1970s due to career concerns (Yale President Kingman Brewster referred to the decade as exemplifying "grim professionalism"), apparently in part because 1970s college students were the first cohort whose parents were themselves college educated and pressuring students to choose career-oriented majors and finish college quickly.[25]

One of the major books about higher education in the 1970s was 1973's *Does College Matter?* (subtitled *Some Evidence on the Impacts of Higher Education*), as if there were some doubt among either those who were answering the question (a long list of contributors to the book, edited by Lewis C. Solmon and Paul J. Taubman) or those who might be asking it (parents? students? employers? politicians?). The answer, naturally, was that college does, or at least did, matter, based on studies during the late 1950s to early 1970s.

Relief over no-nonsense students was short-lived, as the emphasis on careers meant obtaining good grades and letters of recommendation: "Afraid of alienating their professors, fewer students raised basic questions in class." Administrators and professors reported increases in cheating and campus crime, a decrease in students' civility, and a new "consumer mentality" among students who increasingly complained about fees, library hours, foreign teaching assistants who did not speak

English well, and so on. Even dating among students diminished, re-placed by informal group parties and movie attendance. In the late 1970s, student culture became more like the early 1960s, but some characteris-tics had changed permanently. The Greek system was still losing popu-larity, and extracurricular activities had become career- or at least goal-oriented.[26] The political pendulum also started swinging back toward the right, both on campus and off. In 1978, the U.S. Supreme Court ruled in *Bakke*, known to the general public as the "reverse discrimination" case, that admissions quotas for minorities were unconstitutional. On campus, College Republicans were more popular and, for the first time, conserva-tive students launched numerous "alternative" student newspapers.

1980s: Reaganite Themes Pervade Higher Education

By 1980, higher education had dramatically changed in ten years. An extensive nationwide network of community colleges was operating, 60 percent of all high school graduates were starting college (this has since increased to about 75 percent), and 38 percent of all college students were twenty-five years old or older. If by democratizing education, its proponents meant increasing the percentages of Americans (particularly older Americans) attending college, then certainly this process was under way. The numbers of students meant that historically elite colleges could continue to be selective, but many made concessions to achieve a "well-rounded" student body.

As states faced sometimes shrinking revenues and more programs mandated by Congress or courts, state legislatures looked hard at how much they allocated to higher education. Budget increases leveled off, and colleges increased tuitions by an average annual rate of 7.8 percent throughout the 1980s. Legislatures had noticed that between 1975 and 1985, public institutions' total expenditures increased 141 percent unad-justed for inflation—15.4 percent after adjusting for actual inflation.[27]

By the late 1980s, the concept *in loco parentis* had been abandoned; perhaps this was because, as Horowitz wrote, students' primary goal be-came quickly achieving their parents' lifestyle. Overwhelmingly materi-alistic, late 1980s students no longer experienced "group pleasures of college life," "individualist expressions of rebellion," or "sparks of in-tellectual life," she lamented.[28]

Herant A. Katchadourian and John Boli, in their *Careerism and Intellectualism among College Students* (1985),[29] divided 1980s students into careerists, intellectuals, strivers (who were both intellectual and career-oriented) and the unconnected (who were neither intellectually nor career-oriented). Study results, by gender, ethnic group and socioeconomic status, showed in part:

	% Careerists	% Intellectual	% Strivers	% Unconnected
Men	29.0	15.3	25.2	30.5
Women	16.2	34.3	25.7	23.8
Blacks/Chic.	24.1	13.8	34.5	27.6
Asian-Am.	21.4	14.3	35.7	28.6
Whites	23.7	26.9	22.0	27.4
Lower SES	28.8	13.7	27.4	30.1
Middle SES	28.1	26.3	22.8	22.8
Upper SES	20.0	36.4	18.2	25.5

It is interesting to note that contrary to historical stereotypes of men being more intellectual than women, this book suggests otherwise. Also note that minority students tended to be more polarized into being strivers or unconnected, while white students were more evenly distributed among the four groups (with white women accounting for most of the even distribution). White male students were distributed fairly similarly to male students generally. Katchadourian and Boli's typology of college students is discussed further in chapter 3.

1990s: Conservatives Mount the Offensive

By the 1990s, the number of Americans in institutions of higher learning continued to increase slowly—helped by part-time, evening, weekend, on-line, and other accommodating course schedules. Attending college was seen as a given by most middle-class children, who—in some families—by the late 1990s were often the third or fourth generation to attend college. Funding for universities seemed less controversial in the state legislatures, with the notable exceptions of New York and California. In the 1990s, the number of women, minority, physically disabled, non-traditional age, part-time, and gay/lesbian-identified college students continued to increase, and colleges had made adjustments in facilities, curricula, schedules, and other aspects of their operations to accommodate them. Many students insisted that they were not as materialistic or career-driven as students in the 1980s.

In the 1990s, many colleges and universities began serious efforts to develop specialties and related reputations for certain departments or degrees, and to drop or merge other departments and degrees. Most of this restructuring did not attract media and public attention, and generally college curricula were not an issue to the typical American. However, pressures from conservatives for a greater voice in forming the agenda of higher education was fomenting. Starting with Allan Bloom's book, *The Closing of the American Mind: How Higher Education Has Failed Democracy and Impoverished the Souls of Today's Students,* higher education was hit with a barrage of indictments bearing such names as: *ProfScam: Professors and the Demise of Higher Education,* by Charles J. Sykes (1988); *Tenured Radicals: How Politics Has Corrupted Our Higher Education,* by Roger Kimball (1990); *Illiberal Education: The Politics of Race and Sex on Campus,* by Dinesh D'Souza (1991); and *Imposters in the Temple: American Intellectuals Are Destroying Our Universities and Cheating Our Students of Their Future,* by Martin Anderson (1992).

Legislatures further cut appropriations to public institutions in the early 1990s, with a slight uptick finally in 1995; late 1990s observers predicted that future appropriations generally would not exceed the inflation rate—and that was before the nationwide state budget crises of 2002 and 2003. While education supporters claim increased expenses were needed primarily to support student services and comply with increased government regulation, critics claimed increased funds were being spent on ways to increase an institution's prestige, administrative excess, and light teaching loads.[30] The U.S. Department of Education attributed much of the costs to a 123 percent increase in "administrators" over fifteen years, which included computer analysts, public relations and marketing personnel, fundraisers, financial aid specialists, counselors, accountants, and coaches.

In the nearly sixty years since the G.I. Bill was passed by Congress, the number of colleges and the number (and percentage) of Americans attending college has jumped tremendously. About 28 percent of American adults hold a two- or four-year college degree, placing the United

States in the top three countries in the world in higher education achievement. Attending college has become virtually automatic for children from wealthy homes, and the overwhelming majority of children from middle-class homes also start college. At the same time, the number of students from ethnic and other groups that traditionally did not attend college has risen substantially overall, as has the number of "nontraditional" (older) students and part-time students. For students, however, college campuses also have become primarily a place to get a degree to get a job. The percentage of students working while attending college has climbed, and professors and administrators report less student involvement in traditional campus activities and organizations. In other words, for many students, the center of their lives has shifted off-campus.[31]

The percentage of professors with terminal degrees and those who are required to conduct and publish research for tenure has increased and, as intellectual historian Russell Jacoby argued,[32] it also would appear that a higher percentage of authentic U.S. intellectuals now teach on college campuses. Students, their parents, and other citizens should be pleased at educators' increased credentials. However, if students and their parents are interested only or primarily in "vocational" education for boosting students' career choices, this may be irrelevant to them. Moreover, conservative authors, politicians, and others are attacking what they perceive as entrenched liberal politics both in faculty offices and classrooms. In the early twenty-first century, state legislatures cut appropriations for, and raised tuitions at, public colleges and universities, precisely the opposite of what employers should have demanded to strengthen their domestic workforce, and therefore the U.S. position in the world economy. In many states, higher education outlays were cut primarily because of healthcare costs for the elderly and the rapid growth in the number of jails and prisons, which had been overwhelmingly driven by conservative legislatures passing mandatory minimum sentencing laws and facilitating dramatically increased arrests and convictions for often minor drug offenses. That many young men and women are being sent to prison rather than to college is only one indication that the future of U.S. higher education is conflicted and uncertain.

Chapter 1
"How Smart Is Too Smart?"

Both before and since George W. Bush was elected president in 2000, more than one columnist, commentator, and Web site asked some variation of what Roger Simon asked in the July 19, 1999, *U.S. News & World Report*: "How bright do you have to be to be president?" Christopher Hitchens observed in the October 9, 2000, *Nation* that the Republican Party "packages and presents a provincial ignoramus who can neither read nor write." Eventually, E. J. Dionne, in *The Washington Post* (March 13, 2001), told Bush's opponents, "Now is the time for a moratorium on calling the president of the United States stupid"—not because he thought Bush intelligent, but only because he didn't want the public to have low expectations. In fact, some pundits had gone so far as to ask the lowest common denominator question: Is George W. Bush too stupid to be president?

Bush's intelligence (or lack thereof) presents political scientists, campaign strategists, and journalists with numerous fascinating questions: Why would the Republican Party's biggest donors, most of whom supported George W. Bush from the beginning (at which point, a significant percentage of Americans did not know "W" from his father), support an ignorant presidential candidate? What percentage of the public has realized Bush is vapid, when did they realize it, and why did apparently at least some of them vote for him anyway? What percentage of the electorate is itself too dim to realize or understand how dull-witted Bush is? What percentage of the public is in denial, allowing cognitive dissonance to give themselves a more favorable assessment of their president than the evidence suggests is warranted? And so on.

After a terrorist attack on New York City on September 11, 2001, and the launching of a surprisingly easy "war against terrorism" in Afghanistan and elsewhere, the American public's esteem for Bush increased dramatically although Bush's limited vocabulary and the simplicity of his impromptu statements showed that the president had not changed. (Archconservative Alan Keyes, in an interview published in the January 27, 2002, *New York Times Magazine*, refused to answer a question about Bush's speaking skills.) During the country's months-long patriotic fervor, Chris Matthews, host of the "Hardball" television program, was almost alone among politicians, pundits, and prominent journalists in pointing out that Bush was still the same man he was before—more focused, generally more serious, and more emotional, but no more intelligent, educated, nor articulate than he had been previously. Writing in the January 20, 2002, *New York Times*, David E. Sanger pointed out that Bush's use of "black-and-white terms," serving him well in war, still wouldn't work very well during peace. Sanger noted, "Mr. Bush's phrases seemed simplistic" and his vocabulary simply "blunt." In the February, 2002, *Vanity Fair*, even Christopher Buckley's mostly favorable article noted that Bush "probably last consulted a thesaurus at Andover" (a college preparatory school); that Bush finally had more "gravitas" than before September 11, when he was a "frat boy who choked on his tongue talking about 'subliminable' advertising"; and that Bush displays "quaint, Manichaean simplicity." Just for good measure, Buckley reminded his readers, "during the presidential campaign, Bush could not name the leader of—among three other countries—Pakistan."[1]

By late 2002, two former Bush administration officials, one of whom was John J. DiIulio Jr, former head of the White House Office of Faith-Based and Community Initiatives, were confessing the truth about the Bush administration's anti-intellectualism. DiIulio told the

January, 2003, issue of *Esquire* magazine that he had essentially been the White House staff's only intellectual or policy wonk on domestic issues. DiIulio said he hadn't even witnessed "three meaningful, substantive policy discussions....There were, truth be told, only a couple of people in the West Wing who worried at all about policy substance and analysis....[T]he lack of even basic policy knowledge, and the only casual interest in knowing more, was somewhat breathtaking." The article's author, Ron Suskind, quoted another "senior White House official" still working there, as saying, "certainly in domestic policy, there has been almost no meaningful consideration of any real issues. It's just kids on Big Wheels who talk politics and know nothing. It's depressing. Domestic Policy Council meetings are a farce." Shortly thereafter, former Bush speechwriter David Frum's book, *The Right Man: The Surprise Presidency of George W. Bush*, admitted that with the exception of political director Karl Rove and Office of Management and Budget Director Mitch Daniels (who later quit to run for governor of Indiana), "conspicuous intelligence seemed actively unwelcome in the Bush White House."[2]

Thus, those with a broader view of history—such as historians, sociologists, political scientists, anthropologists, and others—can appropriately ask another group of questions centered around this one: How did presidential politics and nominees decay from Adlai Stevenson and John F. Kennedy, two intelligent men who—to greater and lesser extents, respectively—eagerly posed as intellectuals, to Jimmy Carter, who de-emphasized having been a nuclear engineer and instead emphasized his Plains, Georgia, roots, and Bill Clinton, a Rhodes Scholar who downplayed Georgetown, Yale, and Oxford in favor of Hope, Arkansas,[3] to George W. Bush, who has continually bragged about having been a "C" student and who attended Harvard Business School (in an experimental program for students whose undergraduate degrees were in the humanities) only when his application to his home-state University of Texas law school was rejected?

A direct relationship, in fact, exists between the public and media asking, in effect, if Adlai Stevenson was too smart to be president and less than fifty years later asking if George W. Bush was smart enough, or too dumb, to be president. The American public's long-time anti-intellectual attitude eventually was reflected in and by a presidential candidate, and then president, who was perhaps the least intellectual occupant of the White House in more than seventy-five years and perhaps the most anti-intellectual one in about 165 years.[4]

The American public's comfort with, if not demand for, the "common touch" is not limited to presidential politics, of course. Even in the competitive government civil service system, and the supposedly ruthless—Darwinistic—business world, executives and managers are not always seeking out the best and the brightest, even in a high-tech economy called the Information Age.

For instance, on June 6, 1997, newspapers around the United States published an Associated Press article about an applicant for a police officer's job in New London, Connecticut, who wasn't scheduled for an interview—because he scored *too high* on a standard intelligence exam. The *Athens* (Georgia) *Daily News* headlined the article, "How smart is too smart to be a police officer?"

The applicant, Robert Jordan, told reporters, "I know I would be a good cop, but I had the misfortune of selecting too many correct answers. What kind of a message does this send to children? Study hard, but not too hard?"

New London's Deputy Police Chief, William C. Gavitt, and the city's attorney, Ralph J. Monaco, told the mass media that police officer applicants who score too high on the intelligence exam could get bored with police work and quit after costing the city $25,000 each in police academy training. "We're looking for bright people, but we're not looking for people that [sic] are so bright to an extent that they're not going to be challenged by the job," Monaco said. (At least Bush is being challenged.)

A representative of Wonderlic Personnel Test Inc. of Liberty, Illinois, producer of the exam, confirmed that New London is not the only employer that screens out potential employees who are found to be "too smart," but wouldn't release names of others. (Wonderlic confirmed that the exam is administered to about 3 million people every year by government agencies and Fortune 500 companies.)

Despite (or, more probably, because) the easily documented ignorance of so many Americans (check the results of any standardized exam, or watch "Jaywalking" on The Tonight Show), news coverage of ignorance as ignorance (the case of George W. Bush) or tangible results of hostility toward, or skepticism or fear of, intelligence or intellectuals is rare. Conversely, while the mass media may sometimes portray intellectuals regarded as "theoretical" or "abstract" as overly idealistic, out-of-touch, and so on, others who are highly educated and often quite intelligent (physicians, engineers, lawyers, MBAs, and so on) are shown as valued for their skills—while their education and intelligence often go unremarked. More commonly, intellectuals are simply not covered at all. News media are not likely to hear about the very bright being discriminated against, not least because it may be difficult to prove, probably seems trivial compared with other forms of discrimination, and because victims of anti-intellectualism (often due to their own internalized anti-intellectualism) are not likely to publicize it. For the news media, where is the "news peg" for either ignorance or intelligence?

Surely part of this picture is Americans' common confusion of education with intelligence, professors and experts with intellectuals, an extensive education system with public support of and interest in real education, earning degrees without becoming educated, and so on. Although this point will be detailed at length in this book, one example will help introduce this predicament. *The Public Pulse* in January 1996 described 31 percent of Americans as people who "love learning" because they are interested in learning more about current events, investing, medicine and health, computers, economics, other countries and cultures, and history (in that order or priority). However, most of these interests relate to specific outcomes such as short-term financial and/or physical benefit. In other words, even this third of Americans interested in learning are not interested in the areas of traditional learning (humanities and sciences), such as philosophy, literature, politics, mathematics and the physical sciences, religion, or the applied and fine arts.

The concept of intellectuals/"intellectualism" has long resided uneasily in American culture. Historian Richard Hofstadter, in his *Anti-intellectualism in American Life* (1963), found U.S. culture to have been anti-intellectual since the early nineteenth century. He defined U.S. culture in terms of its relationship to anti-intellectualism, which is a:

> complex of historical relations among a variety of attitudes and ideas that have many points of convergence. The common strain that binds together the attitudes and ideas which I call anti-intellectual is a resentment and suspicion of the life of the mind and of those who are considered to represent it; and a disposition constantly to minimize the value of that life.

Hofstadter defined intellect as the "critical, creative, and contemplative side of mind," and intelligence as that which:

> seeks to grasp, manipulate, reorder, adjust, intellect examines, ponders, wonders, theorizes, criticizes, imagines....It is an excellence of mind that is employed within a fairly narrow, immediate, and predictable range; it is manipulative, adjustive, unfailingly practical quality—one of the most eminent and enduring of the animal virtues. Intelligence works with the framework of limited but clearly stated goals and may be quick to shear away from questions of thought that do not seem to help in reaching them. Finally, it is of such universal use that it can daily be seen at work and admired alike by simple or complex minds.[5]

This book employs Hofstadter's definition of U.S. anti-intellectualism as its working definition of that term and, similarly, knowledge sociologist Daniel Rigney's 1991 theory of U.S. anti-intellectualism is used as a basis for investigating how and why anti-intellectualism manifests itself in institutions, philosophies, laws and policies, practices, and processes.[6] Chapter 3 goes into great detail on various definitions of "intellectuals," but this book always assumes, at the least, that an American intellectual is someone who is intelligent and independent enough to be a critical, creative, and contemplative citizen, if not also such a worker. It is important to note, before this book goes any further, that it considers only Western definitions of anti-intellectualism and intellectuals primarily because the book is about American magazine coverage of American higher education, but also because anti-intellectualism is less obvious in many or perhaps most Eastern countries. Persons of color are represented by John McWhorter, an African American; Edward Said, a Palestinian immigrant; and others, in addition to white writers such as Leon Fink and Russell Jacoby who highlight the most recent group of new American public intellectuals, who are overwhelmingly African American.

Finally, this book may strike some readers as nearly omitting female voices, but—with the notable exceptions of Hannah Arendt, Heidi K. Goar, Helen Lefkowitz Horowitz, Aimee Howley, Myrna N. Klobuchar, and Betty Jo Hyde Welch—women scholars, unfortunately, have been generally absent from the research on American anti-intellectualism or theories of intellectuals.

Based on his analysis of Hofstadter's book and others' research, Rigney suggested that U.S. anti-intellectualism comes in three flavors:

1. "religious anti-rationalism," the view that emotion is warm

(i.e., good) and reason is cold (i.e., bad) and/or a belief in absolute systems of belief (primarily evangelical Protestantism);

2. "populist anti-elitism," public skepticism first toward the patrician class of "gentlemen politicians" and old money, later hostility to progressive politics and support of such figures as Joe McCarthy or George Wallace, and;

3. "unreflective instrumentalism," beliefs and behavior indicating that knowledge is worthless unless it immediately and directly leads to material gain, such as profits or higher wages.

Rigney did not overstate Hofstadter's case, but instead carefully analyzed Hofstadter's evidence. In fact, Rigney's theory is narrower than Hofstadter's evidence in one area: the role of gender. However, Rigney also pointed out Hofstadter's neglect of the mass media's role in U.S. anti-intellectualism, citing media commentators such as Edward S. Herman, Noam Chomsky, and Neil Postman,[8] and presenting media's role as a significant topic for research. Following Rigney, the research into magazine coverage conducted for this book hypothesized, even assumed, that signs of anti-intellectualism in U.S. culture are ubiquitous in terms of media content and other sites. Thus, this book, which investigates media content, is the first step toward a comprehensive study of the role of media in U.S. anti-intellectualism that would answer two general questions. First, are mass media a primary actor in creating and/or perpetuating anti-intellectualism? (Today, for instance, perhaps journalists should be asking themselves to what extent their profession is at fault for a man such as George W. Bush becoming a presidential nominee and then president.) Second, do the mass media have significant potential to resist pervasive American anti-intellectualism?

To begin investigating these questions, this book examines articles about higher education published in several mainstream, enormously popular magazines starting in 1944, the year of the "G.I. Bill" — which provided education benefits to veterans and doubled, almost overnight, the number of U.S. college students. In analyzing such coverage, the basic question was how articles, headlines, photographs, photograph "cutlines" (captions), and other elements of such articles covered or otherwise portrayed higher education, with a special eye to intellectuals and would-be intellectuals (faculty, students, and others), professors, students, and the characteristics and manifestations of anti-intellectualism identified by Hofstadter and Rigney (see appendix).

General interest, mass circulation magazine coverage of higher education since the G.I. Bill in 1944 provides an entry point for investigating popular print media's contribution to the ongoing formation of anti-intellectualism in the United States. Informed by aspects of British and American cultural studies, European critical theory, and the social and intellectual history of the United States, this book crafts a theoretical approach and supports an argument that U.S. mass media play a specific and decisive role in (and do not simply report on) the shaping of societal views toward intellectuals, "intellectualism," anti-intellectualism and other aspects of U.S. intellectual life. This book also illustrates, through the popular magazine content, the plight of U.S. intellectuals, the recent history of U.S. higher education, and the crisis (particularly acute for the mass media as part of diversified, publicly held corporations) between the intellectual possibilities and responsibilities in a democracy (media as the Fourth Estate) and the anti-intellectual demands of an advanced free market economy—tensions that Daniel Bell (1976; 1996) called the "cultural contradictions of capitalism." In other words, profit-driven media seeking large audiences naturally tend toward lowest common denominator content and audiences, which would be nonintellectual anywhere and likely anti-intellectual in a broadly anti-intellectual culture.

Little empirical research investigates the ways in which mass communication, intellectuals, higher education, and popular culture intersect in practice in the United States (see chapter 2). Specifically, relatively little research has been conducted on media coverage of higher education (examples are found in chapter 3), or on the impact of higher education on the quality, effectiveness, and profitability of media industries. Critical theory has not engendered a realistic, concrete agenda through which U.S. journalism might advance democracy, or free U.S. culture from the constraints of late capitalism. (One attempt at proactive democratic news media, civic/public journalism, stems from Dewey's pragmatism.) Likewise, journalism/mass communication is rarely mentioned in histories of higher education, and only recently has research into the history of mass communication education been conducted.[9] In fact, mass communication researchers have paid little attention to higher education beyond the specifics of pedagogical practices.

The relative paucity of scholarly research on the intersections of mass media, intellectuals, anti-intellectualism. and/or higher education is due partially to specific historic trends and partially to the development of journalistic routines. Media have covered higher education in the United States from the earliest days of both higher education (usually tied to Harvard College's founding in 1636), and mass media themselves (which reached a critical mass in the mid-nineteenth century), but the term "intellectual(ism)" has had a rocky history in Western cultures, and an even more dubious one in the United States. Moreover, mass media typically cover events, trends, issues, locations, and organizations that are recognized by government agencies, economic actors, religious organizations, scholars or educational institutions, social movements, or other journalists. This has meant heavy coverage of some aspects of higher education, and little to no coverage of other aspects that are as important or arguably more important, as we shall see. For instance, news media have rarely covered intellectuals *as intellectuals* or even employed the word "anti-intellectual." Its relatively recent coining aside, mass media surely have been unlikely to use such a clearly negative-sounding word to label themselves, their readers, their advertisers or their news sources.

In the United States, given the rare usage of "intellectual(ism)," the term remains vague, sometimes confused with "professor," "college teacher," or "expert," and is rarely used in reference to authors, artists or others who might warrant it. Further, standard histories of U.S. higher education seldom discuss the role of "intellectuals," and many standard "intellectual histories" of the United States devote relatively little consideration to higher education. Recent calls for a more active role for "public intellectuals" may therefore fall on dead ears. Certainly, it is only since Hofstadter's 1963 book that the terms "anti-intellectualism" and "higher education" have been linked more than rarely, although the debate regarding the extent to which colleges should prepare students for jobs versus give them a broader education had been raging for decades.

Moreover, we may never know whether in the past mass media workers thought of themselves as "intellectuals" (it's rather doubtful, considering the largely financial interests of owners and the working-class backgrounds of most journalists until well past the mid-twentieth century) and the evidence that readers thought of themselves as intellectuals is anecdotal at best. While journalism education in higher education dates to the mid-nineteenth century (the first journalism courses taught during Reconstruction; the first journalism school opened in 1908; the first graduate journalism school in 1911), mass communication as a social science can be traced back only about fifty years. Media studies and communication studies as interdisciplinary fields influenced by the humanities as well as the social sciences are even more recent. Finally, journalism education in the nation as a whole still tends to be more professionally than academically oriented. It is quite likely that many journalism professors would not call themselves "intellectuals."

A Few Scholars' and Journalists' Renewed Interest in U.S. Anti-Intellectualism

When anti-intellectualism in U.S. culture is occasionally covered or discussed explicitly in the news media, it is typically in a newspaper's syndicated or guest column, analysis-type articles on primary and secondary education, or in book reviews. Since the publication of Hofstadter's book in 1963, several subsequent works also have directly addressed anti-intellectualism—most notably *The Last Intellectuals* (1987) by Russell Jacoby, and *The Closing of the American Mind: American Culture in the Age of Academe* (1987) by the late Allan Bloom. Bloom's work was a surprise bestseller and prompted two direct responses: *Essays on the Closing of the American Mind* (1989), edited by Robert L. Stone; and *Beyond Cheering and Bashing: New Perspectives on The Closing of the American Mind* (1992), edited by William K. Buckley and James Seaton. *The Opening of the American Mind: Canons, Culture, and History*, by Lawrence W. Levine (1996), parodying Bloom's title, further contributed to the discussion. By 1997, when a conference was held at Bloom's former employer (The University of Chicago) marking the tenth anniversary of the book's publication, scholars agreed that Bloom's work, for all of its discussion in the media, had had little impact on U.S. higher education or the broader culture.[10]

Conversely, Hofstadter's Pulitzer Prize–winning book may be in the process of being rediscovered. In the November, 1998, *Atlantic Monthly*, Greenburg reflects on the persistent popularity and influence of Hofstadter's first book, *The American Political Tradition and the Men Who Made It* (1948). Greenburg also commends both Hofstadter's scholarship and his integrity, describing the scholar's persistent search for the middle ground between radicalism and conservatism, and his intellectual honesty, which made him (according to fellow historian C. Vann Woodward) "critical of many aspects of American life" but never "join[ing] the fashionable cult of anti-Americanism."[11]

Hofstadter's scholarship is historical in approach. In *Anti-intellectualism in American Life* (apparently at least nine years in the making) he collected and analyzed mountains of evidence of anti-intellectualism in U.S. politics, education, religion, and business, and — having produced a comprehensive work — he moved on to other subjects. Hofstadter's book was followed by related works by Coser (1965), Shils (1972), Jacoby (1987), Bloom (1987), Fink, Leonard and Reid (1996), Fink (1997), and others.[12] More recently, though, education scholars (primarily those who study secondary schools) have begun revisiting Hofstadter in an attempt to explain attitudes, issues, and outcomes in U.S. education.

In 1993, Edward W. Said delivered a series of lectures in the United Kingdom later collected in the volume *Representations of the Intellectual*. Said called for a new generation of public intellectuals in the United States who would speak and write their consciences on diverse matters of importance, regardless of whom they offended or whose interests they threatened. Leon Fink also emerged in the 1990s as a major scholar of U.S. intellectuals and, to a lesser extent, anti-intellectualism. His 1997 book, *Progressive Intellectuals and the Dilemmas of Democratic Commitment*, argues that in order to understand today's "new public intellectuals" ("most notably associated with a prominent, if diverse, group of African American writers and critics"[13]) one should study the "first" generation of public intellectuals in the early twentieth century. Fink's conclusion is similar to Hofstadter's guarded optimism, which Fink characterizes as confident about the abilities of experts and cautiously hopeful due to the election of President John F. Kennedy. (However, Fink may not be aware that when Kennedy was nominated for president, Hofstadter blurted out, "Mencken was right. We are a nation of boobs....We're a nation of boobs."[14])

John H. McWhorter's book, *Losing the Race: Self-Sabotage in Black America* (2000), devoted two entire chapters to anti-intellectualism in the United States' African American community and culture.

Focusing on why black Americans often perform poorly in schools, standardized exams, and so on, McWhorter omitted any comment on American anti-intellectualism generally—almost as if only African American culture is anti-intellectual rather than perhaps only one of the most anti-intellectual groups in American society. (If one were to measure anti-intellectualism largely by high school and college graduation rates, one would have to argue that Latino culture is even more anti-intellectual than African American culture.)

Philosophy scholars William Irwin, Mark T. Conard, and Aeon J. Skoble included a chapter, mostly on the most intellectual member of a television family ("Lisa and American Anti-intellectualism" by Skoble), in their 2001 book, *The Simpsons and Philosophy: The D'Oh! of Homer*. Anti-intellectualism is hypothesized as part of American philosophy—in addition to politics, religion, education, and popular culture—by these scholars.[15]

Most recently, Judge Richard A. Posner's book, *Public Intellectuals* (Harvard University Press, 2001) attempted a mostly economic analysis of public intellectuals, essentially examining the supply of and public and media demand for public intellectuals, the types and relative quality (including, most notably, the accuracy of their predictions) of their work, and public intellectuals' incentives and motivations. The law professor's 408-page book, while including much *dicta* of interest to those studying anti-intellectualism, avoided using that word and primarily attributed the public's lack of interest in, and the media's lack of scrutiny of, public intellectuals to the allegedly low and declining quality of public intellectuals' work. But, as Posner admits with understatement, his book "do[es] not emphasize history," and therefore cannot integrate cultural factors into his analysis. However, Posner's assumptions and conclusions about the mass media and public intellectuals are relevant here, and are discussed in chapter two.

To date, the only scholarly analysis of U.S. anti-intellectualism informed by critical theory has been a 1992 master's thesis written by Heidi K. Goar (*Anti-intellectualism as a Social Control: Reflexivity and Conformity*), which was grounded in the writings on anti-intellectualism by Hofstadter, Jacoby, and others, and critical theory from C. Wright Mills, Marcuse, Marx, Chomsky, and others. Goar's contribution was initiating an exploration of the contradictions inherent in relationships between U.S. anti-intellectualism and American elites. As she wrote, "rarely does one find in these already rare pieces speculation on why American society has developed in this way." Goar, although no better than Hofstadter at proposing solutions to persistent U.S. anti-intellectualism, provided updated reasons why anti-intellectualism must be fought, and why discussing anti-intellectualism matters.

Goar believed that anti-intellectualism's negative effects are clear: anti-intellectualism limits social progress, makes the culture less diverse and less interesting, and damages the self-esteem of intellectuals, who are nonetheless necessary for social progress. She explained, "Members of this society internalize these anti-intellectual ideologies and are controlled through the fear of being seen as deviant and therefore ridiculed or ostracized."

Goar's thesis implied that anti-intellectualism lulls U.S. citizens into a false sense of security, and suppresses any possible broad-based efforts to improve education or make the economy more just. This is just fine, with current elites, she points out: "If it is admitted that there are other countries in which freedoms are similar, or that a foreign country is more appealing than the United States, the grip of control loosens."[16]

Goar omitted reports from the United Nations and think tanks concluding that the United States no longer has the highest material standard of living, the best primary or secondary education system, or the healthiest population; instead, the United States has one of the world's highest incarceration rates and treats its inmates the poorest of any western, industrialized country. Moreover, in 1998, Congress made a temporary exception in its tough immigration laws to allow 100,000 more immigrants into the United States for highly paid technical work in its computer-related industries, for which not enough Americans were available. It must be noted that this exception was made not only because of those industries' growth, but because relatively fewer Americans are interested in scientific and technical jobs — even those with high salaries, good job security, and long-term career potential.[17] The potential of the culture being negatively affected by anti-intellectualism in other ways seems high as well, as evangelicalism and materialism proliferate.

Scholars are not alone in revisiting Hofstadter's tenets, as George F. Woodworth pointed out in 1995: "These charges of 'anti-intellectualism,' particularly those directed toward educational issues, continue to appear in the press, in newspapers and journal articles, and the concept itself appears to have entered popular as well as professional discourse." In 1994, the late William Henry III, then at *Time*, wrote in his *In Defense of Elitism* that he agreed with anthropologist Margaret Mead, who observed a "brand of 'anti-intellectual' popu-lism...running amok, eerily reminiscent of the nineteenth-century Know-Nothing movement." He noted that anti-intellectual Americans had come to "revile an emphasis on the talented as 'elitist'—as though the mere invocation of the word should be enough to taint the thought and so end the debate. The very essence of school is elitism" because schools' inherent idea is that "knowing and understanding more is better than knowing and understanding less."

As we shall see, one wouldn't necessarily know that from exam-ining the coverage by popular news media—whose historical purpose was providing information—of colleges and universities—whose his-torical purpose was education, whether in theology, philosophy, medi-cine, or any other discipline.

Chapter 2
American Intellectual History, Anti-Intellectualism, and the Mass Media

Not all intellectuals in the United States work on college campuses, and not all professors and administrators or students are intellectuals. Thus intellectuals and anti-intellectualism need to be situated against the broad backdrop of U.S. culture even more than if one could make contrary assumptions. The term *intellectual* is strikingly absent from the discourse of both U.S. intellectuals and the general public's vocabulary. An examination of a twelve-year period of Education Abstracts (April 1986 to April 1998), a large and widely used scholars' database, showed that even the use of the word, *intellectual*, is declining in written communication in the United States. *Intellectual* is a "key word" for only 100 articles (slightly more than eight per year, on average), despite Education Abstract's indexing of every article in *The Chronicle of Higher Education*, and dozens of other periodicals. Of that total, one-third were citations to the (London) *"Times* Higher

Education Supplement." Many of the remaining were either book reviews of Henry A. Giroux's book *Teachers as Intellectuals* (1988) or Russell Jacoby's *The Last Intellectuals* (1987), or appeared in publications from Canada, China, or Germany. The term "intellectual" also is often misused or abused, such as in the title of Heather Mac Donald's 2000 book, *The Burden of Bad Ideas: How Modern Intellectuals Misshape Our Society*, which criticizes ideologues who happen to be intellectuals (or vice versa) and does not, nor cannot, indict all intellectuals. (Note, for example, that Mac Donald herself is a "modern intellectual," but the book contains no *mea culpas*.)

Fortunately, many intellectual histories of the United States have been a little more interested in battling anti-intellectualism or being "pro-intellectual," although Oscar Cargill's *Intellectual America: Ideas on the March* (1941)—an early important intellectual history of the United States—was not one of them. Ironically, Cargill himself was often guilty of anti-intellectualism. For example, in his chapter, "The Intelligentsia," he criticized University of Chicago President Robert M. Hutchins by observing, "Under his unimpeded direction the new monasticism, one fears, would create a small and privileged society completely cut off from the world," and added that the "monastic character of American higher education is suggested...by the trivial pursuits of their thousands of scholars." In contrast, Richard Hofstadter's professor, Merle Curti, addressed intellectuals as such, and traced anti-intellectualism (he used the term) back to the late eighteenth century in his *The Growth of American Thought* (1943). He attributed it primarily to the typical American's being possessed of little education, while burdened with a lot of work, and harboring jealousy of well-educated lawyers, physicians, and ministers who prospered in bad times. He pointed out that frontier anti-intellectualism, facilitated in part by "unlettered preachers," "encourage[d] some educated men to conceal their learning."[1]

Sociologist C. Wright Mills wrote in 1963 that intellectuals were marginalized, caught between the public's anti-intellectualism and the efforts of corporations, marketers, advertisers, and political candidates, campaign managers and pollsters, to influence (or outright manipulate) the public. As Edward Said summarized it in 1994, to Mills, intellectuals were "faced either with a kind of despondent sense of powerlessness at their marginality, or with the choice of joining the ranks of institutions, corporations or governments as members of a relatively small group of insiders who made important decisions irresponsibly and on their own."[2] Mills understood that unmasking the status quo and providing alternatives meant loneliness for intellectuals, rather than alignment with the rest of society, and that being an intellectual means engaging with politics, not only culture or economics or scholars' theorizing. Even so, Mills wrote that intellectuals and artists were the last groups that could resist "mass-art and mass-thought."

Henry Steele Commager, in his landmark book, *The American Mind: An Interpretation of American Thought and Character since the 1880's* (1950), barely addressed formal education, and shied away from the term *intellectual* in favor of discussing individual authors, scholars, and other figures. In his conclusion, however, Commager complained bitterly about "pressure for intellectual conformity and the growing intolerance with independence and dissent" starting in the 1940s, adding, "The new intolerance was distinguished not only by its quasi-official character but by a certain moral flabbiness, a weakening of intellectual fiber."[3]

While Crane Brinton (1950) claimed that anti-intellectualism referred to man's seeming unwillingness or inability to learn what he could learn that would improve his life, Broudy's definition (1955) was similar to Hofstadter's eight years later—"the explicit or implicit, intentional or inadvertent disparagement of theoretical activity and knowledge in life and in the school," as well as a certain inability to implement rationality in one's life. Jacques Barzun wrote in his 1959 polemic that anti-intellectualism results in intellectuals coping with "[m]isfortune...[and] degradation" that have "overtaken the mind in western civilization. They blame capitalism, liberalism, the machine, the masses—everything outside themselves, and thus attain the desired status of victim. The beleaguered intellectual—it is a badge and a position in life." He believed that intellect is hated because it is envied, and envied (as George F. Woodworth put it in 1995) "because it is felt to be a sign or pretense of social superiority." Wrote Barzun, "We should expect that in an age of egalitarian democracy 'anti-intellectualism' would increase, for everyone now has the right to resent whatever looks like privilege and eminence."[4]

Jules Henry's *Culture Against Man* (1963) also addressed U.S. anti-intellectualism. Henry complained that the U.S. educational system discourages children from being creative or inquisitive, and instead teaches them to be "stupid" and "absurd." He wrote, "the function of education is to prevent the truly creative intellect from getting out of hand...Creative intellect is mysterious, devious, and irritating." Henry, noting the irony of a system claiming to be educating while actually creating "idiots," argued:

> creativity is the last thing wanted in any culture because of its potentialities for disruptive thinking; that the primordial dilemma of all education derives from the necessity of training the mighty brain...to be stupid; and the creativity, when it is encouraged (as in science in our culture), occurs only after the creative thrust of an idea has been tamed and directed toward socially approved ends.[5]

Other intellectual histories since those by Curti, Henry, and the others also have addressed, directly or indirectly, anti-intellectualism in American culture—even if they also sometimes didn't use the term—but none had the impact of Richard Hofstadter.

Richard Hofstadter's Contributions

Rarely cited, Hofstadter's first published writing on anti-intellectualism was his 1953 article in *Michigan Alumnus Quarterly Review*. Written for the alumni of a top public university, it defended intellectuals and their "play of the mind for its own sake, for whom it is one of the major ends in life" and responded to complaints that intellectuals are impractical in this way:

> I can think of some intellectuals like Thomas Jefferson and Robert Owen and John Maynard Keynes who have been eminently practical, and I consider the notion that the intellectual is inherently impractical to be one of the most contemptible of the delusions with which the anti-intellectual quiets his envy—the intellectual is not impractical but primarily concerned with a quality of ideas that does not depend upon their practicality.

Hofstadter's primary accomplishment was to warn his readers against confusing form with function: he said that he would not "make the mistake of identifying higher education in general with intellectualism" (indeed, he wished to emphasize "the extent to which anti-intellectualism is rampant within the educational community"). Conversely, Hofstadter added, Jeffersonian democracy's interest in education was "aristocratic," while "Jacksonian democracy, whatever

its benefits in other areas, was identified with a widespread deteriora-
tion in the standards of professional education, masquerading under
the ideology that easier access to these privileged areas of life must be
made available to the people."[6]

However, after criticizing professors, he then accused popular
movements for too often having "fail[ed] to understand the place of
learning in our culture, or even on occasion for their hostility to it."
In particular, he wrote, Protestantism's first "Great Awakening" of
the mid-eighteenth century caused the founding of more colleges, all
with administrators dictating the "right brand of theology." Moreover, in the twentieth century,

> The movement that destroyed the old classical curriculum and made Ameri-
> can universities, especially our state universities, the nurseries of all kinds
> of sub-intellectual practical skills of less than university grade was in its
> impetus very largely a popular movement; and while many of the conse-
> quences of that movement must be set to its credit as compensations, the
> undercurrent of vocationalism and anti-intellectualism was undeniable.

Hofstadter singled out William Jennings Bryan as "one of the most
genuinely popular, and I believe democratic, political leaders in our
history," and yet "the sort of respect he showed for science and academic freedom is familiar to you all," a comment on (among other
statements and positions) Bryan's anti-evolution arguments in the
"Scopes Monkey Trial."[7]

Written as a response to McCarthyism and as a plea for U.S. citizens to wake up to and fight their own anti-intellectualism, Hofstadter's Anti-intellectualism in American Life in 1963 suggested that U.S.
anti-intellectualism must be checked, and the author held out the possibility that some forms of intellectual civil life can be encouraged.
However, Hofstadter's book clearly showed that he believed the
country was likely to continue to be anti-intellectual. His thesis was a
fundamentally scathing, depressing indictment, and one that has stood
the test of time, as subsequent authors suggest. Among his major ac-
complishments was rejecting both myths of perfection corrupted by
historical decay, which have yet claimed subsequent writers such as
Neil Postman,[8] Allan Bloom (see below) or Donald N. Wood (see below), and visions of utopian inevitability.

Hofstadter believed that it was in educational institutions that anti-
intellectualism in other spheres of life crystallizes and converges. A

fervent critic of those who interpreted in anti-intellectual ways the generally pro-intellectual writings of John Dewey, he targeted for criticism the "deintellectualized curricula" in U.S. schools that place a higher value on social and affective development than on the cultivation of capacities for learning and critical analysis. Hofstadter observed U.S. educational institutions de-emphasizing "book learning," jeopardizing high academic standards, neglecting the brightest and most creative students, pushing narrow vocationalism, discouraging purely theoretical work, and devaluing intrinsic rewards of learning. Robert D. Cross observed in 1990,

> As Hofstadter sadly but indignantly concluded, the educational establishment has contributed a great deal—perhaps even more than evangelical religion, democratic politics, and the cult of practicality—to the overwhelming "anti-intellectualism" of American life. "Anti-intellectualism" has been pandemic in American life; a "useful intelligence" has been the watchword.[9]

Lamented Hofstadter:

> A host of educational problems has arisen from indifference—underpaid teachers, overcrowded classrooms, double-schedule schools, broken-down school buildings, inadequate facilities and a number of other failings that come from something else—the cult of athleticism, marching bands, high-school drum majorettes, ethnic ghetto schools, de-intellectualized curricula, the failure to educate in serious subjects, the neglect of academically gifted children.[10]

Hofstadter already had noted that even though other countries are democratic, with public schools and diversified modern economies, U.S. schools were (and are) peculiar:

> American education can be praised, not to say defended, on many counts; but I believe ours is the only educational system in the world vital segments of which have fallen into the hands of people who joyfully and militantly proclaim their hostility to intellect and their eagerness to identify with children who show the least intellectual promise.[11]

In contrast to other scholars before and since who have claimed that anti-intellectualism was cyclical (if not unique to their own time), it was Hofstadter's mandate to demonstrate persuasively his thesis that the United States had almost always been anti-intellectual, and no less so after the advent of universal free public schools than before. As

Rigney's subsequent theory neatly summarized, if it was anti-elitism and religious fundamentalism that originally caused the U.S. population to be anti-intellectual and uninterested in (or even hostile to) formal education, economic considerations perpetuated it. Hofstadter was convinced that reformers such as Horace Mann were forced to "market" universal public education on the basis of "public order, political democracy, or economic improvement," not developing minds or learning culture:

> To the rich, who were often wary of its cost, they [education reformers] presented popular education as the only alternative to public disorder, to an unskilled and ignorant labor force, to misgovernment, crime, and radicalism. To the people of middle and lower classes they presented it as the foundation of popular power, the door to opportunity, the great equalizer in the race for success...
>
> [P]ride was expressed that American colleges and universities, unlike those of Europe, were not devoted simply to the acquisition of knowledge but to the moral cultivation of their students. The American college was complacently portrayed as a place designed to form character and inculcate sound principle rather than to lead to the pursuit of truth.[12]

Like George S. Hage (but unlike Rigney later), Hofstadter found both sexism and fear of homosexuality to be causes of anti-intellectualism and anti-education sentiment:

> There were often not enough male models or idols among their teachers whose performance will convey the sense that the world of mind is legitimately male, who can give them masculine examples of intellectual inquiry or cultural life, and who can be regarded as sufficiently successful and important in the world to make it conceivable for vigorous boys to enter teaching themselves for a livelihood.

Hofstadter complained that populist (mis)interpretations of John Dewey's writings had ironically degenerated into a new elitism by the 1940s and 1950s: curricula were "deintellectualized" as 60 percent of children were deemed "in some sense uneducable." Much of the justification for "life adjustment" originated in psychological theories rather than Dewey's philosophy, prompting Hofstadter to quip acidly, "Life adjustment educators would do anything in the name of science except encourage children to study it."[13] He also complained that disciples of Dewey (the so-called life-adjustment educators) dismissed much of college curricula as "education-for-more education studies," and believed that universities taught "unusable and unteach-able traditional subjects" such as algebra and foreign languages only because of faculty members' vested interests and higher education institutions' need to stratify students into the brighter and the dimmer. The result, Hofstadter wrote, was that all students were "in large mea-sure get[ing] the kind of training originally conceived for the slow learner." Moreover, "life adjustment" was ultimately not only capi-talistic but obviously materialistic; it "help[s] them [students] learn the ways of the world of consumption and hobbies, of enjoyment and social complaisance—in short, to adapt gracefully to the passive and hedonistic style."[14]

The question remains as to why, in Hofstadter's chapters on anti-intellectualism in U.S. education, he wrote so much about primary and secondary education, and so little about higher education. Possibly, it is because he had already written about higher education in previous books.[15] Probably, it was because the historical evidence shows that anti-intellectualism in primary and secondary education was originally a cause, and perhaps only eventually also the result, of anti-intellec-tualism in higher education.

Research into anti-intellectualism in American life since the publi-cation of Hofstadter's book may be categorized in several ways—by academic discipline; chronologically; and into those who have gener-ally agreed with Hofstadter's definitions and conclusions and those who have not. (Only one article has attempted to recap his entire ca-reer.[16]) However, as Hofstadter's work was history and, to a limited extent, contemporary cultural criticism (both Hofstadter's introduc-tion and conclusion describe and comment on contemporary phe-nomena as of the early 1960s), it is useful to organize subsequent scholarship by first considering commentaries on current events since 1963; then historical research that builds on Hofstadter's work; and, finally, on broader work of social scientific and historical significance.

In the historical period immediately after Hofstadter's book, sev-eral scholars used the term "anti-intellectualism" in ways inconsistent with Hofstadter, suggesting that they had not read Hofstadter carefully or that they proposed alternative definitions.[17] Little else was written about U.S. anti-intellectualism until Russell Jacoby's *The Last Intel-lectuals* and Allan Bloom's *The Closing of the American Mind* were published in 1987. Jacoby followed narrowly in the tradition of Mills's *The Sociological Imagination* (1959) and many of the cynical journalist H. L. Mencken's columns about higher education, which addressed anti-intellectualism among U.S. intellectuals.[18] Jacoby asserted that an entire generation of Americans was devoid of public intellectuals (i.e., almost no new nationally known, nationally respected intellectuals emerged between the early 1960s and the late 1980s). Potential new faces during the 1960–1986 period—on a par approaching Lewis Mumford, Dwight Macdonald, Edmund Wilson, Alfred Kazin, Daniel Bell, Irving Howe, and so on—ended up getting "lost in the universities," he wrote. This wouldn't be so bad, Jacoby implied, except that universities are not conducive to (and often actually discourage) the development of traditional public intellectuals. He also alleged, contrary to the popular vision, that the often-lauded "beat" period in fact spawned no new urban intellectuals. Universities increasingly demand specialization (which traditional public intellectuals have resisted) and even once-leftists such as Todd Gitlin sold out to university life. Finally, campuses were silenced or co-opted after the McCarthyism period by grants and contracts from the federal government and big business.[19]

Jacoby's case has major limitations, among them that he discussed almost no intellectuals living outside New York City. His apparent belief that one may be intellectual only by hanging out in bohemian coffee shops and resisting university employment also ultimately was—or at least is—not convincing. Jacoby wrote a new "Introduction" for his book when it was republished in 2000, but he used it only to deny being a "hopeless romantic" (i.e., essentially arguing that sometimes the past really was better), to complain that academic life continues to be increasingly specialized and segregated from society, and to simultaneously express enthusiasm about the "new black public intellectuals" and a "group of science writers [who have] more or less filled the space vacated by humanists."[20]

Bloom's The Closing of the American Mind may never have used the words "anti-intellectual" or "anti-intellectualism" but Goar (1992) and others have cited it as a significant study of anti-intellectualism in U.S. culture. The major theme of the book, which is subtitled, "How Higher Education Has Failed Democracy and Impoverished the Souls of Today's Students," was consistent with Hofstadter's work.[21] In sum, Bloom believed that U.S. higher education was failing to provide students with a broad, liberal education, and that universities have degenerated into assembly lines for the manufacturing of "skilled" graduates. He was horrified by what he observed to be a general lack of interest in arts and humanities and a general conformity to popular culture (Bloom was particularly critical of rock music). In addition to its specific arguments, Bloom's book was notable for two reasons. First, its popularity suggested that Americans were eager to read (or at least to possess) an intellectual's commentary on higher education. Second, Bloom's book almost immediately inspired a firestorm of defensive and counteroffensive tomes.[22]

In contrast to Hofstadter's well-documented history, though, Bloom's book consists largely of personal observations and mini-essays. Sharing Hofstadter's resignation to widespread anti-intellectualism, Bloom pleaded that the elite, research university be allowed to maintain (or regain) its position as an island of intellectualism in a country of anti-intellectuals. Bloom was not specific about how this might be accomplished, though he cited Aristotle, Descartes, Freud, Hegel, Heidegger, Hitler, Hobbes, Kant, Locke, Machiavelli, Nietzsche, Socrates, de Tocqueville and Weber, and others, to support his views and/or attack others. He also promoted a specific canon (Plato, Rousseau, Shakespeare), and lost many potential allies due to his vitriolic attack on rock music. Hofstadter recognized that in the life of the mind, it is simply exposing oneself to ideas at all that is important: which ones, within reason of course, is of no great matter.

David Bromwich (1996) also followed up on Hofstadter, asking, "Has anything happened since 1964 to change our view of intellectual life in its relation to American society?" He concluded that it hadn't. Impressionistic rather than evidence-based, Bromwich's article asserted that "a clash of views over 'merely' intellectual matters is rarer than it used to be." Journalists provide the public with a "mass means of distraction," he wrote, simultaneously asserting they had once considered themselves the "informal educators of the society." Bromwich added that, "social adjustment" has become the predominant task of primary and secondary schools and anti-intellectualism received a big boost from debates over both Vietnam and the "dogma of cultural identity...[which] has done something terribly demoralizing to us." He concluded that "anti-intellectualism that emerged in its fury in the fifties...has been incorporated as a normal element of the organized system of our politics. It dominates now without a challenge from the mass media and with only the memory of a challenge from the system of mass education." A number of other scholars also made passing references to anti-intellectualism in the youth movements without affixing that label concretely to any person, group or idea.[23]

Leon Fink, a history professor at the University of North Carolina at Chapel Hill, in the mid-1990s began writing extensively about the history of intellectuals, particularly during the Progressive period of the early twentieth century, obviously always with an eye out for anti-intellectualism. His chapter, "Joining the People: William English Walling and the Specter of the Intellectual Class," in his 1997 book, *Progressive Intellectuals and the Dilemmas of Democratic Commitment*, focuses on anti-intellectualism among (American socialist) intellectuals around World War I.

In 2000, John McWhorter, an African-American linguistics professor at the University of California—Berkeley published *Losing the Race: Self-Sabotage in Black America*, the third and fourth chapters of which were "The Cult of Anti-intellectualism" and "The Roots of the Cult of Anti-intellectualism," respectively. In Chapter 3, McWhorter asserted that "black students do so poorly in school decade after decade not because of racism, funding, class, parental education, etc., but because of a virus of anti-intellectualism that...permeates the black community, all the way up to the upper class."[24] McWhorter backed up his argument by detailing SAT scores of middle-class black students being lower than scores of white students living in poverty, SAT scores—if anything—overestimating black students' college performance, and his own experiences with black students at Berkeley (they are neither stupid, nor lazy, they simply don't believe in education). McWhorter went on to argue that black students aren't interested in learning about even important black historical figures, if they are dead, and that black students rarely perform better in schools with mostly or all black teachers or professors. In Chapter 4, McWhorter argues that black students were intellectually uncreative and inflexible yet "leery of precision," asserts that black students are anti-intellectual and therefore hypocritical even at elite black schools, and connects anti-intellectualism with anti-elitism because African-American culture connects education with whites.

McWhorter, in Chapter 4, asks whether African-American anti-intellectualism is "a 'Black' problem or a 'Black American' problem," by contrasting children of Caribbean immigrants with descendents of American slaves (the former look better). Unfortunately,

McWhorter's endnotes and index suggest that he was totally unaware of any scholarship on American anti-intellectualism except that within the African-American population, even noting the lack of "black students in the sciences" without mentioning the decrease of all native-born Americans in the sciences. Thus, he never asks nor answers the real question about anti-intellectualism as simply an "American problem."

Anti-Intellectualism in U.S. Mass Media

Hofstadter's 1953 article, along with the books by Oscar Cargill, Henry Steele Commager, and Merle Curti, inspired the late George S. Hage to write his 1956 doctoral dissertation on U.S. anti-intellectualism, the first and one of only two dissertations (at least in the United States) that have specifically addressed anti-intellectualism in the U.S. mass media.[25] Hage's dissertation analyzed newspaper coverage of the presidential elections of 1828 and 1952, and found that John Quincy Adams had been criticized for "book learning" and support of a national observatory, while Adams and Adlai Stevenson were both ridiculed for their "gifts of language." Hage called references to candidates' "unreflective" traits, primarily those "concerned with physical action and development, with knowledge gained through the senses or intuitively, and with exaltation of the heart or the head" as "not anti-intellectual in themselves" but "divorced from reflection and valued above it by the anti-intellectual." Press appraisal of Stevenson's intellect was overwhelmingly positive, while it had been negative for Adams, but Hage concluded that this probably was because Stevenson was a "wit" while Adams was a "theorist." However, Dwight Eisenhower's and Andrew Jackson's non-intellectual and anti-intellectual qualities both received more coverage than Stevenson and Adams' intellectual qualities.[26]

Hage, like Curti and George Santayana, also had found that "The insinuation of effeminacy was designated an indicator of intellectualism from the viewpoint of the anti-intellectual."[27] Hage was the first to trace the linking of effeminacy and anti-intellectualism back to Adams' time: the *Albany Argus* called Adams's clothing "the climax of affectation and dandyism"; the *United States Telegraph* said he "fights best by 'midnight lights'"; and the *New York Enquirer* described his supporters as "very accommodating... in their disposition" and as speaking French. Similarly, Hage pointed to editorials referring to Stevenson as "Adelaide" or "Adeline," calling his voice "fruity" or "trill[ing]," his vocabulary peppered with "teacup words," his role as assistant to the navy secretary as "a lacy sort of dilettante," and one of Stevenson's supporters as a "typical Harvard lace-cuff liberal." Hage noted that these kinds of insults had been common since before 1828, but he also echoed a 1955 analysis by David Riesman and Nathan Glazer when Hage observed:

> How powerful, then, is the political consequence of combining the image of the homosexual with the image of the intellectual—the State Department cooky-pusher Harvard-trained sissy thus becomes the focus of social hatred and the Jew becomes merely one variant of the intellectual sissy—actually less important than the Eastern-educated snob!

Hage was particularly concerned about the future effectiveness of intellectuals if they continued to be associated with homosexuals and/or traitors.[28]

At least in part because Hofstadter apparently was unaware of Hage's dissertation, Hofstadter rarely mentioned the mass media in his 1963 book, and when he did, it was often in passing—such as the following passage (immediately following that one above on "underpaid teachers, overcrowded classrooms," and so on):

> At times the schools of the country seem to be dominated by athletics, commercialism, and the standards of the mass media, and these extend upwards to a system of higher education whose worst failings were underlined by the bold president of the University of Oklahoma who hoped to develop a university of which the football team could be proud. Certainly some ultimate educational values seem forever to be eluding the Americans. At great effort and expense they send an extraordinary proportion of their young to colleges and universities; but their young, when they get there, do not seem to care even to *read* [emphasis in original, citation omitted].[29]

Disappointingly, even the ten pages on the mass media in Jacoby's 1987 book were shallow, rife with conspiracy theories, and contained several factual errors, and Bloom paid little serious attention to the news media or other mass media—again with the exception of his diatribe against rock 'n' roll music. Books, articles, and academic papers such as *The Experts*, by journalists Seymour Freidin and

George Bailey (1968) have tried to assess the American news media's use of "experts" and "analysts." Their anecdotal findings—which didn't focus exclusively, or even primarily, on "intellectuals," "public intellectuals" or university professors—showed that "experts" quoted by the news media were often, occasionally usually, wrong about what they were quoted on. Apparently fearful that the public would too readily believe, perhaps even act on, "experts' opinions," their book is contrary to one major tenet of journalism—seek out numerous different sources that are, or should be, knowledgeable about a news subject (and in some ways anti-intellectual) would journalists or their consumers fare any better by quoting sources who have no discernible credentials or expertise rather than those who do? (Note: Freidin and Bailey also managed to misspell Hofstadter as "Hofstetter" throughout the book, although the Columbia University historian was still living when the book was published, and it is likely that Freidin and/or Bailey had met him.)

Jeffrey C. Goldfarb's 1998 book, *Civility and Subversion: The Intellectual in Democratic Society*, also is conscious of the interaction between the mass media and anti-intellectualism. Goldfarb claims that the news media's standards in both competence and ethics have declined, resulting in less "serious discussion" in the media generally, and that broadcast soundbites inhibit such serious discussion more so than did or does newspaper and magazine articles. Most significantly, Goldfarb understands that the modern mass media potentially give intellectuals access to a larger audience than ever, while at the same time the public (and, apparently, scholar Stanley Aronowitz) is content with giving their roles to Oprah Winfrey and Phil Donohue. Concludes Goldfarb,

> "fail[ing] to draw the distinction between the intellectual and the entertainer, between empty talk and deliberation....makes sense only when informed discourse is confused with talk performance; important distinctions concerning cultural quality are not made. When they are made, the room for the intellectual would appear to be small indeed."[30]

Goldfarb, however, only tangentially addressed anti-intellectualism per se, and wrote relatively little else about the news media.

The most significant published work building explicitly on Hofstadter is Daniel Rigney's 1991 theory article, in which he wrote:

In retrospect, Hofstadter fails to anticipate the power of mass communication to shape American cultural life and to influence attitudes toward intellect. The power of the media to define the terms of public discourse has not, however, escaped the attention of more recent social critics. Postman (1985), for example, examines public discourse in an age dominated by entertainment industries, concluding that the electronic media have not produced Orwell's dark vision of an externally imposed oppression after all, but rather something more akin to Huxley's vision of a brave new world, a trivialized culture that creates an almost limitless appetite for amusement and diversion. News and education are now essentially popular forms of entertainment, competing with situation comedies and video games for the fun-consumer's shortened span of attention...

Rigney cited the Edward S. Herman and Noam Chomsky argument that public opinion is now a "manufactured product" controlled by corporate media and, while concluding that Herman and Chomsky exaggerate somewhat, added,

The effects of mass media on attitudes toward intellect are certainly multiple and ambiguous. On the one hand, mass communication greatly expand the sheer volume of information available for public consumption. On the other hand, much of this information comes preinterpreted for easy digestion and laden with hidden assumptions, saving consumers the work of having to interpret it for themselves. Commodified information naturally tends to reflect the assumptions and interests of those who produce it, and its producers are not driven entirely by a passion to promote critical reflection.[31]

Although many scholars have written since Rigney about the "dumbing down" of American popular culture, negative depictions of teachers in television and film, and so on, none of them have taken into account either much of the history of American anti-intellectualism (most scholars seem to believe it is a new phenomenon) or integrated anti-intellectualism in the mass media, as Rigney suggested be done, into a comprehensive theory or other explanation of American anti-intellectualism.

Developing a Theory of U.S. Anti-Intellectualism

In 1977, Richard Gillam conceded that Hofstadter (and this book suggests, concepts of anti-intellectualism as well) is difficult to place ideologically, as he "remains for some a liberal, for others a conservative." However, Gillam, who compared and contrasted Hofstadter with sociologist C. Wright Mills, found many more similarities than differences between them. In fact, he wrote, their differences were matters of emphasis that stemmed primarily from differences in their "temperaments." Gillam also suggested that Christopher Lasch (although it was Lasch's 1978 and 1991 books that greatly enhanced his stature) was a successor to both, as an "engaged thinker" who possessed "Hofstadter's sensibility" and Mills's politics. Although Hofstadter was the more brilliant analyst and theorist of the two and eventually not as negative as Mills, both held: that intellectuals live for ideas, not off them; unshakeable belief in the critical ideal; that power in the United States had become concentrated and oppressive; that a mass society had developed; that "extrarational" culture developments had "new and invidious significance"; an eventual belief in elitism to counter "disruptive and anarchic" status politics or populism as well as "democratic hope"; and opposition to anti-intellectualism (Hofstadter took on the entire U.S. culture, whereas Mills critiqued only anti-intellectual intellectuals).[32]

Further complicating our understanding of anti-intellectualism in U.S. culture is that anti-intellectualism has been found in numerous, sometimes surprising, sites, including environmentalism, science, the military, legal research and judges' opinion writing, and efforts by the government and economic elites to control social deviance.[33] Drawing on theories of social control (from Marx, Max Weber, Mills, Marcuse, and Peter Berger), conformity (Hagan and Simpson, Scheff, de Tocqueville, Henry), self-image and reflexivity (Morris, Cooley, Mead, Goffman, Thomas), Heidi K. Goar's in-depth interviews successfully probed for how anti-intellectual ideologies may be internalized by Americans "through the fear of being seen as deviant and therefore ridiculed or ostracized." She also found that being an intellectual in U.S. culture is tantamount to being un-American and thus unpatriotic: "The prevailing *mise en scene* of this country is 'my country, right or wrong, love it or leave it.' Oddly enough, this position opposes democracy and its tenets."[34]

Donald N. Wood's 1996 book, *Post-Intellectualism and the Decline of Democracy* proposed that "Intellectualism," was the cause and effect of the "Enlightenment," but that it has been replaced by "post-intellectualism." Wood defined intellectualism as consisting of a search for knowledge, critical thinking, social criticism, and broad liberal arts, all of which he said have been replaced by ignorance, "dumbth" (a decline in analytic thinking), establishmentism (reluctance to change the status quo), and specialization, respectively. Wood, who referred to Hofstadter only once, believed that "post-intellectualism" started with the dilution of universal education in the 1870s (that at a time when only about 2 percent of the population had a high school diploma!), and continued with the 1890s labor movement, the burgeoning popularity of movies and television (in fact, a major reason for Wood's "post-intellectualism" was the replacement of the "Written Word" by the "Electric Media"), and the growing role of government during the twentieth century.

Wood's book also was not a worthy successor to Hofstadter. Although he could point to hundreds of phenomena that he claims are post-intellectual, or at least along the trajectory from intellectualism to post-intellectualism, Wood failed to provide a convincing body of evidence for most of his specific charges. Against mass media, he made a laundry list of such plausible but unproven accusations: artistic exploitation; corruption by commercial support and special interests; being wracked by mergers; a lack of substantive content; the construction of [unrealistic] "reality"; damage to democracy; the promotion of escapism; the propping up of elites; invasions of privacy; an overemphasis on, or promotion of, violence; and being partially responsible for copycat crimes, suicides, aggressive behavior, desensitization, "mean world syndrome," and "narcotizing dysfunction." Ultimately, the cause-effect relationship between an "intellectual" world and a "post-intellectual" world was not clearly supported, nor was the unavoidable implication that the United States was once an "intellectual" country.

Relatively little research on anti-intellectualism in U.S. education has focused on higher education. One exception, Barnett Singer's 1977 article, charged that the tremendous growth in the number of professors had resulted in the lowering of quality and standards in higher education, and that "infelicities of the social science style have spread into many other disciplines, including history, law, journalism, and even mathematics. The rot runs deep."[35]

In more recent years, anti-intellectualism has been a charge thrown back and forth in the "culture wars," such as conservatives' labeling of cultural and ethnic diversity efforts on college campuses as part and parcel of "political correctness." In 1992, Joan W. Scott charged anti-intellectual conservatives with "misrepresent[ing]...the way universities actually operate" in order to whip up even more anti-intellectualism among the general public than was already present. As she explained,

> if Hofstadter is right (and I think he is), [Lynne V.] Cheney, the NAS [National Association of Scholars], the highly visible band of journalists and publicists who are promoting the conservative agenda, have in common the intention to control thought, to prescribe its contents and boundaries, to police its operations, and, above all, to reign in the critical spirit that must be unfettered in a truly free society. That this is all done in the name of democracy is, according to Hofstadter, a characteristic of anti-intellectualism.[36]

Many recent authors, such as George Dennis O'Brien's *All the Essential Half-Truths about Higher Education* (1998), discuss anti-intellectualism without using the word, and—like O'Brien—obviously are torn between opposing it in principle and appreciating it in practice. A former president of both Bucknell University and the University of Rochester, O'Brien, for instance, defended both the core values of liberal arts and research universities, while also praising business schools (perhaps the most anti-intellectual part of a large and/or public university) for their narrow focus on the teaching of their exclusively practical courses.

Starting with Hofstadter's definition, Betty Jo Hyde Welch's 1980 doctoral dissertation sought manifestations of "anti-intellectualism" in order to ask questions about influences on high school students' decisions to attend college. She hypothesized that "anti-intellectualism will relate negatively with the decision to attend college." North Carolina high school students planning to attend college reported fewer anti-intellectual friends, parents, and teachers than did other students.

Almost all of the research since Hofstadter on anti-intellectualism in U.S. education was been concerned with primary and secondary education and even one article about librarians! Numerous other scholars have linked education to anti-intellectualism in various ways not relevant to this discussion.[37]

Although surprisingly no articles or books on anti-intellectualism in U.S. business have been published since Hofstadter's book, several scholars have picked up where Hofstadter left off in studying anti-

intellectualism in U.S. religion,[38] politics and business. S. A. Newman's article is particularly salient because, in a 1993 reprinting and
updating of a 1973 article, he commented on changes in anti-
intellectualism among Southern Baptists over a twenty-year period.
The anti-intellectual trend already under way in 1973 still continued
in 1993, he wrote, and the number of anti-intellectual church members "increased appreciably" during the period. Newman also noted,
"anti-intellectuals get peculiar satisfaction from the consternation of
the moderates." Anti-intellectual fundamentalist leaders today often
admit their own ignorance of theology. Worst, anti-intellectuals have
largely succeeded in excluding from church positions persons who
aren't anti-intellectual. A good example of Newman's argument is
J.M. McCain's 1995 master's thesis. McCain, himself a Southern
Baptist, found members of an Atlanta-area Southern Baptist Church to
be anti-gay, citing the Bible as the authority for their anti-gay views.
However, McCain also found that most of them had only the vaguest
notions of what the Bible supposedly says about homosexuality; many
couldn't even name which book(s) allegedly condemn homosexuality
(primarily Romans and Leviticus). McCain's conclusion argued that
homosexuality is no worse a sin than any other, and directed Southern
Baptists to continue to condemn homosexuality—but simply be more
"knowledgeable" about why they are doing so.

Daniel Rigney and Thomas J. Hoffman's 1993 article on anti-intellectualism among Catholics is the only scholarly research that reported findings different from Hofstadter's book. The authors found
U.S. Catholics much less anti-intellectual than did Hofstadter, which
may be largely due to changes in the U.S. Catholic population between 1962 and 1993. Their data showed that Catholics and non-
Catholics are "virtually indistinguishable in their intellectual orientations even when education, birth cohort, and sex are controlled."
However, they "found Catholics to be significantly more positive on
some measures of intellectual orientation than fundamentalist Protestants, but significantly less so than nonfundamentalist Protestants, Jews,
and those with no religious affiliation." Rigney and Hoffman also
concluded that "nothing here is to suggest that American Catholics
should be satisfied with their current level of intellectual vitality."

Four research articles published since Hofstadter's book have begun addressing evidence of anti-intellectualism in U.S. literature and,
generally, in U.S. popular culture.[39] All are relatively brief, isolated

pieces of research, which could easily be woven into a larger and more significant project.

Two studies of anti-intellectualism in U.S. politics are a 1976 article by Malcolm J. Sherman, who concluded that federal court decisions on teacher qualifications have been anti-intellectual, and R. D. Froome's 1965 master's thesis, *The Anti-Intellectual Case of Articulate McCarthyism*, an attempt to point out that not all anti-intellectual rhetoric is advanced by figures who are clearly dim-witted. Froome's study discussed events surrounding anti-intellectual Senator Joe McCarthy, who was supported by intelligent conservatives such as James Burnham, John Chamberlain, Max Eastman, and William F. Buckley, Jr. (The fact that some anti-intellectuals may possess impressive academic or professional credentials hadn't escaped Hofstadter, either.)

Primarily, the research on anti-intellectualism since Hofstadter takes a scattershot approach to extending Hofstadter's arguments, providing more evidence for some of his points, and exploring more fully areas that Hofstadter only touched on. But no sustained effort has been made to analyze critically Hofstadter's theses. It is, in fact, quite easy to develop a list of topics and issues related to anti-intellectualism that remain to be explored. The most obvious gap is the mass media's role in anti-intellectualism, the caesura identified by Rigney and that this work begins to fill. Other gaps, though, also exist: As noted, the literature on anti-intellectualism in popular culture, the military, the business community and even modern politics, is extremely limited. However, several spheres of U.S. culture have not been examined at all: anti-intellectualism in voluntary associations, in the home environment, in athletics, within other leisure time pursuits and organizations, and so on.

Mass Media's Role in U.S. Intellectual Life and Anti-Intellectual Culture

Given the lack of attention to the mass media by scholars studying anti-intellectualism, it may be valuable to review extant scholarship regarding the mass media's role in the intellectual history of the United States. In other words, how have the mass media proposed political, economic, literary, and other influential ideas in the country's history? Likewise, what role has the intellectual development of the

United States played in the development of the mass media industries? Certainly the protection of mass media by the U.S. Constitution's First Amendment means that from the very beginning, a free press was central to the idea of the new democracy. Starting with the penny press of the 1830s and especially since the development of modern national mass-market magazines in the 1890s, one may easily argue that for their own survival media depend on certain educational and intellectual levels among the public. In the case of education, the print media link literacy with sales.

Intellectual history as a specialty among historians reached its zenith in the United States in the middle of the twentieth century, after film, radio, and television had been invented and at least the first two media were widely available. Yet Hofstadter in his *Anti-intellectualism in American Life* was not alone in assigning a minimal role to mass media in the history of U.S. intellectual life.

Merle Curti's *The Growth of American Thought*, first published in 1943, virtually ignored the mass media's role in U.S. history, despite its length (793 pages of text by its third edition in 1964) and, incredibly, the inclusion of a section titled, "The Problem of Communication," in the last chapter ("Dialogues in Our Time"). This section primarily addressed the gulf between scientists, politicians and intellectuals, and the public. Earlier in the book, Curti discussed the colonial press for just over a page, the mass-produced "Penny Press" starting in the 1830s for a page, and the press's role in the Spanish-American War in one sentence; the *New York Tribune* was mentioned once, *The New York Times* not at all. Magazines received similar short shrift, as did books. Commager, eulogized in the mass media as a "legendary historian,"[40] also dispensed quickly with the mass media in his 1950 landmark, *The American Mind*. He assigned only fourteen of 443 pages of text to changes in journalism from the mid-1880s until the mid-1920s; media were almost never mentioned after page 81.

Lewis A. Coser's *Men of Ideas: A Sociologist's View*, in 1965, considered mass media more seriously, devoting a ten-page chapter to "Intellectuals in the Mass-Culture Industries," most of which addressed print media. Furthermore, his vignettes of several intellectuals' experiences working for mass media uniformly conveyed frustration at media's political and other biases, and overall assembly-line (hence the word "mass") work environment. Warren I. Susman's *Culture as*

History (editions in 1973 and 1984) integrated discussion of media into his Harold Innis—inspired worldview, including one chapter titled, "Culture and Communications." A rambling critique of mass communication research at first, it eventually becomes a fascinated, and fascinating, commentary on how mass media are deeply interwoven into life in the United States. Norman Birnbaum's *Radical Renewal* (1988) also attributed more significance to the mass media's roles, although primarily to argue that media (particularly television) have a negative impact on a country's intellectual life. Birnbaum also believed that the media's emphasis on consumption helped make the United States more individualistic and that print media had begun to "supersede...community, church, family, and school" before radio and television were even invented. He pointed out that both media and conversation have experienced a "dreadful vulgarization" and concluded that the media were superficial, for example, underestimating the 1960s liberal movements (this will be news to those conservatives who say the media are still pushing supposedly discredited liberal ideas). He wrote that today's journalists have become like career foreign service bureaucrats in that "they combine abject servility to power and complacent ignorance in equal measure."[41] Many other books on American intellectual history omitted almost entirely any consideration of the mass media.[42]

As Daniel Rigney pointed out in 1991, U.S. mass media's role in U.S. anti-intellectualism has received almost no scholarly attention. As noted already, one of the few examples of such research by mass communication scholars was Hage's 1956 doctoral dissertation, of which apparently Rigney, like Hofstadter, was not aware.[43] Among mass communication scholars, however, scattered evidence hints that mass media fulfill some sort of intellectual role in U.S. society. In 1952, journalism education giant Frank Luther Mott wrote, "If significant news is done in large quantities, if it is done skillfully... [readers] are likely to feel the challenge of it and a certain pride in being 'intellectual.'" One must ask today what Mott meant by "intellectual" (he may simply have meant "well-informed" or "intelligent" considering the context), and if the U.S. is not "intellectual," whether the media are at least partially responsible.

As University of Tennessee journalism professor Edward Caudill found, and wrote about in 1989, U.S. media coverage of intellectuals and their ideas is a virtually untapped area of study for scholars of mass communication. Further, Caudill obviously believed that the intellectual history of the U.S. mass media, though barely begun, is an important area for him and others to research: "News responds to, reflects, and defines the values of society...Ideas, as they are presented in the press, simultaneously are changed by the press and are changing culture." Reflecting on the concept of "ideas as news," Caudill acknowledges that ideas in and of themselves are inherently difficult for journalists to cover:

> The organization and process of news gathering, interpreting unfamiliar concepts and language, and news values are among the challenges...A theory may have little inherent newsworthiness. It usually lacks both timeliness and immediate significance for the audience. In addition, such stories could harm the newspaper if readers thought the publication was ignoring their values (i.e., they would quit buying the newspaper or magazine)...Although a theory may pertain to all things at all times, it does not have the urgency, event-of-the-moment aura, that news favors. Proximity is another common news standard that ideas fail to meet. The theory may pertain to all places, but because it does not belong to a particular geographic or governmental entity, it does not have the advantage in any news medium of being uniquely local...
>
> Additionally, even if such a theory entered the news process, the reporter still has the problem of converting the information into "news." The idea, in the unlikely event that it comes a reporter's way, must overcome the effort required to make it fit into an appropriate news category. Stories about ideas and theories lose potential impact by being categorized as "soft" or feature news rather than hard news, which implies immediate importance...Just because an idea is important does not mean it is exciting or even interesting by news standards, such as timeliness, proximity, novelty, or conflict. Concepts relevant to everyone are difficult to make relevant to anyone...
>
> The new idea also may bring the problem of unfamiliar concepts and language, unlike a typical police or political story.[44]

Unlike Caudill's research, which traced the media coverage of a particular idea—in his case, evolution—this book does not investigate the coverage of a particular idea. A check of indexes indicates that the idea of anti-intellectualism is almost never discussed in popular media, even after Richard Hofstadter won the Pulitzer Prize for a book with the word in its title. Instead, this work locates and analyzes evidence of anti-intellectualism in magazine coverage of higher education—evidence of an attitude or philosophy toward all ideas and in particular, persons who have ideas and for whom ideas are of central importance.

Caudill wrote that his own work fits into the overall scheme of scholarly research because

> the history of an idea, as opposed to individuals and institutions, is the exception rather than the rule in journalism history. The case has been made for a history of the press, and the case is made for the history of ideas. However, explorations at their intersection are rare.[45]

Caudill cited only three works—by Donald L. Shaw, Michael Schudson, and Gerald J. Baldesty[46]—as examples of such scholarship and suggested two other types of "intersections": analyzing concepts of news and reporting as they existed in other spheres of U.S. life besides journalism and the law; and more research such as his own, investigating how the media have covered and portrayed specific ideas. Caudill may not have envisioned research such as this book, but it easily complements his ideas; he discussed the importance of the idea of democracy and the need to examine it "from a multitude of perspectives." One can compare this with the importance Hofstadter bestowed on anti-intellectualism and his examination of it from several perspectives. Caudill also mentioned the importance of studying elites, and this book, in part, examines evidence of anti-elitism in the media. Moreover, while Caudill had to contend with the reality that only a limited number of typical U.S. citizens even knew about Darwin's theory of evolution, let alone had read his work or that of his students (such as Thomas Huxley), this book safely assumes that millions of U.S. readers have been exposed to coverage of higher education in the most popular print media.

Therefore, Caudill would most likely support this work. In devoting the final four pages of his book on the press coverage of evolution to "the history of ideas and press history," he pointed out that "newspapers and magazines are critical sources in the historian's assessment of an idea's impact on society because the press disseminates ideas to society," and more dramatically, "In becoming public, any idea, however noble or humble, intelligent or inane, provincial or universal, is filtered through the press."

Finally, Caudill would not be discouraged by the potential vagueness of studying a topic such as the "evidence of anti-intellectualism in U.S. magazines." Summarizing his own obstacles, he explained:

> [T]he history of ideas presents a problem of defining what is being studied.

Darwinism was a cultural phenomenon as well as a scientific one. Thus, one doing a history of Darwin or evolution faces the task of dealing with the many aspects that became Darwinism, studying those ideas as they applied to both nature and society. An idea typically has no clear boundaries, no distinct points in which it is born, lives and dies, no physical limits on its time and place of existence...The problem of definition grows as the number of messengers multiplies, and in the press there were not only numerous messengers but numerous interpretations of the idea.

So, ultimately, Caudill issued a call for, and encouraged confidence in, more research like his own:

The study of ideas in the press is critical to understanding the mass societies that emerged in the 19th century. The state and evolution of mass culture is not amenable to simple explanations or ideas from a single person or source. The people are gone, but their messengers remain. We cannot know how individuals interpreted the message, but we can know what the messengers told them.[47]

Richard A. Posner's *Public Intellectuals*

Richard A. Posner's book, *Public Intellectuals: A Study of Decline*, published in 2001, cannot properly be described as a study of the mass media's role in U.S. intellectual history, because it admittedly does "not emphasize history." It also does not offer a cultural, social, political or religious theory of anti-intellectualism, only a poorly supported economic theory of public intellectuals that avoids using the term *anti-intellectualism* and implies that any anti-intellectualism is rational and increasingly prevalent over the past fifty years, if not a recent phenomenon altogether. Moreover, *Public Intellectuals* is not a study of the mass media's role in the country's intellectual life, because the mass media are treated superficially and, therefore, not completely accurately. However, Posner himself is an important judge, professor, author, and public intellectual (for instance, an earlier book, *Sex and Reason*, gained a wider audience and is brilliant—sometimes maddeningly so to religious conservatives), and his book incorporates mass media content both in its own data collection and his analysis, so his book cannot be ignored.

Posner's book also was written from much the same perspective of journalist David Brooks in the "Intellectual Life" chapter of his 2000 book, *BOBOS* [Bourgeois Bohemians] *in Paradise: The New Upper Class and How They Got There.* Brooks claimed that while the group of American intellectuals dominant in the 1950s and 1960s—interested in profound issues such as religion, capitalism, and middle-class culture—was overrated and out of touch, today's intellectuals are more realistic but also worse in a sense. They develop, Brooks writes, policy and research niches, then market themselves to and through television appearances, op-ed pieces (allegedly sometimes ghost written for them) and conferences, often ending up making high incomes while still not saying or writing anything original, helpful, or even interesting. Then, Brooks observes, they feel "status-income disequilibrium," wondering why they don't make more and scheming on how to do so.

Unlike so many scholars who de-emphasize or ignore the role of the mass media in American society, something like a fish ignoring the water, Posner (like Brooks) understands that the primary—if not only—way in which an American public intellectual can be "public" is through mass media. (His book has certain similarities to Freidin and Bailey's *The Experts.*) In other words, although he recognizes public intellectuals' other outlets—such as teaching, lecturing, consulting, testifying, letter writing, meeting, and so on—he knows they reach relatively few people. ("My interest is in the expressive dimension of public-intellectual work, that is, in communication with the public on intellectual themes by means of books, magazine articles, op-ed pieces, open letters, public lectures, and appearances on radio or television.") Posner gathered evidence on public intellectuals from three sources: "web hits," which he defined as searching for a person using the Google search engine on the World Wide Web; "media mentions," which he defined as being referred to in the "Major Newspapers," "Magazine Stories," and "Transcripts" databases in Lexis/Nexis; and "scholarly citations," for which he used the *Science Citation Index* and the *Arts and Humanities Citation Index.* Other scholars and book reviewers have detailed the problems with his method (starting with the selection of indexes and databases as a way to weight public intellectuals and ending with the biases and omissions of the sources he chose), and so they aren't detailed here. One point must still be noted: considering that so much of *Public Intellectuals* is about the mass media, it is notable that none of the databases used by Posner index the major scholarly publications in mass communication, such as *Journalism & Mass Communication Quarterly, Critical Studies in Media Communication, Journal of Communication, Newspaper Research Journal, Journal of Media Ethics, Journal of Media Economics, Mass Communication and Society*, and others. (Thus, there was extremely little chance that a journalism professor, even one who recently was or still is also a journalist, would make Posner's list of public intellectuals—unless he/she has written important books for a general audience.)

Posner's definition of public intellectual is limited to a "person who, drawing on his intellectual resources, addresses a broad though educated public on issues with a political or ideological dimension."[48] Thus, he excludes, for example, Carl Sagan, who probably was the greatest American popularizer of science from the mid-1960s until the late 1990s (and whose work was not strictly apolitical or nonideological). Posner includes *some* journalists: "William Buckley, Andrew Sullivan, George Will, Christopher Hitchens, Gregg Easterbrook, and Leon Wieseltier."

Posner frustrates his readers by being almost entirely descriptive in his comments about the media, so he tells us, "some nonacademic magazines have able and selective editors, [but] few editors are competent across the entire range of subjects covered by their magazine"[49]; he doesn't tell us whether this situation can be or should be different, although one can assume, based on his economic arguments, that if it should be different, it would be.

Posner observes that some public intellectuals' fame is demand-driven by television and radio, and apparently to a lesser degree in his view, "magazine editors..., editors of newspaper op-ed pages, book publishers..., [and] reporters seeing quotable commentary," because of "their insatiable demand for expert commentary on matters of public concern." He also knows that individuals seeking the modern American public intellectual's role are highly likely to pursue an academic career and unlikely to pursue journalism—both because generally "journalists are not in a good position to acquire specialized knowledge" and, Posner seems to believe, because public intellectuals are too specialized to work in most journalism jobs. He reasonably points out the "sheer impracticability of creating a corps of journalists who know enough about the range of academic disciplines that produce knowledge or opinion...to be able to write competently about them," although he obviously doesn't realize that if public intellectuals' work were in higher public demand, such a "corps" *could* be assembled by organizations such as the Associated Press. Posner appreciates journalists who are knowledgeable specialists (clearly he doesn't want to give the media a free pass to employ uneducated and unintelligent journalists) and does not argue that unspecialized reporters be stopped from writing on scientific, social scientific, legal, artistic, or other developments.[50]

Posner's evidence collection by database, though a flawed methodology, produced results that at least ring true: media tend to quote the same public intellectuals over and over again, like a herd instinct; nonacademics are mentioned more than academics; liberals and conservatives get about the same number of citations; media mention academics with little regard to their scholarly standing; academics who have served in government are mentioned more often; and living public intellectuals are mentioned more often than dead ones.

On the other hand, Posner takes his economic analysis to assumptions and conclusions about the news media where it can't go. Believing that the media both know exactly what the public wants, and gives that to the public—no more and no less and ignoring journalism's own practices, processes, ethics and goals—he writes that "media...wouldn't fill up newspaper and magazine space and airtime with the words of intellectuals unless the public wanted to read and hear those words." (Posner would be surprised to know that, although U.S. daily newspapers devote the most space to sports news, sports news is rarely in readers' top ten types of newspaper content when it is divided into fifteen to twenty components.) To be sure, he later concludes that the "media's demand for public intellectuals is derived from the demand of the educated general public for intellectual information *best supplied by public intellectuals* concerning issues of a broadly political character" (emphasis in original). He "suppose[s]" that a "reputable journalist...might...be the greater expert in communicating [economics] experts' findings to the public than an academic economist would" although, for example, a slightly jargony story by an economist probably would serve the audience better than an inaccurate and incomplete television report. Much later, he observes that "as specialization increases, we can expect more and more of the responsibility for translating academic ideas for the general public to devolve on journalists, as specialists in communication"; this may be logical, but he doesn't address whether journalists are willing, in addition to the uncertainty over being able, to assume that responsibility.[51]

Posner also has some confidence—still too much—that the media, on behalf of the public—"pay close attention to the quality of the inputs, that is, of the public intellectuals themselves," later calling it "some screening, but not much" (perhaps because if journalists were educated enough to scrutinize public intellectuals, *they* would or could be public intellectuals). Again, scholarly literature on the sociology of news (deadline pressures, reporter-source relationships, reporters' personal characteristics, reporter-supervisor relationships, and so on) and the imperatives of objectivity, has informed us that sources—not only public intellectuals, and perhaps especially public intellectuals—are quoted by news media for a lot of reasons besides their intrinsic "quality."[52]

Still later, Posner uncharacteristically differentiates between media when he writes that, "Since success in the electronic media is not well correlated with intellectual quality, there is no reason to expect the expansion of the [electronic] media to lead to an increase in either the number or the quality of public intellectuals, though it should increase the aggregate output of the public-intellectual market."[53] But Posner, although having earlier listed a string of intellectual magazines (his book contains no list of intellectual television or radio programs), doesn't follow up on differences between media; mostly in *Public Intellectuals*, all media are just media.

Posner also doesn't understand the media audience very well: he claims that "Newspaper readers...know that reporters write to tight deadlines and therefore cannot be trusted to be highly accurate, and so take journalistic accounts with a grain of salt."[54] In fact, newspaper readers believe that poorly written articles stem from incompetence and/or bias, that journalists should hold a story and make it better rather than rushing into print with a poor one, and—with the exception of claimed political (and sometimes religious) biases—still would like to—and usually do—believe what they read in the newspaper.

Posner demonstrates his ignorance of the mass media most in the following paragraph:

> There is a norm of accountability in journalism that has no counterpart in academics' public-intellectual activities. Newspapers employ ombudsmen, publish corrections and retractions, and publish critical letters from readers. They worry about criticism for being biased and inaccurate, and about the occasional libel suit. They realize that they are in the public eye, that they

are suspect in some quarters, and that they are inviting targets. Reporters report the news of the day, and if their reports are grossly inaccurate this is discovered eventually and they are fired.[55]

The judge apparently didn't know that only about 2 percent of all U.S. daily newspapers employ an ombudsman, that newspaper editors usually resist publishing any more corrections than they absolutely must, and that staffers designated to choose publishable letters to the editor are highly selective and then often literally edit the letters. It also should be noted that journalists—especially in broadcasting—are often rather sloppy and nearly willfully incompetent considering how many people might notice, and that news reporters being fired for being incompetent and/or unethical is a lot less common than someone such as Posner would guess.

Ultimately, Posner's book tells us a lot less about the relationships between public intellectuals, higher education, and the mass media that it could or claims to. One need look no farther than his conclusion than his economics-based conclusion: that the American public doesn't pay much attention to public intellectuals because the quality of their work is relatively poor and is declining. Considering just the fact that the public has access to most goods and services of public intellectuals at little to no cost (public intellectuals' ideas and opinions account for a small percentage of the content of paid media, such as newspapers and magazines, and are widely available free or at low/indirect costs borne by an entire public—through broadcast media, the World Wide Web, public libraries, public education, public lectures, museums, etc.), citizens shouldn't be upset by either the money or time spent on/with public intellectuals. It also can be pointed out that the American public continues to voluntarily consume large quantities of other low-quality raw data, other information, formal journalism, arts, and entertainment, some of which they pay for and some of which is free.

Again, Posner's economic analysis of public intellectuals has been widely criticized in book reviews and elsewhere. Suffice it to say here that ideas in the mass media in a fuller historical and cultural context are critical to understanding the twentieth and twenty-first centuries. Moreover, even though many people who appeared in a study of the twentieth century are still with us, exactly what they knew or believed or said or did in 1950 or 1960 or 1970 or 1980 or even 1990 is not.

In short, we can learn a lot about American anti-intellectualism and Americans' ambivalence toward higher education by examining popular media coverage over a sustained period of time.

Chapter 3
Media Among Society's Institutions: The "Most Prominent and Dynamic Part"

Any study of the U.S. mass media's construction of higher education, intellectuals, and anti-intellectualism must draw on the disparate literatures of critical and cultural analyses of the mass media, higher education, intellectuals, and anti-intellectualism. Extensive research has been conducted on the role of intellectuals in U.S. higher education and the role of universities in the country's intellectual life.[1] However, relatively few scholars—especially in the United States—have examined the nexuses of mass media and intellectuals, mass media and anti-intellectualism, or higher education and anti-intellectualism. Indeed, in this country, terms such as *intellectuals* and *anti-intellectualism* are often used so loosely as to be meaningless for analytical purposes. Conversely, European theorists have been more discerning in their analyses. Thus, it seems appropriate to fashion a theoretical perspective by first reviewing American theory and research findings, and then comparing, contrasting, and linking them with British and

European works when and where possible.

Many critical scholars of mass communication have deconstructed images (verbal and visual, in genres ranging from war news to car advertisements) presented by the media—at the least, challenged the objectivity of journalism, the idea of objectivity itself, and that media fairly cover all news and all groups—of women and ethnic, religious, sexual, and other minorities. Such analysis is usually grounded in the theories and research methods of the German Frankfurt school or British Birmingham school scholars. However, several U.S. scholars have developed critical theories of the mass media that are not Europe-oriented and that take into account concrete political and journalistic processes and practices in the United States. The best known of these is the "Propaganda Model," developed by Edward Herman and Noam Chomsky, and most clearly developed in their 1988 book, *Manufacturing Consent*. To them, the traditional debate over the U.S. mass media's power and content typically could be reduced to two sides: the first, that the media should be less free because they have abused that freedom and now threaten the democracy that facilitated their existence, and the second, that the public should continue to enjoy unregulated media because such media are worth the risk. Chomsky and Herman believe that both sides of that argument incorrectly assume that the mass media are in all ways independent. As Milan Rai summarized, "Chomsky and his colleagues have argued that the mass media in the United States, far from being defiant of ruling circles, are in fact supportive and compliant towards those who hold power."[2]

Chomsky, in his 1989 book *Necessary Illusions: Thought Control in Democratic Societies*, added that the modern mass media perform the "societal purpose served by state education as conceived by James Mill in the early days of the establishment of this system: to 'train the minds of the people to a virtuous attachment to their government,' and to the arrangements of the social, economic, and political order more generally [including] protecting privilege from the threat of public understanding and participation." As Rai further explained, "In other words, the purpose of the media is to cultivate public stupidity and conformity, in order to protect the powerful from interference by the lower orders. This is an 'unsettling' interpretation of the media, no doubt, but argument and evidence are offered in support, and there is a case to answer."[3]

Hanno Hardt, one of the more prolific (along with Robert McChesney and the late Herbert Schiller) U.S. critical scholars of the mass media, neatly summarized a litany of hard issues in the critical analysis of today's U.S. mass media. Hardt charged that rather than skeptically and analytically covering politics, media workers increasingly are simply "fascinat[ed] with social and political power." At the same time, media also are increasingly responsive to the capitalist economy (resulting in an emphasis on profits, and thus, marketing), as most major media companies are publicly owned. One result, Hardt agreed with *Washington Post* media critic Howard Kurtz, is that, "Controversial [story] ideas are pasteurized and homogenized until most of the flavor has been drained"; in an effort to keep from alienating a single reader, the newspaper industry is instead boring them all. Moreover, Hardt charged, even initiatives credited with improving traditional journalism that is valuable to citizens, such as civic journalism (using newspaper pages and staffers explicitly to help their public become more involved and influential in politics and community affairs, especially identified problems), are controlled by corporate-minded foundations and pre-empt more fundamental debates about journalism.

Hardt even accused journalism educators of having become extensions of media corporations through facilitating recruiting and by making their teaching increasingly responsive to corporate demands. Rather than naively agreeing with utopian views of new technology, Hardt asserted, journalists and journalism educators must concentrate on the core issue of serving the general public by, in part, continuing to believe in the "relationship between knowledge and conduct." Rather than simply teaching traditional "skills courses" (news writing, news editing, advertising copywriting, and so on), Hardt recommended "sharing practical knowledge [which] refers to understanding the cultural and historical conditions of labor, the economic consequences of commercial practices, the material circumstances of newswork, and their impact on the ideological framework of journalism."[4]

Based on the writings of Chomsky, Todd Gitlin, Hardt (1992), Hardt and Brennen (1995), and others, the question is raised as to whether U.S. media coverage of higher education, intellectuals, and anti-intellectualism increasingly reflects economic pressures for corporate relationships and vertical integration—both in mass media and higher education—one result of which might be less controversial, less interesting stories.

The overwhelming importance of the mass media and the education system (rather than focusing entirely on politics, economics, religion and/or the family), and the relationships between the two institutions has long been recognized in Europe. The Italian Antonio Gramsci, who notably elaborated the concept of "hegemony"—the dominance of society by one group or class through the unspoken consent of other groups—believed that the "press" and the education system are the only two institutions in modern societies capable of favorably transforming the cultures and politics within which they operate. His writings discussed the importance of the press and the involvement of intellectuals with it (including detailed histories of several intellectuals' media involvement). Gramsci posited the press audience (i.e., readers) as ideological elements and/or economic elements and insisted that media cover "all intellectual centres and movements."[5] He even predicted that journalism schools would become increasingly common, believing that editors should set up de facto in-house journalism schools that would provide working-class journalists with politically based journalism training.

Although Gramsci's descriptions of the press were specific to post—World War I politics (especially with respect to the possibility of a communist revolution in Italy) and the technology of the time, he well understood the potential impact of mass media in western democracies. Himself a former journalist in Turin, Italy, he wrote that within the "dominant class," the press is the "most prominent and dynamic part." He hoped that a communist press would articulate the interests of a mass democratic movement and reach a broadly based readership. Subsequent cultural theorists—such as Simon and Mouffe—have retreated from Gramsci's arguments about how much control media have or can have over a society,[6] but they still believe that the media are a "battleground fought over by opposed social forces." Thus the media can be a site for struggle over the definition of intellectuals, higher education, anti-intellectualism, and knowledge among groups that have interests in how such concepts and practices are defined. Gramsci's writings also prompt questions such as what intellectuals' role is in today's mass media, and whether and how media cover "all intellectual centres and movements." However, Gramsci wrote when it was still possible for individual editors to be independent, and when privately owned newspapers and magazines could be more easily in-

fluenced by readers and/or their own staffs. Michel Foucault's recommendation that individuals throughout society be agents of resistance and institutional change was more relevant for the latter part of
the twentieth century, when corporate consolidation of media and ad-
vertiser demands, rather than readers' or employees' preferences, increasingly drove media content.

Steven Best and Douglas Kellner have charged the late French
theorist Michel Foucault with a "neglect" of "media power." They
summarized (without necessarily endorsing) Baudrillard's argument
that Foucault simultaneously underestimated media's historical significance by failing to consider mass media in his work, and indirectly
overestimated media's role by continuing to locate power in institutions, one of which is the media (Baudrillard believes that power is so
abstract that it no longer is located in any institution). Nonetheless,
Best and Kellner and other scholars do not dismiss Foucault from
relevance or usefulness in media studies. The overarching theme of
most of Foucault's work was that the Enlightenment produced highly
regulated "disciplinary" societies and binary divisions that "brand"
deviants, and these charges can be "tested" within media studies research. For example, to gather evidence of Foucault's theories from
the mass media (similar to the evidence found in Foucault's histories
of prisons, mental illness, and sexuality), the media's complicity with
government, social scientists, and medical scientists might be linked
with the media's historical quest to be "objective," and their reliance
on official and credentialed sources. Media also tend to accept and
publicize such institutionalized dualisms or dichotomies as "mental
illness" and mental health, function and dysfunctional, and so on,
thus complying with the regulatory prerogatives of other powerful
institutions.[7]

Evidence from the mass media for Foucault's theory of power
and knowledge (primarily, that powerful individuals and organizations
produce and define what is and is not knowledge, such as in medicine,
psychiatry/psychology, other sciences, even among professors), and
how the power/knowledge axis is directly and indirectly responsible
for regulation and branding, could be organized along the lines of the
"Circuit of Culture" model advanced by Paul Du Gay, Stuart Hall,
Janes, Mackay, and Negus (1997) in their *Doing Cultural Studies: The
Story of the Sony Walkman*. For our purposes, the moment—the essential, constituent component—of the text would answer the question

of how various "deviants" have been represented in the media. More specifically, the relevant question is how the media (re)produce and/or resist concepts of intellectuals, anti-intellectualism, and higher education—specifically, of course, whether intellectuals and/or "anti-intellectuals" are portrayed as deviants. A second question based on the culture circuit would ask what kind of identities are developed for such "deviants" and what roles media content plays in their construction. Thus, this book may question whether mass media construct—that is, create through the way they arrange ideas or terms—intellectuals or anti-intellectuals as the norm, what images intellectuals or anti-intellectualism citizens obtain, and how citizens obtain them, as a result of media text constructions. A third question could focus attention on how representations and identities further regulation in a society; in other words, what is the overall impact of the ways in which media texts represent intellectuals, anti-intellectualism, higher education, and so forth? A fourth question would concern the production of media content: What do media workers know about the supposedly deviant individuals or organizations, and how does this knowledge, anticipated reader/viewer reaction to certain kinds of representations, personal prejudices, and so on, enter into the ways in which supposedly deviant individuals or organizations are represented by the mass media? Such a production question is outside this book's scope, but media workers' knowledge of, and attitudes toward, intellectuals, higher education, anti-intellectualism and so on, merit study in the future. A fifth question to be answered is how readers or viewers receive the media's representations of intellectual and anti-intellectual individuals or organizations, whether the representations are accepted, rejected or both, and whether such a negotiation process is active or mostly passive. Audience-related questions also are outside this book's purview, but how audience members negotiate media representations of intellectuals, higher education, anti-intellectualism and so on, might well be studied in the future.

David J. Sholle in 1988 argued at length that Foucault's theories also offer the opportunity for critical media studies scholars to move away from theories of ideology and toward theories of power/knowledge. For example, he concluded, television content, in excluding some types of information and ideas and including others (of course television is not the only mass medium that makes such choices) collectively "constitut[es] the domain of that which is discussible."

Sholle observed that Foucault and others have "redefine[d] a process of defining the semantic field, not as the imposition of a set of ideas"—a description similar to framing theory. (Framing theory generally refers to selecting some aspects of perceived reality and making them more prominent or conspicuous, with the result that, as Robert Entman writes, "a particular problem definition, causal interpretation, moral evaluation, and/or treatment recommendation" is "promote[d]".) This combination of gatekeeping (editors' selection of certain news and opinions), agenda-setting (primarily, media influence on what subjects the public, politicians, and media workers are thinking about) and ideology construction (such as implicit endorsements of capitalism, democracy or Judeo-Christian religions) means that not only information or opinions contrary to the political or economic status quo, but "deviant" content of any kind, is at issue. For the purpose of this investigation then, Sholle—based on Foucault's writings—would suggest examining conflicting constructions of intellectuals, higher education, anti-intellectualism, and so on in media content, and omissions of certain philosophies, opinions, sources, and discourses (language as used in specific social contexts) from coverage. However, Foucault's attention to mass media was too narrow to definitively suggest other lines of inquiry, despite efforts to develop a media studies research agenda based on his theories.[8] A fuller picture of possibilities may be gained by reviewing the writings of the theorist with whom Foucault's views are most often juxtaposed.

Jürgen Habermas, like Gramsci, believes that a country's education and media systems are the only two institutions capable of facilitating its transformation. Furthermore, unlike Foucault, Habermas has written extensively about media. For example, in his essay, "On the concept of public opinion," Habermas asserted that media are the link between public opinion and quasi-public opinion, the latter of which terms Habermas defines as formal opinions that are released as "announcements, proclamations, declarations, and speeches."[9] Thus, a question related to this book is whether the media publish or broadcast such "formal opinions" regarding higher education, intellectuals or anti-intellectualism, and when they do, whether they resist (by criticizing those opinions or publishing opposing opinions from other sources) or endorse such "formal opinions."

Habermas has invoked the media most often, such as in a 1989 book, when waxing romantic about a "public sphere" in which conversation and reading were one continuous loop.[10] He is still optimistic about the media's potential for serving the public good, envisioning their very existence as a sort of virtual coffeehouse, where each "customer" is allowed to make his or her own interpretations of text. Conversely, Habermas also has pointed out that the press cannot fulfill its potential for public-opinion formation if not independent from "political and functional elites." Therefore, a question related to this book would be whether media content reflects or resists pressures from such elites in the ways in which it covers intellectuals, higher education, anti-intellectualism, and so on. In addition, Habermas may already have answered this question for himself, as he wrote that the "horizontal and vertical expansion of the educational system does make it easier to exercise social control through the mass media"—suggesting that, even with his emphasis on individuals' abilities to resist/negotiate media content, he is less than absolutely optimistic.[11]

In sum, Habermas has offered a historical analysis of the public sphere (essentially, the domain of voluntary conversation oriented toward pragmatic goals and agreements), including media's role in it, the possibility of preserving/reconstructing that sphere today, and an analysis of the individual media consumer who interacts in various ways for various reasons with both media and the education system (which today are increasingly linked). However, Habermas seems overly optimistic about the future of public spheres, and by orienting his writing most closely with European nations and cultures, fails to provide a concrete analysis of an education/mass media matrix in today's United States.

Cultural and Critical Theories of Higher Education

Critical and cultural scholars generally believe in the important cultural roles of both media and education and the possibilities they hold, separately and together, for transforming society. Therefore, it alone is telling that the field of critical theory-based scholarship in education made a late and limited start in the United States. As noted scholar William G. Tierney wrote in 1991, "higher education literature includes only a dearth of studies that have employed critical methodologies and frameworks." That situation has improved a little in the years since; one important book (by Len Barton and Stephen

Walker) had been published in 1983, but Tierney's 1991 book was followed by many others.[12] In introducing critical analysis of education, Tierney wrote that,

> With regard to education, critical theorists point out that the purpose of schooling is not merely to provide jobs or to create good citizens. Indeed, one central arena where the conditions for empowerment can be constructed is within educational institutions. As Giroux notes, critical theory,
>
> > does not equate the struggle for public life with the narrowly defined interests of one group, irrespective of the nature of their power or the legitimacy of their interest. This is a pedagogy which links schooling to the imperatives of democracy, views teachers as transformative intellectuals, and makes the notion of democratic difference central (Giroux, 1989, p. 6).

Here critical theory in U.S. higher education serves as a counterweight to anti-intellectualism. Higher education should offer more than just a better chance at a better job, and thus Tierney and Henry A. Giroux would adamantly oppose unreflective instrumentalism in higher education. Higher education should be empowering, and so they would oppose the intellectually oppressive nature of religious anti-rationalism. Furthermore, by trying to strengthen higher education, rather than opposing it, Tierney and Giroux are ostensibly not populist anti-elitists, either.

However, U.S. critical analysis of higher education is limited, if its late introduction and limited impact weren't enough, by two other problems. Despite Giroux's insistence that this research is not about group interests, and that it idealizes teachers as transformative intellectuals, in practice almost all such writing has had as a primary goal making the curriculum more relevant to minority group members and more useful to part-time and non-traditional students.[13] While these reforms may have been necessary, much of this literature (in the name of "democratizing" education) appears to be anti-intellectual (instrumentalist and/or anti-elitist) according to Hofstadter's definition and Rigney's theory.[14] A second major shortcoming is that this school of thought has assigned no role to U.S. mass media in the development of current beliefs or knowledge about higher education or intellectuals, nor any role to the U.S. mass media as a potential partner in bringing about desired reforms. In fact, one searches in vain through volumes of critical theory-based literature on U.S. higher education for more than a passing reference to any mass medium. This fact is astounding, considering that John Dewey, the most influential figure in education in the United States, has "ma[de] mass communication (even above power-sharing) the basis for the modern social order."[15] Indeed, one would be hard pressed to argue that the mass media are less influential now than they were when Dewey died in 1951.

Drawing on Gramsci and Habermas, early practitioners of British cultural studies also identified education, especially secondary and higher education, as a key site for intervention that ideally would result in reform-producing changes in education policy and society at large. Paul Willis's 1977 book, *Learning to Labour: How Working Class Kids Get Working Class Jobs* (London: Saxon House), is a landmark book in cultural studies that examines how working class youths have been socialized and rejected while in school and what happens to them when they leave school. The important *Unpopular Education: Schooling and Social Democracy in England Since 1944*, by Steve Baron and the Education Group, Centre for Contemporary Cultural Studies (London: Hutchinson, and the Centre for Contemporary Cultural Studies, University of Birmingham, 1981) is another such work. The education emphasis emerges from the base of cultural studies in practice embodied by political and other practical roles for its researchers and partnerships between researchers and their "subjects." As Nicholas Garnham has explained, intellectuals have a political role in "emancipatory projects that aid progressive and combat reactionary mobilization."

Like the British and European critical cultural scholars, the American James W. Carey also believes that higher education and mass media are the keys to transforming society. In 1992, he wrote:

> while the making and contesting of meaning suffuses social space, two particularly important sites of struggle are the media of communication and the educational system—independent but deeply interrelated agencies for the production, not just the transmission, of culture, as any editor or critic ought to know from experience.

Carey also has been a harsh critic of U.S. higher education. Starting with his doctoral dissertation in the early 1960s, he has complained about what he believes to be the artificial boundaries erected around academic disciplines and theories. Carey has consistently advocated and practiced interdisciplinary scholarship now closely identified with him as American cultural studies. More recently, in "Salvation by Machines: Can Technology Save Education?" (1997), he has taken issue with technology utopians, countering the idea that computers will facilitate more democratic societies and opposing the (over)emphasis on teaching "computer literacy."

Fiercely independent, the intellectual Carey fights anti-intellectualism, although he has used the term rarely if ever. He has accused faculty generally of being silent in the face of efforts by U.S. corporations to influence the curriculum, let alone research, concluding that pressures by corporations, students, and parents have resulted in universities becoming utilitarian and economically driven: "The independence of the university is now pretty much gone, and where it remains is largely a pretense." Worse, Carey has accused faculty themselves of being anti-intellectual; their political squabbles now are anti-intellectual rather than intellectual: "Universities...are not pleasant places to be these days, filled with a lot of ill-natured arguments and uncivil habits that are destroying the possibilities of public life." Moreover, "We have tolerated academic practices that actively contribute to the ignorance of students and fail the most decent expectations of the public," he added, and, finally, "The decadence besetting the academy is not political correctness but a genuine lack of interest in education."[16]

European Critical Higher Education Theory

Gramsci was sharply critical of Italian universities and, not being confident that they would reform, detailed how and why typical workers could benefit from primary, secondary, and continuing education. Habermas outlined what higher education typically accomplishes and what it could or should accomplish in modern nations; in so doing, he took to task both educators who are not meeting their professional and moral responsibilities, and other institutions in society that have been allowed too much influence over higher education. Foucault, although seemingly resigned to most aspects of modern higher education, told professors and students to be aware of the power relationship between them, suggested that professional education be better grounded in traditional social science and humanities disciplines, and discussed how higher education is segregated from society.

Gramsci, of all critical theorists, best explored the relationships between intellectuals, higher education, and the mass media. As he wrote cynically, "Every relationship of hegemony is necessarily an educational relationship."[17] When, in 1914, Gramsci began writing about politics and education, Italy boasted some of Europe's oldest universities, but did not yet offer universal primary and secondary education. With the state not assumed nor expected to be the sole provider of education, a void existed that potentially could have been filled by churches, unions, the press, other businesses, or other institutions. Labor unions' "Popular Universities," however, did not impress Gramsci, because they taught primarily "esoteric information." He argued that it fell to higher education to secure "the attainment of a higher awareness, through which we can come to understand our value and place within history, our proper function in life, our rights and duties." Gramsci supported traditional education that helped students learn to think on their own, because they would not be engulfed in an "inorganic, pretentious and disorienting culture." Without efforts to prevent it, such a culture is likely due to formal education's "badly assorted reading...lectures having more sparkle than substance...conversations and discussions without any meaning." Later, Gramsci added, "University discipline must be considered as a type of discipline for intellectual training capable of bearing fruit in institutions that are not 'university' ones in the official sense." For example, he believed that learning ancient languages (Latin, Greek) has a legitimate intellectual purpose that generally does not reproduce class-based ideology; in fact, he wrote that the replacement of Latin and Greek with professional and vocational education is a "progressive degeneration," explaining:

> The most paradoxical aspect of it all is that this new type of school appears and is advocated as being democratic, while in fact it is destined not merely to perpetuate social differences but to crystallize them in Chinese complexities.[18]

Although the first complete English translation of Gramsci's major work, *Selections from the Prison Notebooks of Antonio Gramsci*, was not published until 1971, and companion volumes not until 1994 and 1995, by the 1980s scholars of the "new sociology of education" began drawing on Gramsci's work to flesh out the role of ideology in (primarily public) schools. The result was a theory of "re-production" that holds that schools are modern society's primary site of reproducing ideologies, and attempts were made to explain how "school knowledge maintained existing and inequitable power arrangements." Early work in this area concentrated primarily on class relations. But reproduction theory "has rarely been extended to post-secondary education" and, in addition, formal education's "relations to civil society are rarely explored."[19] Gramsci's work is no less relevant for these limitations in the literature so far; the key question that Gramsci-inspired reproduction theorists ask—"why, despite consistent efforts at reform, do schools not provide the equal educational opportunity that we expect of them?"—is still an issue at all levels of education. In the United States, an even more basic question is whether "efforts at reform" have even moved in the proper direction. For example, U.S. higher education has undergone tremendous change in the last fifty years (see Introduction), but other than the facts that larger numbers and percentages of Americans start and finish college, and a larger body of pure and applied knowledge exists to be studied, is higher education today "better" than it was fifty years ago?

Gramsci also stood on its head the U.S. debate over teaching a canon of literature; rather than American concerns that a traditional liberal arts curriculum is elitist and being a business major isn't, Gramsci believed just the opposite: professional, technical, and vocational training reflects and exacerbates class and other differences among students.

In contrast to Gramsci's model of all citizens as "specific intellectuals," Habermas holds a more traditional view (not unlike Voltaire, or Hofstadter) of an elite group of intellectuals leading society toward reform and scientific progress, with higher education providing the institutional foundation for intellectuals' work. He wrote, "Mass education systems are perhaps the only organised means, apart from the 'culture industry' and its mass media, on a sufficient scale to reach potential addressees of critique...[B]oth educational academics and teachers possess a degree of institutionalized insulation from social norms and sanctions governing expression of opinion in other contexts in life."[20]

For Habermas, education and intellectualism lie at the very heart of critical theories of society and the human emancipation that both can facilitate and describe: humans are the learning species. Societal reform depends in part on "an increase in the learning power of society." Education is such a central concern that it is a matter of public, not only personal, concern; if the overall learning power of the populace is not increasing, the nation is not moving toward Habermas's state of "emancipation." He believes that both education and news media are part of a "bourgeois public sphere."[21]

Habermas may be too idealistic about a public sphere for policy debate, but he has candidly described much in today's societies as anti-intellectual. He has realized that in our late capitalist economy, it became formal education's "dilemma" to prioritize three sometimes-conflicting goals: teach knowledge and skills that are socially and economically useful; help form democratic citizens; and teach truth. The final goal is the most problematic: while faculty may question what truth is, how much of it they know, how much they can or even should teach, Habermas also understands that young people are not simply empty vessels: "There remains the question of truth, especially at the level of the students' own experience." In other words, students can easily dispute, for example, the typical American economist's claim that an individual consumer, or even consumers as a group, is rational. Complementing his three-pronged "dilemma," Habermas also has listed three functions that have been assigned to or assumed by universities: to socialize students for careers; to transmit, interpret, and develop society's cultural tradition; and to help form students' political consciousness.[22] Of these three functions, the first is strictly anti-intellectual and the second and third may or may not be, depending on universities' cultural and political (or even religious) orientations.

Not surprisingly, Habermas believes that education shifts toward more technical and "relevant" learning simultaneously with capitalist elites' push to "depoliticize" the humanities and social sciences, calling for a return to "traditional" curricula. In other words, anti-intellectual conservatives wrap themselves in a flag of "classical" or "traditional" curriculum because students and professors presumably will be largely unable to use it as ammunition in fighting today's status quo. Finally, Habermas claimed, neoconservatives attempt to revive education institutions as sites for reproducing historical values of nation, families, and morality, thus largely rejecting social science, the critical exploration of values, and "personal development" elements in the curriculum. It is in part for these reasons that Habermas has defined the "crisis of modernity" as a "crisis of learning"—a crisis of learning that is obviously anti-intellectual.[23]

Habermas believes anti-intellectualism must be resisted on an ongoing basis. Late capitalism experiences cyclical crises in its perceived legitimacy due to conflicts between what late capitalism promises and what it delivers—conflicts caused both by shortfalls in societal benefits (such as dramatically increased free trade's lack of promised relief for worldwide poverty) and unexpected, negative results (such as speculative investment leading to stock market crashes in 1929, 1987, and 2001, or periodic deep recessions, a polite term for depressions). For example, Habermas would predict that such legitimation crises would be blamed on "subversive intellectuals" (such as environmentalists who opposed energy deregulation prior to Enron's manipulation of California energy prices in 2000, which was made possible by conservatives' successful demand that the California energy market be regulated) rather than the cyclical nature of capitalism (which produces inflation and recessions) or the public's own unrealistic expectations (which produced the overheated stock markets of the mid-1980s and especially the late 1990s). It is in these cyclical legitimation crises that Habermas has hoped to intervene with facts and with ethical values—disseminated through either "mass education systems" or the mass media.[24] In examining media coverage of higher education, we should therefore ask if intellectuals are portrayed negatively largely for simply being bearers of bad news.

Habermas also wrote about how formal education can be utilized to increase the "learning power of society." Traditionally, students have been treated as objects, not as subjects, he wrote, and they must be recognized as the latter if they are to develop those skills currently thought to comprise "critical thinking." First, schools must eliminate authoritative, manipulative teaching practices, and strive for a balance between "well-adjusted," status quo—oriented students and "rebels without recognition," who contradict the status quo. Habermas also has encouraged students to engage in critical thinking from their first day studying a subject, thus disagreeing with fellow scholars who argue that only experts should be critics; on the contrary, he believes experts rarely are critics: "Uncritical mastery of existing disciplines offers no hope that learners will suddenly undergo a change in attitude, becoming skeptical and analytical about their ideas, or they will suddenly be able to criticize after having hidden this virtue away for so long."[25] In media coverage of intellectuals and higher education, therefore, is critical thinking—one of the primary values of intellectuals to society—valued or devalued?

In sum, Habermas believes that intellectuals inside and outside academia, and professors and their institutions, in the twentieth century were presented with extraordinary opportunities for teaching, learning, and researching in ways beneficial to society and culture, and free from oppressive demands of the economy and government. Overall, he would like to be idealistic about the possibilities and motivations of higher education and intellectuals, but he believes these opportunities are being lost because of increasing pressures from corporations and governments that many scholars are either unwilling or unable to resist. Again, Foucault has provided additional insight into power relationships within the academy, and potential sites of resistance.

If Habermas's theories on intellectuals and knowledge are in the tradition of Voltaire, then Foucault's are in the tradition of Rousseau. Rousseau's overall opinion about intellectuals was that they were (are) misinformed experts who construct cultural and social hierarchies based upon the categories, opinions, and expertise of others. For Michel Foucault, a man who spent his entire life as a student or professor, the primary dynamic in higher education—a power relationship between professor and student—interferes with teaching and learning. Foucault preferred to view himself as a craftsman, and his students as apprentices.[26]

Foucault cynically wrote that the teaching of an individual fact in a school or university means that "piece of knowledge has the right to exercise power." However, despite students' increasing knowledge presumably moving them toward a status quo—oriented elite, Foucault perceived students—as long as they were in school—as temporarily "outside of society." In fact, he believed that students are pushed so far to the political and economic margins as to be neutralized: "rendered safe, ineffective, socially and politically ineffective," later to be again included, if not reabsorbed, by the status quo society.[27]

Foucault, like Jacoby and Said, believed that professors are generally co-opted by elites and, not coincidentally, that the number of "free-floating scholars" in Western countries has declined since the nineteenth century, as an increasing percentage moved to universities or corporate and government laboratories. One could ask here whether media texts suggest that universities are refuges for former, or persons who otherwise would be, "free-floating scholars." Foucault also wrote that the rise in the number and types of medical and scholarly experts—and the amount of knowledge they possessed—meant not only more control over the masses, but also the means by which theorists and supposed reformers built their own social position; ultimately, a sovereign intellectual expert of the modern period (such as Darwin, Freud or Einstein, among numerous earlier and later examples) displaced earlier sovereign powers—especially monarchs and clergy. Foucault's critiques exposed and provoked thought about myriad discourses and, on campuses, he wanted professors and students to understand the heretofore unarticulated power-oriented relationship they had with each other and to act upon that knowledge. Believing that education institutions are both a possible and necessary site of resistance to society's status quo, he also believed that students should resist the claims of science and social science by challenging their professors.

Finally, one must be aware that Foucault was an intellectual who, more than most intellectuals, also was fervently committed to radical political action outside the classroom and the academic conference. He complained as well that the university curriculum is not related to today's problems and admitted that even his own teaching was obsolete and academic—not "erotic." Worst of all, to Foucault, were the narrowly technical, professional programs (among which he surely would have included journalism/mass communication) that, in his view, should be grounded in traditional scholarly disciplines.[28]

Cultural and Critical Theories of Intellectuals

As Edward Said summarized it, one of the twentieth century's most pressing theoretical questions for education policy and other public policy has been, "Are intellectuals a very large or an extremely small and highly selective group of people?"[29]—which in turn requires a definition of the term, "intellectuals." Gramsci, Foucault, and others have met the second challenge with differing definitions, but all have had in common the idea of two types: a traditional or ideal type, and a modern type in business, law, science, education, and/or mass media distinguished primarily by advanced education. Thus the answer to Said's question would be "both."

Said has pointed out that Gramsci was among the first, and eventually the most influential, to point out that intellectuals (not social classes) are "pivotal" to the workings of modern society. (In his early writings, Gramsci tended to claim that intellectuals were necessary for a successful socialist movement and intellectuals were useless in a non-socialist society, but later discussed roles in society for what he believed were two major types.) Said reported this approvingly, explaining, "There has been no major revolution in modern history without intellectuals; conversely there has been no major counter-revolutionary movement without intellectuals."[30]

Gramsci distinguished among intellectuals and also between intellectuals and intellectualism, the latter of which terms he criticized as the idea of "culture as encyclopedic knowledge," resulting in "misfits" who are "crammed with empirical data, with crude, unconnected facts" feeling superior to others. While attacking false intellectuals, he was cautiously idealistic about what true intellectuals could do in a socialist society, being concerned particularly about intellectuals (especially "geniuses") and masses being distanced from each other in many ways. As noted previously, Gramsci theorized two types of intellectuals: traditional (sometimes "great") intellectuals: teachers, priests, and administrators (who he believed perform the same functions across generations and across class lines); and organic (sometimes "pure") intellectuals, who come from any social group and are actively involved in business, politics, and other spheres of society, on behalf of their social group. As Said wrote, Gramsci proposed the latter as "directly connected to classes or enterprises that used intellectuals to organize interests, gain more power, get more control." Gramsci was most interested in organic intellectuals originating in the working class, although he also acknowledged many exceptions.[31]

Gramsci, writing for Italian workers in the period between the world wars, may seem idealistic about organic intellectuals. Even so, he was ahead of his time in, for all practical purposes, predicting the explosion in the number of organic intellectuals, at least in terms of the kinds of professions and crafts they would practice—if less so regarding their political activism. As Said said, contrasting Gramsci's intellectuals with Julien Benda's "crusty, eloquent, fantastically courageous and angry individual":

Gramsci's social analysis of the intellectual as a person who fulfills a particular set of functions in the society is much closer to the reality than anything Benda gives us, particularly in the late twentieth century when so many new professions—*broadcasters, academic professionals*, computer analysts, sports and *media lawyers*, management consultants, policy experts, government advisers, authors of specialized market reports, and indeed the *whole field of modern mass journalism itself*—have vindicated Gramsci's vision [emphasis added].

Gramsci also theorized that "all men are intellectuals, one could therefore say: but not all men have in society the function of intellectuals."[32] Gramsci thus suggests the question of whether, over time, the definition of "intellectual" is broadened to become more inclusive.

As Stanley Aronowitz and Henry A. Giroux pointed out in responding to Allan Bloom's *The Closing of the American Mind*, and as Nancy Warehime understood in analyzing responses to Bloom, Gramsci is important as well because his theories about intellectuals are relevant to both the Left and the Right. In a conclusion suggestive of Gramsci, Aronowitz noted that the conservative, elitist Bloom and his political opposite, Russell Jacoby (*The Last Intellectuals*, 2000/1987), experienced similar "impulses"—"they share the traditional intellectual's hostility to the twentieth century, its cultural and social pluralism, and its loss of tradition." Bloom and Jacoby both believed intellectuals should be countercultural, and yet exercise some authority in public or political life. Both (Bloom explicitly, Jacoby implicitly) were nostalgic for a time "when at least the minority was able to search for the Good and the True unhampered by the temporal considerations such as making a living," and complained of intellectual and moral decay caused by "mass culture, bureaucratically wrought degraded institutions, and anti-intellectualism."[33]

Habermas's mixture of realism and idealism about higher education also has been evident in his writings on intellectuals: idealism about how intellectuals should act, realistic about how intellectuals are marginalized in a late capitalist economy. In a market driven state, he asserted, democratic processes move toward private negotiations, and intellectuals begin to be discredited as unproductive in society; eventually, "intellectuals...ha[ve] been culturally neutralised by the impact of a triumphant positivism." Habermas concluded that today, the social sciences, "especially legal positivism, neoclassical economics, and recent political theory," are proof that bourgeois consciousness has been "thoroughly emptied of binding normative concerns."[34] In other words, he believes that intellectuals need not be, and in fact should not be, relentlessly rational—at least not at the expense of pursuing democracy and other ethical values. (In studying media coverage of higher education, therefore, we might well ask whether academics and/or intellectuals are portrayed as unproductive, rational to a fault and/or amoral.) Habermas rarely has used the word "intellectual" as a noun, but has advocated "experts" reconstructing democracy through "communicative action," critiquing modernity without advocating postmodernism, and ultimately leading the preservation of modernity.

Although Habermas and Foucault usually disagreed (Habermas the optimist and Foucault the cynic as regards the Enlightenment), they largely agreed about the plight of traditional/universal intellectuals. Foucault, believing as already noted that the new social and medical sciences of man have been used as much or more to exercise power as to liberate, also believed that intellectuals have been limited to working in nursing, hospitals, asylums, laboratories, universities, familial and sexual relations. He caustically wrote that, "If intellectuals in general are to have a function, if critical thought itself has a function,... it is precisely to accept this sort of spiral, this sort of revolving door of rationality that refers us to its necessity, to its indispensability, and at the same time, to its intrinsic dangers."[35]

Foucault also theorized two types of intellectuals: the universal intellectual, who is interested, knowledgeable, and active in a variety of social, cultural, political activities and subjects; and the specific intellectual, who is narrowly trained but whose expertise secures him or her a powerful role in society. Foucault thought both types should have their work published in the mass media (lacking that, he probably would have settled for intellectuals' work being reported). Importantly in studying the United States, Hofstadter's intellectual is similar to Foucault's universal intellectual as well as to Habermas's and Said's ideal types.

Foucault believed that universal intellectuals (Said noted that Foucault considered Jean-Paul Sartre an example) are a dying if not extinct class, and that the universal intellectual has had his/her place taken by specific intellectuals. These latter intellectuals' "specificity" is threefold: they have a class position (as petty bourgeois serving capitalism), each one has particular conditions of his or her life and work, and all interact with modern societies' "politics of truth." For Foucault, the political problem for intellectuals is not science nor even ideology, but how to interact with the truth and what kind of philosophies to hold, and decisions to make, with regard to power.[36] Foucault lamented, contrary to what Gramsci predicted, an absence of universal intellectuals because of the status quo's need for, and ability to enforce, hegemony. (He commented that critics are tolerated only because of a "simple relaxation on the part of the system which, aware of its own solidity, can afford to accept at its margins something which after all poses absolutely no threat to it.") But both despite and because of universal intellectuals' absence, Foucault did not oppose specific intellectuals. He understood their value to a society, as long as that society was aware of the knowledge/power axis that specific intellectuals exploit, and attempts by political parties or labor unions to manipulate them were recognized and/or resisted.

Said has conceded that Gramsci's vision of intellectuals, particularly the growth in numbers of his "organic" type and the idea that an intellectual "fulfills a particular set of functions in the society," has been "vindicated." However, he has been more interested in appealing to the responsibilities and possibilities of universal or traditional intellectuals, who he believes are more necessary than ever. Said is impatient that too many scholars are writing about traditional/universal intellectuals and far too few actually acting as such: "In the outpouring of studies about intellectuals there has been far too much defining of the intellectual, and not enough stock taken of the image, the signature, the actual intervention and performance, all of which taken together constitute the very lifeblood of every real intellectual."[37] This book attempts to provide insight into intellectuals' image and performance as perceptions of them are reported in mass media.

To begin with, Said balked at postmodern views of intellectuals (such as suggested by Lyotard, 1984) and sneered that "postmodern intellectuals now prize competence" alone, neither searching for truth nor advocating democracy. Instead, he called for intellectuals who are:

representing, embodying, articulating a message, a view, an attitude, philosophy or opinion to, as well as for, a public...raise[s] embarrassing questions...confronts orthodoxy and dogma (rather than produce them), to be someone who cannot be easily co-opted by governments or corporations...Least of all should an intellectual be there to make his/her audiences feel good: the whole point is to be embarrassing, contrary, even unpleasant... [They are] of a quite peculiar, even abrasive style of life and social performance that is uniquely theirs.

Intellectuals must be on the "same side with the weak and unrepresented," Said wrote (not addressing if and which "embarrassing questions" should be asked about the "weak and unrepresented"), and he implied that their personalities must be compatible with their roles.[38]

The "Western university, certainly in America, still can offer the intellectual a quasi-utopian space in which reflection and research can go on, albeit under new constraints and pressures," Said wrote. Perhaps in response to Jacoby, Said added, "To accuse all intellectuals of being sellouts just because they earn their living working in a university or for a newspaper is a coarse and finally meaningless charge." But he agreed with Jacoby that in the United States, essentially no intellectuals remain outside the academy, and that many professors are not intellectuals. The greatest threat to intellectuals as a class is their "professionalism," by which he meant "thinking of your work as something you do for a living, between the hours of nine and five with one eye on the clock, and another cocked at what is considered to be proper, professional behavior."

Four "pressures" lead to professionalism and "challenge the intellectual's ingenuity and will": specialization; "expertise and the cult of the certified expert"; the "inevitable drift toward power and authority in [professionalism's] adherents, toward the requirements and prerogatives of power, and towards being directly employed by it; and the "system that rewards intellectual conformity, as well as willing participation in goals that have been set not by science but by the government." These pressures and others, Said claimed, result in the "reprehensible" decision of academics to avoid "difficult and principled position[s]" because they do not want to appear too political or too controversial or nonobjective—especially if the scholars are counting on obtaining consulting incomes or honorary degrees or even government appointments. "For an intellectual these habits of mind are corrupting par excellence," he wrote.[39]

Said was well aware of the strength required of his intellectual; for example, to him, intellectuals are more likely today than ever to be accused of being "disloyal" or "unpatriotic"—not only when they analyze a country's politics or economics, but even its corporately created culture. (Said's suspicions were graphically confirmed imme-diately after September 11, 2001.) In fact, Said wrote that many intel-lectuals (by choice or circumstance) are exiles of one sort or an-other—literally or metaphorically. Intellectuals usually are reconciled with their feelings of "restlessness, movement, constantly being unset-tled and unsettling others...The intellectual as exile tends to be happy with the idea of unhappiness." He noted that one "privilege" of be-ing an intellectual in exile is that "of being surprised, of never taking anything for granted, of learning to make do in circumstances of shaky instability that would confound or terrify most people." Said argued that this intellectual in exile is "necessarily ironic, skeptical, even playful—but not cynical." He prompts questions such as how independent, courageous, patriotic, isolated, professional, happy or unhappy, and/or cynical news media coverage of intellectuals and/or academics make them appear.[40]

Although Said did not mention him in his 1994 book, one U.S. scholar who surely filled (and continues to fill) the bill of being an independent intellectual, asking and making uncomfortable state-ments, is Noam Chomsky. It is appropriate that Chomsky's first po-litical essay as an adult was "The Responsibility of Intellectuals," for he has striven during his entire career as one of them to fulfill what he believes are his duties. Including himself, he wrote, "It is the respon-sibility of intellectuals to speak the truth and to expose lies." Much later, he added in *On Power and Ideology* (1987), "I think that what we ought to do is to try to understand the truth about the world. And the truth about the world is usually quite unpleasant." In *Language and Politics* (1988), Chomsky wrote, "Putting it a bit crudely, it is best to tell people that which they least want to hear, to take up the least popular causes, other things being equal." Rejecting the social sciences paradigm (perhaps free market economics in particular), he added, "In some intellectual circles, it is considered naive or foolish to try to be guided by moral principles. About this form of idiocy, I will have nothing to say."[41]

Chomsky believes, of course, that the question of who U.S. intel-lectuals are and how many of them exist depends on how one defines the term. For him, "intellectual" is an ideal entity like Said's. But Chomsky has cautioned that as the word generally is used, it refers to those inculcating or articulating ideas, generally in the service of the university, government or business. So, when Arthur M. Schlesinger,

Jr. in 1992 accused him of betraying the intellectual tradition, Chomsky responded, "That's true, I agree with him. The intellectual tradition is one of servility to power, and if I didn't betray it I'd be ashamed of myself." He complained that U.S. "intellectuals" generally are anti-intellectual in that they are not, and often don't even try, to speak the unpleasant truth. Therefore, Chomsky is not surprised when the U.S. public is anti-intellectual as well, as it is only failing to support anti-intellectual "intellectuals." (Strangely, Judge Richard Posner also is surprised in some ways by the American public's lack of support for intellectuals, if for other reasons.)

Whereas U.S. scholars have been virtually silent on the nexus of higher education, mass communication and intellectuals (one notable exception being Hardt, as noted above), European researchers exploring this three-way relationship have employed critical theories of intellectuals, anti-intellectualism and late capitalism to critique socially transformative possibilities. For example, in 1995 Nicholas Garnham wrote in *Media, Culture & Society* that a "focus on intellectuals enables us to place the system of education in its proper place at the centre of media studies..." He added that such an analysis also "shifts that focus from the consumers, the overwhelmingly dominant concern of recent media and cultural studies, on to the producers, thus striking a more appropriate balance between the autonomy of the reader and authorial intention." This, in turn, Garnham wrote, allows scholars and others to ask who the culture producers are (authors, reporters, playwrights, directors, fine artists, and so on) and what their goals, thoughts, actions, and decisions are, and whether they can be influenced by means other than audience ratings and other feedback. After noting criticisms of intellectuals from Gramsci, Foucault, Bauman, Lyotard, and Rorty, Garnham also grimly explained that,

> This widespread defenestration of the intellectual—at least in her or his amateur mode, the professional intellectuals, of course, proliferated regardless—has four linked results within the media and cultural studies. First, it leaves no ground for critical judgement of media performance on the basis of either truth, beauty or right. Second, while it allows agency to audiences, for what is resistance but agency, it tends, since the notion of authorial intention and its effect is suspect, not to allow it to cultural producers and thus has no interest in studying intellectuals, who they are, what they think, how and why they act. Third, because of the above, it provides no ground for policy intervention in the processes and institutions of cultural production and tends increasingly to evacuate the field of established national represen-

tative democracy in favour of identity politics and communitarianism. Fourth, it leaves little if any room for a pedagogy, whether critical or not.[42]

British and American Cultural Studies and Intellectuals

The United States and Western Europe share the characteristics of late capitalist economies, democratic governments, widely accessible public education, extensive and diverse mass media, and technological sophistication. However, the United States' intellectuals are not identical to those in other countries nor is the environment in which they function; one need only look at the differences between the political interests of U.S. versus German college students, the respect accorded professors in much of Europe, the deference given to time spent in college in much of Europe, and so on. As Said wrote, "to speak of intellectuals today is also to speak specifically of national, religious and even continental variations on the topic, each one of which seems to require separate consideration." Therefore, works such as *Intellectuals, Universities, and the State in Western Modern Societies* (edited by Ron Eyerman, Lennart G. Svensson, and Thomas Soderqvist), which discusses the United States essentially interchangeably with countries such as Sweden or Finland, are problematic.[43]

Despite differences between the United States and other countries, even the United Kingdom, the Briton Raymond Williams has described a historical trajectory for British intellectuals mirroring that of the United States; in short, the definition and role of British intellectuals has been about as problematic as in the United States. Williams wrote that intellectuals—originally associated primarily with faculties for, and processes of, intelligence—were specifically identified in the early nineteenth century, and that during that century the ideal of intelligence clashed with the ideal of democracy because of conservatives' position that the intelligent should govern.[44]

Williams did not and could not trace the entire history of British intellectuals and intellectualism in his *Keywords* book. However, he explained, as Hofstadter had shown and Rigney would theorize for the United States, that in popular usage, the meaning of intellectualism metamorphosed from meaning rationalism to representing coldness and abstractness, and eventually ineffectiveness. Today, Williams claims that in Britain the term "intellectual" is used neutrally, and he has implied that this is perhaps because of public uncertainty about intellectuals generally. Specifically, college professors may now be "specialists" or "professionals," with the word "intellectual" reserved more often for those with wider interests. And it is unclear, at least in Britain, whether intellectuals are automatically considered an elite group (specifically, what is their social status or social function?) and whether they are or must be independent of the culture's established social system.[45]

Cultural and Critical Theories of Anti-Intellectualism

Major critical theorists have not specifically addressed the issue of anti-intellectualism. Perhaps critical theorists—most of whom have been from Germany, France or Italy—have not found anti-intellectualism in their native countries, unlike scholars writing in the United States or the United Kingdom. Perhaps instead critical theorists believe intellectuals are a powerful elite and therefore anti-intellectualism does not exist, or if it does, it is not to be discouraged. This is extremely unlikely. This does not mean, however, that critical theorists have not provided guidance for examining anti-intellectualism above and beyond their writings on intellectuals and education.

Gramsci's work suggests that we ask whether anti-intellectualism is so pervasive in the United States that it now is hegemonic; this book analyzes mass media's role (whether participating in or opposing) in the construction of that hegemony. Gramsci would ask whether anti-intellectualism in U.S. culture is and/or was economically determined, culturally determined, or the product of individual agency. Furthermore, he would ask, assuming anti-intellectualism would be resisted for the society's overall benefit, about the possibility of resistance from the bottom up. Whereas Gramsci would not have opposed top-down reforms that he deemed beneficial, he believed top-down reforms to be at best unlikely to occur and thus societal transformations (originating in the education system and mass media) depended on "organic intellectuals" rooted in the lower classes. In lamenting, at length, the phasing out of Latin and Greek from the Italian schools' curriculum, he wrote in part that "[i]ndividual facts were not learnt for an immediate practical or professional end. The end seemed disinterested, because the real interest was the interior development of personality, the formation of character by means of the absorption and assimilation of the whole cultural past of modern European civilisation."[46]

Habermas observes what Hofstadter and Rigney would call anti-intellectual processes, attitudes or behaviors, even if he does not use the term. Habermas came to believe that scientific advances beginning in the Enlightenment resulted in a decline of critical thought, and that the writings of the Marquis de Sade and Friedrich Nietzsche (who believed the Enlightenment was nihilistic) were reason reduced to instrumentalism; the "bourgeois consciousness has grown cynical" and doesn't respond to normative critique. Further, Habermas has written that the application of instrumental reason to more and more areas of life has included the press, which in turn has become less political. He also believes that distinguishing knowledge that is instrumental from that which is not is important: "The level of development of society is determined by the institutionally permitted learning capacity, in particular by whether theoretical-technical and practical questions are differentiated, and whether discursive learning processes take place." In other words, as Heidi K. Goar would later write, anti-intellectualism limits a society's development.[47]

The three-pronged Rigney theory of U.S. anti-intellectualism already was briefly introduced in the first chapter, but it is helpful here to compare it and contrast it with other scholars' theories of intellectuals, higher education and/or anti-intellectualism to highlight the specific manifestations (mostly, but not entirely, from Hofstadter's book) cited by Rigney's article. Arguably more importantly, Rigney's theory outlines specific manifestations of anti-intellectualism that can be, and have been, used in this book to analyze media content. In his explanation of religious anti-rationalism, Rigney emphasized opposition to, and fear of, reason and the relativism that supposedly results from the employment of reason; discernible opposition to modern science; opposition to, and fear of, traditional sources of authority (primarily religion and government) being challenged or questioned; belief that educational systems should be used for students' social and affective development and to teach students absolute moral or religious codes. In discussing populist anti-elitism, Rigney asserted that its manifestations include: favoring "common people's" interests over those of advantaged classes; support of right-wing populism; support of left-wing populism; the devaluing of book learning, high academic standards, and gifted/talented students; and allegations that intellectuals are snobs. He also pointed out that a "new class" of Americans is simultaneously elitist and "emancipatory." In explaining unreflective instrumentalism, Rigney was primarily concerned with: the suppression of questions about the ends to which increasingly efficient and practical processes (including education, of course) and practices are put; impatience with impracticality, utopianism and theory; narrow vocationalism in schools of all levels, and (relatively recently) the justification of even liberal arts learning based on graduates' supposed "problem-solving" abilities; and the belief that universities can be—even should be—less autonomous.

Goar, although a sociologist like Rigney (and apparently unfamiliar with his work at the time), approached anti-intellectualism from a different angle and with a different purpose, but didn't necessarily disagree with any of Rigney's major points. Relying on selected writings of Hofstadter, Bloom, Chomsky, and several of her own field's giants, Goar argued that anti-intellectual ideologies are ingrained in U.S. social institutions, and our country's intellectuals have little power—especially when compared with corporate executives, religious leaders, politicians, and other prominent figures who are not intellectuals. Further, powerful (status quo) individuals and organizations want to keep it that way and are able to do so; non-intellectual elites continuously work to oppress intellectual elites and thereby solidify their own control. Concludes Goar, seconding Chomsky in his 1989 Bill Moyers interview, about manipulating the public's political (or any other, for that matter) behavior:

> First, control information: this is done through the educational system and the media. Second, control organization among members: this is done by convincing people that those who actively go against the establishment are unpatriotic and dissenters. Third, control actual ability to make decisions or create change: this is done by making the election process nearly irrelevant to the quality and structure of the ruling party and thus create widespread uninterest and apathy.

Goar is "deeply concerned" that Americans do not often discuss intellectuals, intelligence, or even politics—let alone "contemplating the universe," apparently because such persons would be "ridiculed or ostracized." She adds that popular media are a major factor in U.S. anti-intellectualism:

The media influences not only individual tastes and desires, it seems to affect the entire mood of the country. It tells people what they should find important; it shows them how to behave; it informs them what to value and what not to value. What an ideal climate of anti-intellectualism for those in control![48]

Raymond Williams approached the cluster of concepts about intellectuals in his *Keywords*. After writing several paragraphs about intellectuals, intellectualism, and intelligence, Williams wrote only that "anti-intellectualism" in common usage means "oppos(ition) to organized thought and learning." In addition, "intellectual" has a broader meaning than "anti-intellectual"; one can be opposed to anti-intellectualism without being an intellectual, and one who is "anti-intellectual" is opposed to much more than intellectuals. Williams used a cross-referencing system to link the concept of intellectual with related terms: "educated," "elite," "standards," "experiences," "expert," "jargon," "theory" and "rational." Williams's contrasting of "intellectuals" with "experts" was perhaps more stark than even he realized. While "intellectuals" emerged from higher education into politics and the arts, Williams (like Foucault) wrote that the "expert" has replaced the cleric in relationship to laymen. But not all experts, like not all clergy, are perceived by the ordinary person to be intellectuals, and thus persons known as "experts" do not incite the same wrath.

Education researchers also have worked on the issue of intellectuals, intellectualism, and anti-intellectualism among U.S. college students. For example, researchers Burton R. Clark and Martin Trow in 1966 identified four student subcultures, only two of which were intellectually oriented: Vocational, Academic, Collegiate, and Nonconformist. Jonathan R. Warren (1966, 1968), Wilfred A. Pemberton (1963), and Kenneth Keniston (1966) have developed similar student culture typologies.

However, Herant A. Katchadourian and John Boli in 1985 offered the most detailed descriptions of college students' academic orientations and extensive ethnographic data to support them. Their study is directly relevant to the present one because their "Careerism Scale" (on which both "careerist" and "unconnected" students score high) and their "Intellectualism Scale" (on which "intellectual" and "striver" students score high), may be read as an operationalization of student anti-intellectualism and intellectualism, respectively. Career-ism-oriented students generally had the following reasons for attending college: "Specialized preparation for future career; acquisition of marketable skills; preparation for graduate/professional school; establishing professional contacts for the future; future financial security; acquiring technical/preprofessional skills." Characteristics they desired in a major are: "Step toward graduate school; useful in career field; many career options." Characteristics they desired in a career are: "Social status and prestige; job security; high income; public recognition." Intellectualism-oriented students generally had these reasons for attending college: "Learning to think critically; exposure to different viewpoints; general liberal education; developing ethical and moral values; developing artistic and esthetic taste and judgment; making friends; developing skills in dealing with people." Characteristics they desired in a major are: "Interesting subject; intellectually challenging; good teaching; departmental faculty accessible to students." Characteristics they desired in a career are: "Requires creativity and originality; intellectually challenging; service to others; opportunities to work with people." Evidence can be gathered for a book, such as this one, that explicitly or implicitly shows students' motivations toward these various goals.

Mass Media and Higher Education

Little scholarly research has been conducted about popular magazine coverage of U.S. higher education, although newspaper research provides some theoretical guidance. Most research, however, simply reports relative levels of coverage for various higher education topics, staffing levels for education beats, surveys of what readers/viewers want to learn about higher education, and the public relations efforts of colleges/universities. More substantive issues are rarely addressed. Articles in the journalism trade press have not been any more helpful. For example, Carl Sessions Stepp's article, "Higher Examination," in the January/February 2003 *American Journalism Review* concluded, based on anecdotal evidence and interviews with about a dozen reporters and editors, that while higher education reporters are supposedly more "skeptical and probing" than they used to be, news organizations are covering higher education less.

In fact, only three academic research projects (Dzimian, 1953; Neeley, 1994; White, 1996) have analyzed magazine coverage of higher education, with other studies partially focusing on it. Krista E. White's 1996 master's thesis pointed out that *Life* substantially increased its coverage of higher education with the post-Sputnik boom of the early 1960s, and White interpreted *Life*'s stories and photos thusly:

> *Life*'s editors and photographers stressed to the public how much fun college could be, further encouraging attendance, and they did this for women as well as men. For the men, the lure of college came by presenting college women as hot babes. For women, *Life*'s lure was college as a female bonding experience—what I call 'the slumber party aesthetic,' and a hunting ground for the MRS. degree, with lots of eligible young men. Careerism was the main reason for men to attend college—the babes were just an added incentive. Not so for women. In popular parlance, a MRS. degree was the main reason for female college attendance.

In her thesis, White analyzed numerous *Life* photographs and found that most *Life* photos taken on college campuses included both men and women, but the men and women seldom appeared to be together. In a surprising number of photographs, the "women are the focus of the photographic composition. Considering Luce's manifesto and *Life*'s reliance on the Babe shot, this comes as no surprise; a pretty girl should be the focus of the picture wherever possible."[49]

Sabrina M. Neeley (1994) performed a content analysis of coverage—by *Time, Newsweek*, and *U.S. News & World Report*—of student activism between 1961 and 1987. She found that student activism in the 1980s was virtually ignored, despite the involvement of hundreds of thousands of college students in causes such as fighting apartheid, racism, and other discrimination, crime on campus, education budget cuts, and U.S. military involvement abroad. Neeley concluded that news media portrayed such 1980s events as local interest stories, or buried them in the "Education" section, while in earlier years they might have been played as "National" or "National Affairs." She suggested that decisions to downplay or ignore student activism give the public a false impression that students are not politically active, and that news media do not always cover events proportionate to their scope or impact.

Adam D. Dzimian (1953) reported that *Life* magazine seldom

covered education during World War II, but that its coverage dramatically increased after that: from one article in 1944, to fourteen or more per year in 1949–1951; likewise, pages devoted to education coverage went from zero in 1944 to thirty-six or more in 1948–1951.

During the 1940s, 1950s, and 1960s, the U.S. public knew little about higher education, and only a small minority of adults had attended college. As a result, the media may have been particularly influential with the public on education issues during this period. *Fortune* magazine, reporting results of a survey it conducted, concluded in 1949 that, "the subject of higher education is very little understood by the American people generally." A 1960 study by the University of Michigan Survey Research Center came to similar conclusions.[50]

With its launch in 1923, *Time* magazine is given credit for having initiated specialized coverage of education, and both *Time* and *Newsweek* employed full-time education reporters by the late 1930s, followed in suit by other newspapers and magazines in the 1940s and 1950s. In 1954, D. J. Caldwell examined coverage of various topics in the *Ladies' Home Journal* from 1883 to 1953, and she found that most content "question[ed]...educational aims" of women. Although Caldwell drew few conclusions, she did find that coverage was polarized between writers who thought college education not practical enough, and others who thought it too practical.[51]

In 1998, Rochelle E. Stanfield connected magazine and newspaper coverage of college tuition levels and their increases with public perceptions of college tuition. She showed that the news media misrepresented tuition costs and oversimplified the issue of college affordability "primarily by emphasizing the cost at a small number of high-priced schools and by downplaying the ubiquity of financial aid." She was particularly critical of a *Newsweek* cover story, *U.S. News & World Report*'s annual college issue, and a *Philadelphia Inquirer* series (pointing out, for instance, that *Newsweek* didn't even mention community colleges), but also complained about *Time, The Washington Post, USA Today*, and the *Chicago Tribune*. Stanfield concluded:

> The twin journalistic tendency to dramatize a story by emphasizing the shocking elements, such as the price of Ivy League schools, and to overlook or underreport the subtler features, such as college aid and tuition discounting, leaves the public with a skewed perception of the intricacies...
> The emphasis on Ivy League and other high-priced institutions reflects

journalistic elitism, particularly among newsweekly and national daily reporters and editors; and that emphasis causes the public's misperception of costs, documented by polls and focus groups.[52]

An essay by Richard W. Moll and B. Ann Wright in the same 1998 volume, similarly charged that the media, and therefore the public, focus on a "few institutions" while thinking about and covering college tuition levels, and therefore the media—at least when they cover higher education—are elitist. Moll and Wright singled out the *Boston Globe Magazine, Newsweek, The New York Times, The Washington Post*, and *The Los Angeles Times, U.S. News & World Report's Best Colleges* guide, and even the *Chronicle of Higher Education* for complaint, much of which concerned the media confusing selectivity of institutions with the quality of their faculties and/or students (i.e., many excellent colleges have high acceptance rates because only excellent applicants bother to apply to them). (They charged that the media often don't find out, or don't care, about which institutions honestly report the SAT scores of all of their applicants and/or all of their students.)[53]

Also in the same 1998 volume, Don Hossler expressed relief that the impact of college "guidebooks," published by *Money* magazine, *U.S. News & World Report* and others,

on students and institutions is not as pronounced as the popular press might suggest...[M]articulation decisions of only a relatively small proportion of potential college students are strongly influenced by guidebooks and ratings. Similarly, guidebooks and rankings do not exert a strong influence on large numbers of college and university administrators.[54]

Curiously, one of the longest and most well-read statements about higher education by any writer for a major American magazine was William A. Henry III's chapter, "The Museum of Clear Ideas," in his relatively popular third book, *In Defense of Elitism* (1994). Henry, a two-time Pulitzer Prize winner, was a cultural critic, not an education reporter, and it is unknown how much he influenced his fellow *Time* staffers on higher education, or vice versa. Nonetheless, his perspective is worth noting. Henry mostly complained about the "opening the academy" to students who, for academic reasons, would not have been there before World War II and, in his view, shouldn't be in college now. One result, Henry charged, was, "No longer a mark of distinction or proof of achievement, a college education is these days a mere rite of passage, a capstone to adolescent party time"[55]—complete with a steep decline in academic standards. Another result, he argued, was that the "American style of mass higher education" had turned out to be "based on a giant lie." Higher education, Henry said, might be

> to "develop a capacity for critical thinking, enhance an already grounded knowledge of the sciences and world culture, learn further how to deal with other people's diversity of opinion and background, and in general become better citizens. They might go for fun, for friendship, for a network of contacts. They might go for spiritual enrichment or for pragmatic honing of skills.
> In the real world, though, mostly they go to college to make money.[56]

Henry noted, however, that college graduates, who make more money than high school graduates, surely would anyway, since people who are able to be college graduates have characteristics that would make them more successful without going to college. He predicted that by 2005, 30 percent of all college graduates would hold jobs not requiring a college degree anyway, ridiculed the old assumption that all college graduates become a "manager or a professional," and bluntly suggested both that some young people instead attend a community college or vocational school if they obtain higher education at all and that some young people simply aren't very bright—and that college can't fix that.

Henry's primary comment about news media coverage of higher education immediately followed his "make money" line above:

> This reality is acknowledged in the mass media, which are forever running stories and charts showing how much a college degree contributes to lifetime income (with the more sophisticated publications very occasionally noting the counterweights of costs of tuition paid and income foregone during the years of full-time study). These stories are no surprise to parents, who certainly wouldn't shell out the same money for travel or other exercises in fulfillment that do not result in a marketable credential. The income statistics are, similarly, no surprise to banks, which avidly market student loans and have been known to shower new graduates or even undergraduates with credit cards. And of course the stories are no surprise to students, who avidly follow news of where the jobs are and what starting salaries they command.[57]

Education reporting reached its peak relative to other beats in the 1960s, perhaps first because of Sputnik and subsequently due to the growth, controversies, protests, and other dramatic changes in U.S. education. If the quality and quantity of education news in the 1960s were to be critiqued, the fault would be attributed to both the mass media and the institutions themselves. This is despite Ray E. Laakaniemi's finding that in February 1966, the University of Michigan sent out 162 press releases; Michigan State University, 122; Wayne State University, 96; and Eastern Michigan University, 38, and that observed newspapers used anywhere from 34.5 percent of them (*Ann Arbor News*) to only 6.5 percent (*Detroit Free Press*). Newspapers favored intercollegiate sports news, followed by other event previews, and professors' work in government and business. Among Laakaniemi's conclusions were that published "[i]tems pertaining to the growth, financing, or basic purposes of the universities were very rare" and that "[m]ore than 75 per cent of the news was of an immediate reward value, thus tending not to have values which would cause it to be remembered or relied upon in building an understanding of the values of higher education." Peter H. Binzen (1962) and Charles E. Flynn (1966) came to similar conclusions.[58]

Also in 1966, Donald F. Scannell, after reviewing the so-called "Michigan studies" on public attitudes toward higher education, wrote that as a general rule, 65 percent of citizens said they received ideas and information about colleges and universities from friends, 46 percent named newspapers, 26 percent named other unspecified reading, 17 percent named relatives, 16 percent named television and radio, and 12 percent named magazines. Scannell also asked his subjects what stories they read about higher education, according to subject matter; what readers wanted to read about higher education was not necessarily what newspapers were giving them.[59]

A few years later, Robert L. Cox realized that, although hundreds of studies had been conducted on education news (almost entirely on primary and secondary education), no study had asked in what kind of news about higher education the public was interested. Through a factor analysis, Cox found three types of readers of education news in Stillwater, Oklahoma, home of Oklahoma State University: students who preferred reading stories that concentrated on students, whether those stories were positive or negative; readers Cox called "passive," who were uninterested in any education news; and "[a]ll-round" readers, who generally were interested in all types of education news.[60]

As an industry, the mass media's interest in education declined slightly during the 1970s, leading Bonnie Lou Ross to conclude in her 1983 study of *The Los Angeles Times'* education coverage from 1960 to 1975 that education reporting still was a low priority. Roger Yarrington's two studies came to a similar conclusion in the mid-1980s; when he investigated why some papers had a full-time higher education reporter, he found three reasons: the economic impact of universities (such as in Boston, prompting coverage by *The Boston Globe*), reader interest (such as the well-educated readers of *The New York Times*), and/or a publisher's commitment based on the notion that higher education is important to society. Amy S. Wells, after studying education coverage in *The New York Times*, *Chicago Tribune*, and *The Los Angeles Times*, concluded in 1986 that education coverage is greatest when public concern with education's quality is high, such as during the 1961 to 1965 period (by comparison, relatively few stories were published between 1946 and 1955). However, over the course of the forty-year period, Wells noted, education coverage increased, stories became longer, stories increasingly were placed in important news locations, and traditional news stories began to give way to investigative stories, feature stories and editorials.[61]

In 1989, Ernest C. Hynds found that fewer than half of daily newspapers had a full-time education writer and only one-fourth had a staff member designated as "education editor," and in 1986, A.S. Wells found that smaller newspapers were more likely to have a full-time education writer, although fewer than 250 papers in the country had one. William W. Lace found in 1987 that Texas newspaper and television journalists had strongly favorable opinions on what he called "fundamental issues dealing with the basic worth of higher education": its value as a resource to the state, its value to communities as an economic asset (a clearly anti-intellectual criterion), and the value to individual students of the college experience. However, reporters had equally strong negative opinions about four particular issues: the influence of partisan politics on the appointment of state board regents, "[t]he emphasis placed upon and the extent of the resources going to intercollegiate athletics," "[t]he extent to which college courses deal with the theoretical rather than with practical applications," and the use, excessive in reporters' minds, of graduate teaching assistants rather than faculty. Important to this book, Texas (higher) education reporters were obviously anti-intellectual about course content, and this anti-intellectualism cannot be explained away by their insistence that too many resources were being spent on athletics; reporters did not advocate their abolition.[62]

By 1993, William Chance was willing to call California reporters who covered higher education "competent," though he criticized them for shallow coverage (too little analysis of policies or issues) and for being too willing to accept administrators' claims that California boasted the world's finest university system. The next year, Marilyn A. Posner found that reporters discover higher education to be a source of ideas for a wide variety of stories: on politics, economics, race relations, crime, and much more. However, most of all, Posner discovered, reporters considered higher education to be a consumer story: "people want to know what they get for their money." This was confirmed by Gary R. Ratcliff and Roger L. Williams's 1994 content analysis of major newspapers, which increased their coverage of higher education by anywhere from 10 percent to 50 percent between 1987 and 1994. Ratcliff, comparing and contrasting Posner's study with Yarrington's, pointed out in 1996 that reporters in 1984 were "covering trends such as desegregation, open versus closed admissions, and improving educational quality. Words like assessment or accountability, which are now in vogue, were not part of their vocabulary." Philip Walzer, aware that higher education news was a higher priority with some newspapers, editors than others, wrote a 1995 article on how reporters can "sell" their editors on higher education news. He suggested they "seize on issues that draw connections to the outside" (such as racial tensions, financial limitations, or uncertain leadership), and a story on how well colleges are educating students—if not inherently newsworthy—could be further justified on the basis that legislators and other government officials want to know.[63]

Ratcliff's 1996 study examined the coverage of higher education by eight daily newspapers, four that he deemed aggressive in their coverage (*Minneapolis Star Tribune, Rocky Mountain News, San Francisco Examiner, San Francisco Chronicle*) and four that he deemed less aggressive (*Columbus Dispatch, Denver Post, Pittsburgh Post-Gazette, San Diego Union-Tribune*). In on-site interviews with reporters, editors, and university relations practitioners, he found that newspaper editors and owners were most influential in determining the tone of coverage, although reporters were allowed varying degrees of latitude in how they perform their jobs. Reporters were most likely to take advantage of that latitude if their own personalities tended toward risk taking and/or if their editors' expectations were vague or inconsistent.[64]

In 1998, Lynn W. Payne—citing recent studies about corporate culture shock and other results of unrealistic expectations of black college graduates—interviewed black undergraduates majoring in business about their goals and expectations following graduation. He found that all of them had unrealistic expectations—assuming that the students were not about to find themselves in the top 5 percent of all U.S. wage earners. While Payne did not study students' expectations about college, he probed to find out what were students' sources of expectations about their post-college life and, directly and indirectly, what they expected a bachelor's degree to do for them either immediately or in combination with an MBA or law degree. He concluded that TV programs and business and/or popular magazines influenced students' expectations about success, self-image after college, and retirement age and personal savings, and that movies affected their expectations about self-image and retirement age/personal savings. Cross-tabulating students' demographics with their attitudes and beliefs, Payne discovered that "traditional" and lower income students were more likely than "non-traditional," middle- and higher-income students to be influenced by TV, movies, and magazines (middle income students claimed to be only somewhat influenced by business and popular magazines, whereas higher income students claimed to be somewhat influenced only by business magazines), and that students from urban or suburban backgrounds were influenced most by professional magazines, while rural students were more influenced by TV, movies, and popular magazines. In fact, Payne found that internships and guest lecturers were required to disabuse students of the notion of receiving starting salaries of $100,000.[65]

Although many higher education institutions have engaged in public relations efforts since the early twentieth century, most of their efforts might be called amateurish by modern standards until the 1970s, and since then they have become increasingly sophisticated. The body that became the American College Public Relations Association (ACPRA—still later the Council for the Advancement and Support of Education) was founded decades ago. In the 1950s, spurred along by Albert W. Rowland's 1955 doctoral study, ACPRA was engaged in a serious effort to determine the exact role of college public relations officers. Among other points, Rowland concluded that public relations practitioners were concerned only about their own campuses and not about higher education in general, nor about public confidence in higher education. Robert A. Bonfiglio found in 1990 that although the public's image of higher education had been badly shaken in the mid- to late 1960s, ACPRA did nothing to redress this until 1972; even then, public relations personnel were split between putting the 1960s behind them and trying to explain to the public the university's historical role in social criticism.[66]

Most mass communication—oriented studies of higher education's public relations have concentrated on defining the role of college PR. However, few of these studies have discussed mass media in much detail despite Frank A. DeFazio's observation that "media/public information services" are considered the most important task for college public relations officers, and "media/press" the most important "public" by college presidents and public relations officers. In 1987, Lace suggested that many difficulties in higher education news reporting might be traced back to stereotypes held, and misunderstandings experienced, by higher education reporters and institutions' public relations directors. Lace criticized those PR directors who had "somewhat lost touch with the news media members with whom they work and upon whom they depend," and he emphasized that "many of these issues dealing with the organization, governance, and operation of colleges and universities are not as important to the media as thought." Lace feared that institutions might react to their own misperceptions by becoming too defensive (justifying the negative, not promoting the positive) and self-defeating. However, two of his recommendations, made in response to what he implied was public anti-intellectualism, were themselves anti-intellectual: institutions should promote how their institutions "contribut[e] to the economic well-being of the institution's graduates, the local community and the state," and:

> Public relations directors should attempt to disseminate material, not only on successful students, but also on successful alumni. Positive stories or articles on alumni who are successes in their careers would emphasize the value of a degree and also would help to counter the notion that college

courses deal too much with theory and do not prepare students for careers.

Apparently Lace was unconcerned about preparing students for their democratic, intellectual, cultural, or private lives: his focus is solely on the economic.[67]

Finally, in 1991, Gaylon E. "Gene" Murray found that a majority of higher education reporters sampled believed that college PR practitioners "too frequently insist on promoting products, services, and activities which [sic] do not legitimately deserve promotion," act as obstructionists to reporters, "clutter[] the communication channels," have not increased the quality of publicity materials, send out publicity disguised as news, otherwise try to deceive the press, incorrectly believe themselves to be an "extension of the newspaper staff," are not "frank and honest," disseminate so much material that the public can't analyze it all and, simply, are trying to get free advertising for their institutions.[68]

The Momentousness of Fighting Anti-Intellectualism

Although theorists such as Foucault, Gramsci, Habermas, Chomsky, and Said have held differing views about education, intellectuals, and the mass media—in part because of their differing experiences in time and by place—they and others agree that the educational systems and mass media systems are key sites, often the most effective or nearly only sites, for ideological (re)production. They also have agreed that, in modern society, educational systems and mass media systems are closely connected and contested sites. The media cover and otherwise influence higher education, and higher education influences the news media through journalism graduates, public relations efforts, sometimes research, and other functions. At the same time, other institutions in society also are influencing both mass media and higher education. Although theorists have had widely varying ideal visions of intellectuals and, therefore, what constitute intellectuals' prerogatives and responsibilities, they all have believed that modern societies (presumably including mass media organizations and education systems) need intellectuals and vigilance against anti-intellectualism. In today's United States, the hegemony of anti-intellectualism has resulted in distorted views of mass media's reproductions of ideology when they are considered at all, and widespread public sentiment that universities are to be non-ideological, above and beyond the promotion of a democracy of docile voters and a capitalist economy composed of active entrepreneurs and executives but docile workers.

Chapter 4
Religious Anti-Rationalism and Higher Education

Daniel Rigney emphasized four themes in his explanation of U.S. religious anti-rationalism as one of the manifestations of U.S. anti-intellectualism (see chapters 1, 2, and 3). Religious anti-rationalism is not specifically mentioned as a manifestation of anti-intellectualism by other theorists discussed in chapter 3, but all would agree that organized religion is an irrational social institution.

An analysis of magazine coverage of higher education since World War II demonstrates ample evidence of anti-intellectual portrayals, and implicit endorsements of social/affective development in higher education and (usually implicitly) a de-intellectualized curriculum. Particularly during the late 1960s and early 1970s, questioning authority also was portrayed as anti-intellectual. On the other hand, minimal evidence was found of anti-intellectual opposition to or fear of reason, and no evidence was found of opposition to or fear of modern science *per se*.

Evidence for Opposition to Reason

Several articles portrayed professors and administrators as promoting ethics and values, sometimes in connection with religion, and note their observation that their largely anti-intellectual students were interested only in practical facts. A picture emerges of the last gasp of an older generation or the lone sage facing the potentially unethical masses that will ultimately triumph. Although *Time* in particular endorsed the older generation's wisdom, the juxtaposition of the younger and older made questionable the persistence of received wisdom. *Time* led a 1964 story, "Far More Than Grades," by pointing out that "brainy" University of Illinois — Urbana/Champaign freshmen who thought they were becoming "assembly-line workers in ivy-covered fact factories" were surprised by visiting Brandeis University President Abram L. Sachar. He told them, "You demand facts, facts, facts" but a college education should give them values "in a world where the harsh voice of unreason cries down the generous passions," and "the elasticity of your minds will be a shield."[1]

Time's reference to such fact-demanding arguably implied that the more intelligent students eschewed theory or philosophy for "facts." It also called "brainy" many students who surely were not, and the article played casually with concepts such as intelligence and knowledge. By quoting Princeton's Robert F. Cohen, who told students not interested in values to "begin negotiations with another institution," it suggested that many other colleges and universities were less intellectually rigorous about values.

Students were shown as damaged or harmed by being "too" intellectual. For example, in a 1970 *Life* magazine article, "An intimate revolution in campus life: Co-ed dorms put boys and girls together," a college psychologist was quoted at length as asserting that an intellectual upbringing is devoid of feeling, and that intelligent students go to college yearning to make up for their home life deficits. An explicit example of Rigney's observation that anti-intellectualism constructs reason as "cold" or "bad" and emotion as "good" or "warm," the article called Oberlin College students more intelligent than average, but also lonely, contemplative, even introverted. The psychologist, a Dr. Verda, said Oberlin students' rearing had been an "intellectual experience, without much loving or open emotion," with parents relentlessly pushing them "to achieve, to be something, to do something." This resulted in little involvement in extracurricular activities (unlike later, when such activities became a way "to achieve") and a limited social life: "These young people come here wanting desperately to generate warm human feeling, but no one has ever shown them how."[2] In this case, making dormitories co-ed was the college's decision to assist in the affective/social development of these students, intelligent students who supposedly most need such development.

Sometimes intellectuals have been described as reading and dwelling on unpleasant information and ideas. While generally favorable toward the establishment of women's studies programs nationwide (it included only one negative comment), a 1968 *Time* article, "Signs of Suicide," suggested that a healthy person wouldn't want to be a reason-obsessed intellectual. The article's writer(s) concluded that, "Enlightenment can sometimes prove devastating." To substantiate this point, they mentioned a female ("girl") State University of New York at Buffalo student telling a professor after a literature course, "I want you to know that you've ruined my life. Everything I read now fills me with rage." Further, a University of Massachusetts professor claimed that women students developed "depression" (*Time*'s writers inexplicably added the word "deep" in introducing the quote) because each and every novel contained an "essentially negative reflection of women" and "even women authors offer little hope as they show women wasting their lives tied to worthless men or driven to suicide by the very awareness that such a course is trying to develop." The professor added that anger might be substituted for depression, but that anger must be "channel[ed]...constructive[ly]." Likewise, that *Time* article specifically warned of specific suicide signs and noted that college students are 50 percent more likely to commit suicide than are similar age nonstudents.[3] Attending college is apparently risky for one's mental health, but the story did not explore potential explanations for the finding.

Evidence Against Opposition to Reason

Rigney has told us that evidence contrary to religious anti-rationalism would come in the form of material that supports intellectual and democratic ideals, scientific/scholarly inquiry and academic freedom, and a broadening of a "culture of critical discourse." However, as is detailed below, college students exercising free speech and assembly through organized protests in the late 1960s generally were not applauded in the text. In pieces about "mock" or "model" political party conventions on campus, students' activities were seldom treated seriously; media typically made a point of highlighting students' juvenile behavior. In addition, the ideas of intellectuals and/or higher education fulfilling a function of broadening critical discourse, or understanding (if critiquing) and teaching about postmodernism, was only hinted at by one article examined for this book. In "The Other Crisis in Our Schools: Our brightest students are getting a dumbed-down education," *Reader's Digest* author Daniel J. Singal complained in 1992, "Along with impoverishment of language comes a downturn in reasoning skills." Singal cited Smith College's twenty-five—year veteran R. Jackson Wilson, who was finding the latter to be the "greatest change" he had observed. Concluded Singal, "Students are ready to tell you how they feel about an issue, but they have never learned how to construct a rational argument to defend their opinions."[4] These findings also are consistent with the "careerism" (anti-intellectualism) and the manifestations of "intellectualism" theorized by Katchadourian and Boli (see chapter 3).

Evidence for Opposition to Science

No evidence was found suggesting that intellectuals and/or higher education institutions either do or even should oppose developments in modern science. On the other hand, no article examined explicitly stated that it is the function of intellectuals or universities to develop and support modern science. However, this is because of the way in which the sample of magazine articles was selected for analysis in this book; other texts over the years concentrated on the scientific advances made by university researchers.

Evidence for Defending Authority

Rigney argued in 1991, based on Hofstadter's book and his own observations, that opposition to questioning traditional authority is a hallmark of U.S. anti-intellectualism. Traditionally, this "questioning of authority" referred to religious texts and leaders but, throughout U.S. history, minorities and other oppressed groups have questioned other authority as well and sometimes been covered by mass media. The problem of authority, and challenges to it, is found not only in Hofstadter and Rigney's work, but also throughout critical theory: Foucault's experts are juxtaposed to those labeled "deviants." Habermas noted that neoconservatives call for traditional notions of nation, family, and morality. Said called for intellectuals to criticize anything and everything that needs to be criticized. All were aware of the defenders of traditional authority, even if they didn't label these defenders as "anti-intellectual."

Although magazine stories occasionally referred to low percentages of students who attended church regularly, what little coverage of students' religious lives was published suggested that religious beliefs are consistent with intellectual pursuits in colleges and universities. In particular, there was no mention of students questioning or losing their religious faith as a result of attending, or even simply during, college. Instead, for example, *Time* in 1957 reported the results of a Harvard Student Council poll on Harvard students' religious beliefs. The Council was pleased that 60 percent of students agreed that they needed a "religious orientation or belief" for a "fully mature philosophy of life," that 79 percent thought the question of existence of a power higher than themselves to be important, and 40 percent attended church regularly. Its report concluded that religious views are formed before college and *Time* asserted that, "college strengthens and intellectualizes these attitudes."[5]

Occasionally, magazine coverage would emphasize the idea of college students attending church, and the universities' role. The message was that two great institutions—higher education and organized religion—could assist each other in their roles as powerful authorities in the society. In a 1952 article, "Students and Religion," *Ladies' Home Journal* reported that "Universities and colleges are helping students keep in touch with their church groups," and it was implied that this was as it should be. No story objected to public university cooperation with local churches on the basis of separation of church and state. Carefully worded to note that at the University of Minnesota, "students *may* fill out religious-census cards" [emphasis added], the article implied that students who were not interested in organized religion on campus (religious organizations are located "along the edge of the campus") were the deviant ones. Attention was paid to a University Christian Mission director, although he only visited college campuses and was not employed by one. The single element suggesting that a majority of students were not active in organized religion was the fact reported that only one-tenth of students were active in the twenty-four campus religious organizations.[6] Possible off-campus involvement was not mentioned, nor was the level of involvement of the active one-tenth. *Ladies' Home Journal,* by merely publishing this article, constructed involvement with religion as something positive for college students.

An advocacy-type article promoting students' involvement in religious activities even more blatantly, however, was found in 1954 in *Life*: Nine photographs, accompanied by minimal text, showed the students as being sincere in their religion and sincerely interested in the plight of poor children in Waco, Texas. It was pointed out that although attending chapel was mandatory for lowerclassmen, off-campus evangelism was "strictly voluntary." Baylor students were either smiling or speaking in every photograph that depicts students, and poor children also were depicted enjoying their time with the college students. Waco residents not interested in students' street preaching were referred to negatively as "uninterested" and "reluctant."[7]

A 1957 *Time* article about an orthodox Catholic chaplain on campus who had made many extreme but vague attacks on Princeton's faculty and who had been "derecognized" by the university, could be interpreted as either supporting or opposing traditional authority. It reported that a "large majority of the students" agreed with Princeton President Robert Goheen's decision to derecognize the chaplain, but the article also noted that the previous year's senior class had voted the celibate chaplain "least likely to send his son to Princeton" and as the class's favorite comedian.[8] Thus, students were portrayed as not taking seriously an important campus issue, and in so highlighting one action by students, implicitly suggested that the students' ridicule of authority figures generally should not be taken seriously. A 1968 *Time* article, "The Cynical Idealists of '68," also discredited students in part by noting that they weren't reading the Bible and "dismiss institutional churches as irrelevant or unimportant."[9]

College administrators and professors sometimes were covered as advocating not religious beliefs explicitly, but traditional "values." One 1964 *Time* article, for example, suggested that elite institutions cared about whether their students learn "values" as well as "facts." The story, "Far More Than Grades," concludes by covering a Princeton administrator who told students uninterested in values to "begin negotiations with another institution where you can attach yourself to a pipeline of inanimate learning and become full, like a storage tank, sealed by a diploma and otherwise useless."[10] This could be regarded as mere hyperbole but also as an indication of the low regard in which Princetonians held other institutions.

Anti-intellectual media coverage questioning student activism not surprisingly started with the widespread U.S. student political protests and activities of 1964, and it was only at the very end of the decade that the media gave grudging credit to students for critiquing the war. In a 1964 editorial, *Life* first praised early 1960s students for no longer being "greasy grinds" (diligently studying students) and for their interest in the Peace Corps, minority rights, and the Poor Corps. The praise was juxtaposed with a report that Haverford College students were raising money for "Communist Vietcong guerillas." In addition, eighty-seven college men had bought an ad in the *National Guardian* announcing they would not fight. And in New York City, Columbia University students had founded the Sexual Freedom Forum to encourage sexual activity (heterosexual only). Other college students in Greenwich Village were advocating legalized prostitution. These student organizations were not praised; the editorial called the students "prankish to the perverse to the profound" whether they were engaged in political protests or "such traditional pleasures as panty raids." *Life* trivialized the students' political activism (by damning with faint praise their "wrongheadness," which contradictorily was shown as not having enough impact that it warranted censure) at the same time it patronized students by suggesting that they were supposed to be rather noisy: "Given the choice we'll take noisy wrongheadedness before gray-flannel silence, any day."[11]

Other examples in which college students were constructed as wrongly challenging authority all appeared in *Time* in 1968:

* "Most students, as well as many professors, do not believe that smoking marijuana is or should be a criminal offense" in an article about the arrests of forty-three persons at SUNY-Stony

Brook.[12]
* College seniors "hold[] no brief for society's sexual taboos," and "marijuana has become an accepted part of college culture."[13]
* A report that illegitimate births had tripled in the twenty-five—year period from 1943 to 1968, largely because male and female college students could visit each other in dormitories.[14]

Evidence Against Defending Authority

In the mid-1960s to early 1970s, major magazines engaged in extensive coverage of "hippies," student protests, and other student political activism. (A careful reading of much of that coverage is discussed primarily in chapter 6.) Note that only one story in the sample unequivocally praised student activism. A 1960 *Life* editorial about college students' "revolts" in the United States, South Korea, Equador, and Turkey concluded that "most" had been "beneficial," including in the United States. Specifically, black students' "sit-ins" were successfully "demonstrating the silliness of a system which denies the right of humans to eat alongside one another," including obtaining "an impressive amount of support from white students outside," and inside, the South. Such students were discovering that they could not "rationalize or defend these paradoxes," and, as if surprising, improved Southern education "produced a force to make men think."[15] However, this type of praise was rare in the magazines examined, more suggestive in its context of the professional practice of showing two sides of a story; thus, this too reflected anti-intellectualism. To explain the coverage by way of Katchadourian and Boli's intellectualism and careerism scales, students were not encouraged to: think, nor praised for thinking, critically; expose themselves and others to different viewpoints; or develop ethical or moral values of their own.

Evidence for Deintellectualizing the Curriculum

The religious anti-rationalist prong of U.S. anti-intellectualism, according to Hofstadter and Rigney, often manifests itself in the belief that education systems should promote social and affective development, and the teaching of epistemological and moral absolutes (usually evangelical Christianity). The magazines examined have in fact repeatedly constructed the college years as primarily or solely centering on students' social and affective development. The fact that such development of young Americans during college was never tied to particular religious beliefs, goals or preferences of a particular ethnic group or region, worked to make this construction universally applied.

It must be emphasized that in tying magazines' (over)emphasis on college students' social and affective development to American anti-intellectualism, this book is not arguing that college is not or should not be a site of considerable social and affective development for Americans who attend college. The issue is popular magazines' emphasis on students' social and affective development, and their obvious and surprising de-emphasis on college students' intellectual development, and the way such coverage choices can influence the knowledge, opinions, and attitudes about higher education, anti-intellectualism, and even intellectuals among American readers.

A good example summarizing how college as a site for social development was referred to during the entire fifty-five—year period is found in a 1968 *Reader's Digest* article. Here, benefits of attending college were stated as either getting a job, or vague and not particularly intellectual: "[T]he intangible rewards can be even more significant—the lasting friendships, the broadened capacity to serve family and community, the deeper understanding of our modern world, the richer appreciation of life."[16]

Fraternities and sororities, dating and sex on campus, spring vacation, and various pranks and semi-riotous behavior by students all received extensive coverage from the magazines. With the exception of a strongly negative message about campus sex in one article,[17] there was overall support for these activities as key experiences of college years (and not typical experiences for all college-age Americans whether in college or not). Even the coverage of "pranks" on campus that drew condemnation from administrators and the police were covered with a wink of encouragement. Students' juvenile behavior was not condemned.

Starting with fraternities, media coverage was largely stereotypical, nostalgic, unscholarly, and even anti-intellectual. A 1948 *Time* article, for instance, expressed relief that World War II veterans already were graduating, because they were mostly uninterested in either "horse-play" or "comradeship." *Time* was eager to see fraternities return to "old trappings: the college pennants, no-parking signs, barefoot Petty girls and dirty shirts."[18]

Belonging to a fraternity or sorority is portrayed in the magazines, particularly *Life*, as something highly desirable, almost essential, for American college students. None of the coverage examined was clearly opposed to fraternities, although articles published in other years suggested a small movement against them in the mid- to late 1950s, due to purported elitism. Only one possibly negative story about fraternities is an excerpt from *Atlantic Monthly* Associate Editor Charles W. Morton's magazine essay on them, which at first glance appears to be a critical *tour de force*.[19] However, Morton's nearly Menckenesque level of satire could easily be interpreted as a send-up of fraternity opponents' arguments.

By the mid-1950s, how fraternity membership fit into young people's lives overall was receiving less attention and being taken more for granted. A 1956 issue of *Life* depicted as an accomplishment the fact that the University of Illinois had the highest number of fraternities of any college in the United States—fifty-eight, which included 2,900 men of 11,000 undergraduate men on campus.[20] The desirability of belonging to a fraternity was the explicit and implicit theme of the nine-page article, which included twenty-six photos. However, the effects of belonging to a fraternity on students' future was not addressed, and fraternity membership's effects on their college years was barely addressed. How fraternity members' pasts related to belonging to, or especially not belonging to, a fraternity also was mostly only hinted at, and limited to what fraternities wanted in their members, not what members or potential members wanted from fraternities. In a 1960 *Life* article, the Greek system was mentioned repeatedly in anonymous comments by high school guidance counselors about fifty colleges.[21] It was described as an almost integral part of attending a prestigious private college.

Despite protests by magazine writers that fraternities were not as anti-intellectual as they previously had been, articles still constructed fraternities as not particularly interested in intelligent or well-educated members. Four photographs in a 1956 *Life* story were grouped under the headline, "The Rushees Fraternities Seek," and bold-faced two-word, all capitalized phrases started each cutline: "Top Student," "Star Athlete," "Smooth Dresser," and "Big Wheel." The article's first page has informed readers that, "Often considered as anti-intellectual, many fraternities now encourage scholarship by competitive awards," and *Life* placed the "Top Student" first in a line-up labeled "Seek," which appeared at the bottom of the article's fourth page. However, only one other shred of evidence that good students were sought was offered: mentioned in passing was that the "STAR ATHLETE" also was "bright." Many photographs depicted how fraternities attempted to impress and entertain rushees, and these include a "hypnotic stunt," a "jazz trio," "tumbling," singing, playing pool, and a "telepathy trick involving playing cards"; in a sole photo, one fraternity member was posed showing a rushee the house's "scholarship plaques."

The fraternity clearly was a males-only enclave as, for example, no women are pictured in the twenty-six photographs in that 1956 fraternity rushing story. But the scene was still heterosexual, even if rushees and fraternities court each other. One rushee was supported for membership, even though he probably wouldn't engage in typical college male behavior of playing the field: "'He'll never be a dater, he's practically married...' says a [unattributed] voice, 'but I think he's really hot.'" (Unlike the colloquial use of the word now to refer to a sexually desirable person, "hot" was defined in the 1956 article as simply "A sought-after rushee.")[22] In addition, to one rushee, girlfriends were girlfriends, but choosing a fraternity was like choosing a wife: "'[I]t's the biggest decision next to getting married.'"[23] In fraternities it is expected that men judge other men and accept being judged. One rushee indicated that he was sought after in part because fraternities thought him to have "'good taste in clothes.'"

That some fraternities did try to end the male-female polarity on campus was made more apparent in the news media in the mid-1960s; news coverage made little reference to anyone trying to do so before then, but that of course does not mean it was not attempted. In early 1968, *Time* thought it newsworthy that Stanford University's Lambda Nu fraternity had just made plans to go coed in the fall. Buried after a story twice as long about tiny Rockefeller University, the story largely concerned coed living's exact logistics: shared dining room, living room, and "other facilities," but women sleeping in a distinct wing and the whole fraternity supervised by a live-in university administrator.[24] Despite *Time*'s emphasis on minimizing parents' fears about the arrangement, the students were nonchalant and optimistic: one junior hoped members would spend more time together in activities other than watching the news on television, while others hoped that students "will be less inclined to idealize the opposite sex"—mostly that women would be less likely to idealize men. Sexism still shined through.

Parties and other rituals at fraternities received extensive coverage, mostly in *Life*, where they made for great photography:

*Yale University's annual Derby Day—twelve photos splashed across four pages in 1948.[25]

*Again note that University of Illinois rushing was the subject of *Life*'s 1956 "Fraternity Rushing." As noted above, fraternities wanted the "top student," "star athlete," "smooth dresser," and "big wheel," but its "fraternity glossary" included slang directly related only to the "star athlete," and much attention to whether rushees were thought to be physically attractive. ("Face man" was defined as " A rushee who is good-looking but not necessarily sharp," while "Furniture" was defined as "A rushee not thought good enough to pledge but personable enough to make [a] house look full.") The glossary was brutally exclusive: students who are "hot," "sharp boys," and "jocks" were desirable, while those who were "crocks," "40-pound robins," "furniture" or "closet cases" (the latter referred to an extremely undesirable rushee, with no modern connotation about sexual orientation) were not.[26] Fraternities were to be taken seriously: Students who "rushed the wrong fraternities" were shown as anxious, even depressed, and then relieved when given the chance to rush others.

*A 1960 *Life* feature photo spread on University of Michigan students depicted them frolicking in hay in the Phi Sigma Delta fraternity house.[27]

*In the late 1970s, fraternities held their own "toga parties," prompted by the popularity of the motion picture, "*National Lampoon*'s Animal House." Placed in *Time*'s "Economy & Business" section, most of a 1978 article was about the high profitability of this hit movie, remembered for John Belushi's "outrageous cries of 'toga, toga.'" However, the third paragraph added that late 1970s students were creating a "craze" because they were "fad-starved." It further explained, "For many, dressing up in a bed sheet is simply a means of venting the pressures of academia; for others, toga parties represent a search for something to be remembered by, even if that token of remembrance is borrowed from the '50s generation."[28]

Fraternities and sororities were not the only campus organizations covered for their various events and rituals, a trend that suggested college students spent a majority of their time involved in such activities. *Life*, in particular, published dozens of articles, with plenty of photographs, showing college students engaged in all types of fun, goofy, immature, silly, humorous, whimsical, and other nonserious, nonacademic and nonintellectual behavior.

The "pantie [or panty] raid" craze first received coverage by *Life* in early April 1952,[29] and by mid-May, it was reporting that University of Nebraska students were copying earlier, panty-raiding University of Michigan students.[30] *Time*, for its part, published articles on May 26 and June 2, relatively far forward on pages 27 and 22, respectively (much closer to the front of the magazine than usual) about what it called "the newest and noisiest college craze—the pantie raid."[31] The May issue referred to the raids as part of a revived "spring riot" phenomenon, and the June issue condemned them, noting that "pantie raids...made night hideous at 52 different" institutions and resulted in "arrests, expulsions, editorial blasts, and the best efforts of police riot squads." Conversely, the conclusion included an approving comment calling the craze the "first really daffy outbreak by U.S. college students since the days before World War II"—and noted that one teacher condemning them had himself swallowed sixty-seven live goldfish in 1939. The May 26 *Time* story juxtaposed the headline "Girls! Girls! Girls!" directly beneath the standing head, "Manners & Morals." The same day's issue of *Life* included a two-page spread of photos, "Campuses enjoy a riotous spring: The fad for lingerie and bruises worries deans and psychologists" followed by another two-page spread, "Ice cream argument is enough to start a Yale free-for-all."[32] Note how close to the front (pp. 28—29 and pp. 30—31) of the *Life* magazine also were these articles, especially in a 140-page issue.

A five-page (excluding advertisements) *Life* photo essay in 1954 about Michigamua, the "top senior honor society" at The University of Michigan, depicted a series of events around an annual initiation. One ritual involved older "braves" literally ripping the shirts off junior "palefaces." Another involved "beer and dirt massaged into [the] face" of "palefaces" who were forced to lie prostrate and na-ked on the ground. After spending hours taking each other's clothes off, applying and removing greasepaint from one another, and so forth, the end of the weekend (covered with photos at the article's conclusion) featured (heterosexual) couples taking canoe rides and dancing.[33]

Other stories about students' sometimes bizarre rituals or vacation activities included:

*"*Life* Goes to a Foresters' Ball in Montana: Portable Forest and Stolen Moosehead Enliven College Party," a three-page, ten-photo *Life* story about a 1954 party at Montana State University.[34] That the party was in a little-populated, rarely visited state such as Montana added to the aura of strangeness.

*"Light turns for spring fancy," a collection of *Life* photos of students' wacky activities during spring vacation 1957: College of Pacific students trying to break a seesawing record, two Princeton stu-dents dribbling a basketball from their campus to New York City and back, a Claremont student playing the guitar as he headed down the highway on a unicycle, Caltech students playing pranks on seniors (such as stabling a horse in one of their dorm rooms).[35] *Life* did not state nor even imply that such events were unusual.

*A two-page *Life* spread concerned a single Harvard student's 1957 spring vacation in Bermuda and all of the dates he had there.[36]

*"Spring + Youth: A Case with Complications" headlines anoth-er 1957 *Life* photo spread of riotous behavior at St. Olaf College, Bowling Green State University and the University of Illinois at Urba-na-Champaign. One photograph showed several dozen students grieving at the grave of the campus mascot dog, the suggestion being that adults would not necessarily grieve *en masse* an animal's death. The article also reported that Bowling Green students burned an ef-figy of the university's president on his lawn and then took fire hoses away from firefighters, something *Life* does not portray as a serious matter. Finally, four photographs taken at Illinois illustrated thirty-two students being arraigned after a "seven-hour free-for-all involving 3,000 students," which required 200 state, county, and city police of-ficers and 150 tear gas grenades to end. *Life* depicted this event with the arraignment photo, a grinning female student, a crowd shot, and

"a muscular rioter, scantily clad for the fray," about to "heave a pail of water."[37] (Life regularly noted it in cutlines when persons pictured were scantily clothed, even though this fact was always obvious.)

*Life's 1957 story, "Surprise Rise for a Rocket" presented the same type of picture: University of Maryland students had taken a fifteen-foot, hollow model of a high-altitude research rocket, out of the student union and hid it on the roof of a nearby building. Back at the student union, they had left a sign, "Farewell Earth People." A dean was quoted as saying, "Panty raids are one thing, but this shows a clear disrespect for the advancement of science" and a fingerprint was lifted off the recovered model and sent to the FBI. However, Life gave no indication that the FBI had fingerprint files on Maryland students.[38]

*In 1960, Life published four photos on two pages about a completely silent "musical" concert given at the University of Detroit.[39]

*Also in 1960, Life included a three-page photospread about residents of identical eight-story, eight-room wide, men's and women's dormitories playing games of chess in their windows with pieces of paper representing the pieces. Life negates the popular impression of chess as an intellectual game: The second-page's photo was of men students delivering pizza to female students, and the third-page photos concerned a male student, having met a female student through chess, making a date with her by Morse code message after telephones had been shut off at 11 p.m.[40]

*Big Ten schools' fashions and rituals were the subject of a 1954 Life photospread. The Midwest schools were said to be "more restrained" than those on the West Coast, and not as "sloppy" as those on the East Coast. One color photo featured honorary groups' "beanies" at Purdue, including one for a "freshman scholastic group." However, other photos featured "cords," suede women's clothing, men's "loud shirts," "oversized" walkways at Michigan State, rain slickers, stuffed toys, bagpipers, a festival float, taps for Ohio State students killed in World War II, a twenty-first birthday party, a "pinning" of a sorority member, an Illinois student dozing while leaning on a statue, a student couple kissing in an Indiana well house, and Indiana "Belles" singing accompanied by harp and violin.[41]

The text also constructed college life as revolving largely around dating and sex. For example, a 1948 Time article was not much more than an advertisement for a book, *Weekend, A Girl's Guide to the College Weekend*, by William B. Jones and Richard H. O'Riley, already authors of *For Men Lonely*, a guide to women's colleges. Their new book was touted as for the "distressed girl come up for a Dartmouth weekend with the wrong clothes, the wrong expectations, the wrong attitude."[42] Later articles are devoted to a favorite place to meet for dates, and the relay race by bicycle from Yale to Vassar ending with the Yale men meeting their Vassar girlfriends.[43]

A 1957 *Life* article made it look as though college students spend much of their time kissing (nine out of ten photos are couples embracing, most of them also kissing) and ridiculously debating where kissing should be allowed. At the University of Michigan, the Stockwell Hall dorm council has voted to ban kissing in a lounge, but opponents have said that students would simply kiss outside in frigid temperatures. They have briefly considered putting time limits on kissing in the lounge (twenty seconds each), but then realized attempted enforcement would be absurd. An anonymous parent was quoted about students kissing, "Animals, nothing but animals," and faculty and administrators were not represented.[44]

A seven-page article in a 1957 *Ladies' Home Journal* issue was nothing more than the extended history of one couple's romance. Steve Ambrose (the Pulitzer Prize—winning and plagiarizing historian who died in 2002) was quoted at the very end of the article as saying that he's thinking about obtaining a Ph.D., but the photograph on the article's first page was more indicative of its overall tone: he and the then Judy Dorlester are pictured in the Wisconsin football stadium, he in his uniform, her with his letterman's jacket on. The cutline read, "Varsity man Steve (with stripes for two years as guard) gave his jacket to Judy. She works part time in State Historical building, found her tenderness dawning 'when he used to come into the library all bruised.'"[45]

Also in 1957, in *Reader's Digest* reprinted from *Harper's* an article about college students' dramatic change—to dating one person at a time! It is written by Charles W. Cole, president of Amherst College, who is bemused by students "going steady," noting that it was a return to nineteenth-century practices and just the term had the "ring of rural America under President Cleveland."[46] Overall, Cole is concerned about less successful marriages being entered into by younger, less experienced daters/partners, and wrote that the phenomenon must be a result, illogical by 1957, of the shortage of men during World War II, as well as Depression men's concerns about getting something in return for their "investment" in dates. No mention of any other activity of college students besides dating was mentioned.

"Too much sex on campus" was the two-page polemic by a Massachusetts judge about how and why colleges needed to educate their students not to have premarital sex; not only should colleges monitor their students' sexual behavior, she wrote, but she also suggested that colleges should expel female students who drink too much or have sex. She simply complained that male students were almost never disciplined by their colleges for "illicit sex," but did not advocate their expulsion, at least not in print.[47]

A 1972 *Reader's Digest* article attempted to knock down twelve common perceptions about college that the author considered to be myths. Concerned about colleges' 60 percent transfer, fail or dropout rate, author Loren Pope wrote his article originally for *Potomac* magazine, and addressed results of students' and parents' anti-intellectualism; for instance, his discussion of "Myth 2" ("A big university offers a broader, richer experience") revealed Pope's assumption that students often tended to choose large universities for better dating opportunities, eschewing the closer contact with faculty assured at smaller colleges.[48]

After the novelty of co-ed dormitories wore off, magazine coverage of campus dating and sex changed from being a staple of higher education coverage, to occasional stories on new wrinkles. For instance, a 1980 *Time* article covered male students at Penn State and the University of Maryland offering a "tuck-in" service to women willing to pay for it (99 cents). The Maryland students, calling themselves Pillow Talk Inc., attributed their service's popularity to their "father image." University of Maryland administrator Patricia Orndorff, who "recalls being tear-gassed and locked in her office during the more obstreperous 1960s," commented on the "fad": "It's great that the students are doing nice things for a change."[49]

As dormitories (and even one fraternity) all over the United States went co-ed in the 1970s, journalists covered this change, writing about the topic as a major issue on campus, and positioning the issue as partially about platonic friendship between men and partially about dating and sex. For example, in late 1970, *Life* devoted ten full pages (with no ads) to "An intimate revolution in campus life: Co-ed dorms put boys and girls together." Overall, the magazine reassured those who might object, and anti-intellectually concentrated on the issue as an example of higher education as a site for affective and social development. Times have changed, the magazine indicated, from the days when 1970s parents had gone to college, which had been a time of "traditionally strict segregation of sexes," and "limited visiting hours carefully clocked." In 1970, it observed, "Parents sometimes anxiously conclude that sex in its most urgent physical manifestations will overwhelm the rest of college life," students' morals were "under constant assault," and earlier years' "good clean fun" was being replaced by "pleasures more ominously orgiastic." The magazine mentioned in passing the possibility that "academic interests will suffer badly," before refocusing on Oberlin College's claims that coed living arrangements there were so successful that the campus' environment was one of "ease" and "naturalness."[50]

A succession of photos then showed men and women in pairs or larger groups, eating, playing "slide flutes," washing clothes, cooking, talking, cutting hair (a female German graduate student cuts a male American's hair), studying (but only one of twenty-one photos), hugging, and staffing a radio station. Four mugshots of college officials verified that students were handling the situation well and that they should be allowed, even expected, to do so. The associate admissions director, Bill McIlrath, explained, "Some parents expect the Oberlin campus to be full of bomb-throwers, perverts and free-lovers. It's not." (McIlrath didn't explain what he meant by "perverts.")

Articles about fraternities and sororities sometimes, though rarely and indirectly, touched on the topic of friendships formed in college. Katchadourian and Boli found that "intellectualism"-oriented students were more likely to include "making friends" as a college goal, and therefore anti-intellectual coverage would de-emphasize friendship, which the magazines did. One exception, published in the format of memoir, was an April 1984 *Reader's Digest* article, condensed from a December 23, 1983, *The New York Times Magazine* article, which *Reader's Digest* headlined, "The Reunion: Arm in arm, we three aging musketeers felt young again, and strong. Only later would we understand why," by Paul Gottlieb. He described his first encounter at Swarthmore College with his now life-long friends by recalling meeting Hugh, who was holding forth on John Dunne's metaphysical poetry, and Charlie, who was blowing smoke rings. Gottlieb, who noted that he then could do neither, thought at the time that Hugh and Charlie, each two years older, seemed "vastly more knowledgeable," surely "represent[ed] everything college was supposed to be." Gottlieb remembered that the three of them talked "incessantly—about God, about literature, about the nature of man—and we talked an awful lot about girls," and that all-night conversations are related to the "intensity of friendships formed in early years."

After a reunion with Charlie fifteen years after Hugh and Gottlieb had last seen him, Gottlieb wrote that he and Hugh questioned how the three "had all influenced one another," concluding that Charlie had taught "wit" to his two friends. When Hugh and Gottlieb asked their friend what he learned from them, Charlie looked at them and said: " I thought you knew...Love."[51]

Magazines examined for this book included only one article specifically about platonic relationships (an intellectual pursuit according to Katchadourian and Boli) among women. Headlined "Passport to Popularity," the 1948 *Ladies' Home Journal* piece consisted of a short introduction and then a "quiz" for college women. Most of the test underscored the segregation by gender on campus by being oriented most toward how college women can get along in a single-sex environment. Three photos and their cutlines introduced the piece more than the headline or the introduction, however. The largest of three photographs portrayed nine women (three sitting and six standing), all looking at a single woman sitting at a desk, indicating that she is a popular woman. This is framed by two large headshots, one of a woman advising other women to join campus groups and the other advising women to "Avoid campus gossip—unless it's complimentary!" The "story's" introduction told college women that they should seek excellent grades, a popular roommate, and proof of their attractiveness (such as a "clipping from the campus paper headlining you as beauty queen") but, better yet, all three because, "to shine in only one of these departments is symptomatic of a lopsided personality." Quiz questions had only two answers, suggesting that one is clearly correct and the other clearly incorrect. "Question 1" asked women what they should do if their roommate is a top dancer and athlete and they, by comparison, are neither. Answer A was complaining about "show-offs" while Answer B was to "cultivate a special talent" even if obscure. Another question suggested that women on dates be deferential to their boyfriends' wishes and finances, and that college men were interested only in women's "figures." Question 20, the final one, asked whether a woman who is an expert knitter should help a fellow knitting student trying to finish socks by a birthday, or keep studying for her classes. The correct choice on this one was A, regardless of the woman's situation. In fact, the correct choice on #10, a dating question, was to show "Academic Annie" that "school means beaus as well as books." The only question primarily about education was #13, which asked whether a woman should go out on a date and then cram in poor-quality studying late at night, or go to the library for better study time.[52] This article was about games and tricks, not the sincere friendship that Katchadourian and Boli had in mind.

Evidence Against Deintellectualizing the Curriculum

Articles studied for this book included no evidence explicitly or implicitly stating that all college-aged Americans, not only college students, undergo social and affective development during those years. Neither was any evidence found specifically opposed to the curriculum that had been deintellectualized in favor of the teaching of absolute values or knowledge. However, Daniel Singal, in his 1992 article in *Reader's Digest* "The Other Crisis in Our Schools: Our brightest students are getting a dumbed-down education," complained about what an emphasis on social/affective development has done to U.S. education. Referring first to the 1960s, he recalled that the time's "educational gurus" were specifying "essentially non-academic schools, whose main purpose was to maximize spontaneity, creativity and affection for others. To the extent that logic and acquired knowledge interfered with that process, they were devalued." This populist tidal wave receded by the late 1970s, but the mediocrity remained, Singal complained, adding the 1960s gurus' "mentality" shifted the education establishment's interests from "high to low achievers." This, in turn, implied that it was "much better to give up the prospect of excellence than to take the chance of injuring any student's self-esteem." The result, Singal wrote, was that teachers were devoting themselves to ensuring that slow learners did not feel like failures, and observers could "often sense[] a virtual prejudice against bright students."[53]

Evidence of one type of American anti-intellectualism—anti-rationalism (whether directly related to religious beliefs or not)—demonstrates that during the period from the mid-1940s until at least the late 1990s, American families were given a model of higher education that in many ways reduced it to a finishing school and a dating club. Students apparently were to join fraternities, make friends, and date extensively in college, all of which are normal activities, but—according to the magazines—not study, think, talk with each other about intellectual matters, listen to professors, or learn academic content in any other way. Various pranks were permissible, as long as they were relatively harmless, probably because students infantilized themselves that way, which meant they ultimately were easier for professors, administrators, and prospective employers to control. That the media apparently didn't cover younger students, nor older adults, engaged in pranks, practical jokes, "dares," etc., suggests that American culture has established the college years as the first, last, and only period of life when antics of various kinds are socially acceptable. That college-aged Americans not in college also weren't covered "playing" in this way suggests that these activities are perhaps a luxury of the middle and upper-middle classes, but also their "last hurrah" before settling into responsible and sedate positions of power in their communities. Regardless of how individual readers of the mass market magazines interpreted all of the various stories on the Greek system, vacations, "capers," and dating, the public—based on the articles discussed in this chapter—would have been hard pressed to have any idea what, if anything, college students do in a classroom, library or laboratory.

Chapter 5
Populist Anti-Elitism and
Higher Education

The standards and goals of U.S. higher education were under broad and continuous attack after World War II first as a way of expanding the middle class mostly for white men, and then as a way of expanding the middle class for women and minorities, according to this analysis of the popular magazine coverage of higher education over a period of more than sixty years. (Ironically, at least older students—including veterans—and women would turn out to be generally better students than "college-age" white men, and therefore did not need lowered standards to succeed academically.) As this chapter will show, "common people's" interests overall were favored, as was the lowering of standards and the phasing out of traditional "book learning." However, there is minimal evidence that the magazines' higher education coverage supported left-wing or right-wing populism; weighed in (at least not explicitly) on whether intellectuals are or should be snobs; or constituted intellectuals as a new, simultaneously emancipatory and elitist, class of Americans.

Evidence for Advocating "Common People's" Interests

One of the most common manifestations of anti-elitism in the media coverage of higher education reflected one of the most common definitions of anti-elitism: advocating or defending the interests of typical Americans vis-à-vis the interests of what Rigney and the European critical theorists would generally refer to as the self-serving advantaged class. Sometimes this took the form of giving a great deal of credit to the potential and extant skills, knowledge, and common sense of the "common people." Sometimes it took the form of giving them a little help to challenge or join the elites. Sometimes it took the form of criticizing elites, and sometimes it took the form of redirecting "blame" from the "common people" if there was blame to be assigned.

The most important trend in U.S. higher education since World War II has been the nearly constantly increasing enrollment and, generally, the diversification of student bodies—what some scholars and politicians have referred to rather idealistically and carelessly as the "democratization" of education. Magazine writers and editors had to decide whether they were for or against the "democratization" of higher education, and could display their biases based on what topics they covered and whom they quoted. For example, in early 1948, *Time*'s writers began an article with, "Any boy or girl who doesn't go to college will soon be considered un-American. That day isn't here yet—but the plans are being laid for it."[1] That fall, *Time* reported Haverford College Vice President Archibald MacIntosh's new book (*Behind the Academic Curtain*) about the country's 655 liberal arts colleges, and the magazine zeroed in on the administrator's finding that more than half of all of those colleges' students dropped out, and most of those in the freshman year due to "academic failure." Despite large enrollment increases, MacIntosh blamed colleges only indirectly for admitting too many students or unqualified students. *Time* explained that students were "partly" to "blame"; quoting MacIntosh in part, it explained that the "'pious sentiment' that everybody should go to college" has resulted in a "'halo'" around the word college and a "blind rush" to attend one. MacIntosh, as *Time* pointed out, mostly blamed colleges because "Many of them fail to learn enough about their students before admitting them, nor do they pay enough attention to them once they are there."[2] *Time*'s message through the editing of MacIntosh's remarks was that it was colleges' fault that so many students drop out, and *Time* did not even hint perhaps students dropping out of private liberal arts colleges may have been transferring to less expensive, more flexible, and more diverse public colleges.

Also in 1948, Harvard President James B. Conant published in *Ladies' Home Journal* what appeared to be a major policy statement, in which he advocated a dramatic expansion of community colleges. He also grudgingly admitted that, even though ex-GIs may have taken up seats in colleges that otherwise would have gone to students with more and traditional qualifications, educating ex-GIs "was, of course, their [colleges'] first obligation." He tied education closely to democracy so as to suggest that the fate of each was tied to the other, even though what he seemed to have meant instead is that the fates of capitalism and education are linked. In any case, Conant lauded "certain uniquely American ideals: equality of educational opportunity, the minimum of class distinction, the maximum of individual freedom, wide distribution of centers of initiative," which he believed worked only within the context of optimism about the capitalist economy (he went so far as to specify "private ownership" and the "profit motive"). Conant ended by making an argument that is an excellent example of a reference to what Habermas called a "cyclical legitimation crisis," the concept of the gap between what late capitalism promises and what it delivers. He wrote that the U.S. education system had the power to "strengthen or destroy our characteristically American ideals," the latter through creating a "caste system." Conant believed that sending more young Americans to college than the economy could absorb in jobs that required a college degree created such a "system," while apparently believing that his solution—asking high school counselors to tell students whether they should go to college or not, and directing many high school graduates to community colleges rather than four-year colleges—did not create a social caste system.[3] (This issue is as, or more, relevant now than it was in 1948; despite elites' talk about the United States requiring a highly educated population for the Information Age and a global economy, U.S. Department of Labor statistics continue to show many more college graduates than jobs that require college degrees.)

Throughout the 1940s, 1950s, and 1960s, coverage of college admissions focused on previous difficulties students faced in gaining admission to the minority of colleges of colleges that were elite (and how such admission was getting easier), with less attention to how easy it was to get into all of the others. By 1978, however, a decline in the number of eighteen-year-olds prompted a shift in college admissions issues: many colleges were beginning to recruit aggressively rather than decide whether to raise or lower admissions standards. An article in *Time* that year was apparently prompted by the publication the previous week of *Hurdles: The Admissions Dilemma in American Higher Education*, by David Tilley (Atheneum). Named as working diligently to recruit students were Coe College (Cedar Rapids, Iowa), Yale, Nathaniel Hawthorne College (Antrim, New Hampshire), Whittier College, University of Texas at Arlington, and Dallas Baptist College. Most intriguing was the lengthy discussion of "yield rates": how many students does a university have to accept in order to fill the freshman class, since not all those accepted will come: the highest yielding public university—San Jose State—boasted 67 percent, while Georgia Tech and Emory were each at only 38 percent.[4] (A *Wall Street Journal* article in 2001 showed that yield rates are still so important that many colleges reject their top applicants if the best applicants are not likely to attend—so that their yield rates increase.)

A one-page article in *Time* in mid-1988 covered colleges with competitive admissions processes wining and dining prospects. Campuses mentioned were Cornell, Columbia, Swarthmore, Yale, Brown, Bowdoin, Harvard, New College (Florida), Sarah Lawrence, Duke, Union, Lafayette, and Princeton. The story's conclusion was a caution from the National Association of College Admission Counselors about students perhaps being too susceptible to marketing, and the proviso that, "A college education is, after all, not cornflakes."[5] The report, though, suggests precisely the opposite: that beyond a few premium-brand colleges, the rest of higher education was (is) just like cornflakes. Institutions of higher education, like all commodities, were already relatively interchangeable and thus there was an institution for anyone.

College tuition typically increased faster than the inflation rate in the 1980s and 1990s, and stories began questioning whether a popular notion of "education for everyone" was becoming threatened. Just as the expansion of college enrollment had been justified as a means to expand, reflect, and preserve democracy, the concept of democracy was invoked when tuitions started becoming less affordable. A *Time* article in mid-1996, more editorial than news story, moved from mentioning historian Frederick Jackson Turner's 1893 vision that public universities would replace the frontier as the hope for democracy, to lamenting quickly rising tuitions and enrollment cuts at California State University in 1992–1993. The article's writer rewrote history by offering evidence that U.S. elites, as well as the general public, have always widely supported public education. In addition to Turner, he cited Lincoln's signing of the Morrill Act, Jefferson's founding the public University of Virginia, Franklin's founding the private University of Pennsylvania, and Harvard President James Bryant Conant's 1943 call for "American radicals" to support public education. Overlooking *Time*'s longstanding obsession with private, elite colleges, writer Nicholas Lemann suggested that if "college" is another word for "opportunity," then colleges should be accessible to all those with "ability and ambition... [A] distinct erosion has taken place." His only nod to the elite schools was that the "opinion-making classes" naturally would discuss issues at universities such as Stanford and Harvard, but frankly "the handful of the most prestigious private schools do not affect very many people and are not a clear public issue." On the contrary, "across-the-board increases" in tuition at public colleges and universities "amount to a major change in government policy," but were "mysteriously underdiscussed." Not a word was mentioned about students obtaining knowledge or skills, and the article simply took it for granted that everyone should go to college (a sentiment that it is extremely unlikely that Turner, Lincoln, Jefferson, Franklin, or Conant would have agreed with). The writer ended the anti-intellectual article revealing his biases for a higher education system that supports democracy and capitalism because it functions as a large, public institution. He complained that changing college tuition from "practically free to expensive changes the bargain between the citizen and the state," even if college education "pays off richly in the long run." (The writer didn't define "pays off," but it is likely that he meant it only in a financial sense.) This was because public education—a "unique and precious national commitment... now diminishing—is the "most important government service" for "most Americans"—"economically," "socially," and "psychically." In fact, he said, public education, literally open to all who meet minimum requirements, "gives a distinctive feeling to this country."[6]

Although the magazines continued to report on events at, and quote professors and administrators almost entirely at private, Eastern elite colleges until well into the 1970s, other words in such articles highlighted middle-class and even working-class aspirations. In a mid-1957 *Reader's Digest* article on college applications, an anonymous dean said, "You do not have to attend college east of the Hudson to be saved," followed by the conclusion that, "Boys and girls of humble background actually enjoy an advantage, for the prestige colleges take rigid precautions to avoid becoming 'class schools.'"[7]

This concept, that even elite colleges were increasingly open, continued to be a part of media coverage through the 1960s and 1970s. A *Life* article in the fall of 1960 about that year's crop of college freshmen clued in more typical college applicants on secrets that may have helped them get into elite institutions: Antioch College was "Not looking for genius," Duke had "a goodly number of spots for athletes," and Harvard had a "Student body apt to be overbalanced with the very bright—needs tempering with the average." Further, Pennsylvania "in admissions seems to consider average student," Princeton's "Selection is overbalanced in favor of high I.Q.'s," Reed gave "Little attention to athletics," and so on. The message was that young Americans didn't have to be particularly intelligent or well-read to get into the elite colleges and universities.[8] Similarly, the *New American Guide to Colleges*, by Gene R. Hawes, in 1964, was paraphrased in *Time* as reporting that a lower percentage of students from families in the *New York Social Register* were attending Harvard, Yale, and Princeton, and more were instead attending other colleges than ever before. Although *Time* provided no evidence that the wealthy students tried to get into the "Big Three" but couldn't, it still reported that "Bright scholars have driven out dull scions." Hawes reluctantly commented (with which *Time* concludes the article): "It could not be said of any period up through the 1940s that most young members of the upper class had to pursue rigorous intellectual training before they could take responsible stations in life. However, this is all too true today. It seems just as well."[9]

A 1988 article narrated a quintessentially American story: Ingenuity leads to admissions into elite schools, even for "everyone." In other words, if one were willing to spend a little money, one could outsmart the system. "Welcome to Madison Avenue U.: Students turn on the hype to win at the college-entrance game" was the headline over a two-page *Time* story that year about college applicants hiring consultants, tutors, test preparation teachers, and others to help them get into top colleges.[10] These extras exemplified ways in which money was shown to be the cache for a fine education.

College admissions policies were not covered regularly by the magazines, but as college enrollment doubled about every ten years—and a prestigious education continued to be upheld as advantageous—admissions received periodic attention. For example, in late 1970, *Time* devoted one and a half pages to the question of admissions policies at the City University of New York (CUNY), which had 190,000 students crammed into eighteen campuses. Headlined "Gambling on Open Admissions," the article presents CUNY officials as progressive but cautious in opening up the university, while at the same time devoting plenty of attention to those who thought CUNY would dumb down too much. Before reassuring readers that "disadvantaged students" wouldn't be "dragging down" quality because they would be placed in noncredit remedial courses and given as much time as they wanted to graduate, *Time* also reported, "Acknowledging fears that the expansion would scare off outstanding students, Bowker redoubled recruiting efforts and succeeded in attracting the same proportion of academic whiz kids that the university has boasted in past years."[11]

Coverage of CUNY seems to have been a catalyst for a renewed, broader discussion of admissions policies, as it was discussed at the 1970 annual meeting of the American Council on Education and in a four-page article in *Time* in late 1970: "Open Admissions: American Dream or Disaster?" The magazine's rhetoric captured the tone, as CUNY's new policy seemed to some "like a triumph of democracy; to others, an omen that colleges may soon be overwhelmed with the 'wrong' kind of students." *Time* called it a "switch from elitism to egalitarianism," and a "most radical response" to changes in major cities. Clearly, the link between education and jobs was on everyone's mind and, therefore, both sides took essentially anti-intellectual positions, with no "pro-intellectual" position represented. A CUNY freshman was quoted as saying, "College is all kids talk about in high school these days. If you don't go to college, you just get any old job," and CUNY had already shifted into needed vocational areas, such as nursing, city planning, and repair/maintenance work.

CUNY Vice Chancellor Timothy Healy praised those who want to attend college only to get a better job: "These are the original American revolutionaries. They want a piece of the action." Much later, however, *Time* noted that

> critics contend that C.U.N.Y.'s new students are being 'overeducated' for nonexistent jobs, and would do better at technical training institutes. Nonsense, says Bowker. The city's economy is rapidly shifting away from manufacturing jobs and he insists that it will need all the service workers and paraprofessionals that C.U.N.Y. can produce.[12]

Irwin Ross's 1972 article in *PTA Magazine*, "College Education: Should It Be a Basic Right for All?"—reprinted in the August 1972 *Reader's Digest*—also focused on CUNY. It was set up as a pro-con debate, with a few pages devoted to each side.

An article in the March 1976 issue of *Nation's Business* was blatantly headlined, "What Recruiters Watch for in College Graduates," as if all college graduates would wish to be employed by the types of mostly larger corporations (a small minority of all corporations) who recruit on college campuses, as if employment is all that counts for college students, and almost as if all corporations should hire using the same criteria.

Keeping college as inexpensive as possible was the theme of an early 1968 *Reader's Digest* article that therefore furthered the idea that college is for everyone. The article described benefits of attending college in two ways: job preparation, or amorphous and "intangible rewards [that] can be even more significant—the lasting friendships, the broadened capacity to serve family and community, the deeper understanding of our modern world, the richer appreciation of life."[13]

In 1978, *Time* updated Americans with a story about how much college was costing ($30,000 for four years!) and how quickly the price was going up (the official inflation rate—based on the federal consumer price index—in 1978 was 7.6 percent). The top ten list was composed of MIT, Bennington, Harvard, Yale, Sarah Lawrence, Pennsylvania, Stanford, Brown, Princeton, and Dartmouth. However, *Time* was finally publishing favorable comments about public universities, and added that in addition to grants and loans to afford college,

"Families can also turn to state schools. Many public colleges offer splendid education for less money, but not all that much less." (It then mentioned that the University of Delaware had cut its tuition, and pointed out what were perhaps surprisingly high costs to attend the University of Vermont, University of Wisconsin, College of William and Mary, and Southern Oregon State College. An accompanying photograph depicted two freshmen at MIT.[14]) Why students go to college, or what the quality of education has to do with its cost, was not addressed.

At least one article suggested that attending college full time need not be a full-time job. "Pink-House Bobos of Atlanta, Ga." in a late 1954 issue of *Ladies' Home Journal* told the story of a husband who had decided to return to college after several years of working. As a married family man of 30, he was working delivering newspapers on a carrier route and attending college to complete his B.S. degree at Georgia Tech before his GI Bill benefits expired. The majority of the article described the trials of a representative young couple without much money. Only the beginning and end of the lengthy article concerned being a nontraditional student. In fact, that he was a college student was not mentioned nor even implied in the article's first page; at the bottom of the second page, the article finally mentioned that a 30-year-old army veteran was delivering the *Atlanta Constitution* in order to pay for his education, and a series of small photos at the bottom of the article's second and third pages showed him sitting at a desk, presumably studying, with his wife hovering over him. The serial caption read, "Barham does his studying at night...sometimes stays clearheaded for weeks...at other times falls asleep at his desk. Tests keep him up. Dottie reminds him: the alarm inevitably rings at 2:30 a.m." A large photo on the third page used a line from the article as the cutline, "At 30, he debated returning to college: 'Suppose I don't try? How will I feel the rest of my life?' Is the current struggle worth it? You get a resounding 'Yes!'" But the headline on the same page made Barham Bobo appear irrational: "Barham left his $100-a-week job to go to Georgia Tech full time. His monthly GI allowance of $120 and paper-route income of $170 support the family while he studies."

For the reader who gets that far, the story ended with a positive note about college for the every-man: Bobo "claims he's getting younger with every term he spends at Tech"; he's "conquered the problems...ranging from reduced income to increased sleepiness and irritability (by now, "it's plain sailing"); and Bobo was facing a win-win choice of going on for graduate work or accepting one of several job offers already in hand.[15]

Not only did coverage suggest that attending college was by then for every American but, over time, a cumulative picture emerged that any barrier to attending college could be overcome. That 1970 *Time* article about admissions at the City University of New York addressed two extreme barriers. Faced with the prospect of students simply not interested in learning, the article pointed out that "gradually teachers found that they could stimulate deep intellectual curiosity with books and materials that illuminated the black experience." No one suggested that interest in learning might be a prerequisite to attending college, as opposed to an attitude that professors were expected and required to elicit. Instead, *Time* offered a lowest-common-denominator type of story apparently as an inspiration to unmotivated students: a two-thirds of a page sidebar told the story of a black man, who spent seven years in prison for robbery, then went to CUNY, and was by 1970 studying for a Ph.D. at Harvard.[16]

The consumer mentality that developed with regard to choosing a college (or a college choosing you) also trickled down to individual departments, professors, and courses at some institutions. For example, a late 1972 *Time* article, "Courses to Turn You On," reported that professors, particularly in disciplines unpopular among students, were responding to student fickleness by marketing their courses, adjusting course content, and even adding into courses components they knew students would like. The University of Pennsylvania geology department sent freshmen a flyer saying, "Give us a chance to turn you on," while an English professor added the movie, *The Godfather*, to his class, which was renamed The Gangster in Film and Literature. Enrollment was also going up in medical-school prep courses such as biology and chemistry (and also in psychology and sociology, for unspecified reasons), and down in engineering and education, because of the job market.[17]

The mystique of the Ivy League is diminished in an article in a late 1992 issue of *Time* about the Massachusetts Institute of Technology and Ivy League universities essentially conspiring with each other in violation of antitrust laws. The Ivy League institutions signed consent decrees pledging that they wouldn't trade information on needy students and offer standardized financial aid packages; MIT has fought back and a judge ruled against it. The Justice Department's lawyer was quoted as saying, "Students and their families are entitled to the full benefits of price competition when they pick a college," while the president of MIT, Charles Vest, claimed that the decision would make it more difficult for the colleges to admit students regardless of financial need.[18] Here the idea of prospective college students and their parents as consumers (consumers of higher education just as they might be consumers of cornflakes) was emphasized.

Evidence Against Advocacy of "Common People's" Interests

Long past the time the majority of young Americans were attending public colleges and universities, *Time, Life,* and other magazines were still giving extensive coverage to Ivy League and other elite schools, conveying the message that prestige and class still counted. Generally, however, the magazines were more interested in economic as opposed to cultural elites. Particularly in *Life*, geographical divisions also were obvious; whereas most articles covered Ivy League and other elite institutions, *Life* occasionally covered a distant, usually public university such as Southern Illinois University or the University of New Mexico. A mid-1960 *Time* article, on increasingly subjective college admissions processes, discussed only Ivy League colleges.[19] The New York–based *Time* in this article and most others in the 1940s, 1950s, and 1960s constructed as undesirable or irrelevant all colleges and college students not in the Ivy League or other prestigious private Eastern colleges. White students over minority students and, as seen above and below throughout the data, male students over female students, continued to be privileged by the media coverage. However, only rarely did textual content defend or promote a curriculum closely associated with the interests of cultural elites.

Even *Reader's Digest,* which for many years had the largest circulation in the United States, celebrated the expensive, private colleges by consistently covering them and quoting their administrators and faculty. In mid-1948, an article (condensed from the March 1948 *Atlantic Monthly*) by Williams College President James Phinney Baxter mentioned only private colleges in the article on colleges' costs. The entire story was a complaint about the rise in colleges' operating costs, followed by a hopeful conclusion out of character with previous descriptions. Asserting that higher education's "opportunities" and responsibilities were "greater than ever," the article framed "big universities" as research institutions, and small colleges as "spread[ing]" that research, "educating men and women for life in a free society, not just teaching them how to earn a living but teaching them the supreme importance of freedom and justice."[20]

An early 1957 article was not atypical of the economic and social class exclusions made by *Time* magazine, several years after most college students were to be found at public institutions and every indication was that public institutions' dominance would grow even more pronounced. That story, about what colleges were doing for superior students—a movement that may well have included all types of institutions nationwide—mentioned only one public university—University of Michigan—and only one west of Chicago—Iowa's Grinnell College.[21] Late the same year, a *Time* article about the pragmatic, anti-intellectual yet graduate school–oriented mood of college students, similarly quoted professors, students, and administrators at Michigan, Kenyon, Princeton, Dartmouth, Columbia, Denison, MIT, Harvard, Amherst, Reed, Chicago, and Virginia. The only non-elite, public universities mentioned were Minnesota, Texas, Iowa, Kansas, and Illinois.[22]

Not just another spring vacation story, a 1960 *Life* piece reproduced the idea of *noblesse oblige* (benevolent and honorable behavior considered to be elites' responsibility) who had both the time and the money to pursue charitable work. Thirty students from Sarah Lawrence College were covered, as the subhead said, "look[ing] into Puerto Rico's problems." Words and photographs combined to show the college women preparing to be mothers and wives in the mainland U.S. and, at the same time, superior to Puerto Ricans (whose island already had been owned by the United States for more than sixty years!). Contrary to earlier reports in *Life*, this article referred to the college women repeatedly as "girls" and photographs depicted them with groups of children, a baby, studying art restoration, discussing family planning with a social worker, visiting the cellist Pablo Casals (who tells them that Puerto Rico's "artistic spirit is free and alive here"), and in sitting in large caned chairs in class; time designated for relaxation was spent at the horse races and snorkeling. Also reinforced were roles such as women as wife/mother figures and whites as superior to other ethnic groups. The women visited Puerto Rico's "big city slums and back-country villages," where one student wrote in her notes, "Nearly all of the villagers are terribly poor and their houses are just shacks, but Puerto Ricans everywhere are warm and dignified and clean—the children are all immaculate." Elsewhere, the women observed clichéd images such as "squalid slums," "population problems," and underpaid fishermen. Another student was pleasantly surprised to find that teachers, officials, and welfare workers "explain the economic facts of life" to typical Puerto Ricans who otherwise might be perceived as having too many children.[23]

Late that same year, another *Life* article followed this with the story of four students from Harvard and one from Yale researching expensive ($452.98) and cheap ($1.98) date weekends in New York City for their booklet, "Ivy League Guide to New York." Again, the wealth of students at exclusive colleges was emphasized; the two photographs on the article's first page portrayed the five at a "high fashion" show and also having just left a rented Rolls-Royce in a no-parking zone. *Life*'s only indication that the story was not to be taken too seriously was its placement at the very end of a 140-page issue.[24]

Also in late 1960, a *Time* article demonstrated economic exclusions by focusing on fifty high-quality but obscure private liberal arts colleges. Prominent in a two-column chart was the total cost of attending each college for a year: only one had total costs of less than $1,150 per year (Berea College, $420, because all students must work on campus), and sixteen cost about $2,000 or more per year. (The U.S. per capita income in 1960, in nominal dollars, was $2,277.[25]) Rather than focusing on the highest-quality public colleges and universities, *Time* perpetuated the idea that a high-quality, private liberal arts education is a highly desirable commodity.

The combination of inflation and competition from state universities affecting private colleges was the subject of a 1976 *Reader's Digest* article by the *New York Times'* education editor. The article barely even referred to students, discussing private colleges as important institutions in a democracy—if only because they could take political and religious positions that state universities cannot. Conceding that only one-quarter of college students were in private schools by 1976, the writer was forced to come up with other reasons why Americans should care about 1,500 private colleges, two-thirds of which enrolled fewer than 1,000 students in 1976. The article led with short vignettes on the closure of Western College in Oxford, Ohio (it was merged into Miami University), New College in Sarasota, Florida, and the near closure of Shimer College in Mt. Carroll, Illinois.[26]

Guides to colleges, first widely published in the 1960s, continued to make news into the 1970s and 1980s, particularly when they said something new or strange. *Time* apparently assumed that students chose colleges based on their social prestige and/or their faculty reputation when its one-third page article, "Snob's Guide: A new way to rate colleges," was published in an issue in late 1978. Prompted by the book, *A New Kind of College Guide that Reports on What You Want to Know Most—and First—About Colleges* by Gene R. Hawes, the article reported, for example, that the University of Cincinnati had more graduates (94) listed in the "Social Register" than did Sarah Lawrence College. (The top ten were Harvard, Yale, Princeton, Pennsylvania, Virginia, Williams, Berkeley, Stanford, Dartmouth, and Cornell.) The book also reported faculty quality using the criterion of median faculty salary. On this one, though, the University of Alaska at Fairbanks was first at $27,800, with Harvard second, and Caltech third. *Time* whimsically pointed out that Kutztown State College in Kutztown, Pennsylvania, paid better than Oberlin, Smith or Yale![27]

In the late 1940s and early 1950s, mass-market magazines' coverage of racial integration in higher education was tied to social, political, and economic mores. After *Brown* v. *Board of Education of Topeka*, with the law shifting in favor of integration, magazines subtly indicated that integration was the way of the future, gently nudging colleges. For instance, that late 1956 *Life* article on rushing fraternities included the fact that all but seven national fraternities had removed "racial eligibility clauses" from their rules. However, it added, "But on only a few campuses has there been any effective move to admit Jews or Negroes—who, in many places, have their own fraternities," and called the situation "improved if far from perfect." So *Life* offered a view that a change from racist rules was progress, even if no change in practices had yet occurred. In so doing, it excused fraternities from admitting blacks or Jews even in 1956. Tellingly, the only minority face shown in twenty-six photos is a black man identified only as the "house porter," dressed in white suit and black bow tie, playing a piano in a jazz trio. To complete a stereotypical image, in the photograph he also appeared to be missing numerous teeth.[28]

The dearth of college students from minority groups was obvious in most magazine coverage, and suggested that higher education was not for minorities. For example, that late 1960 *Life* story about the year's freshmen included photographs of three large groups of students (ranging from several dozen to several thousand) with no discernibly minority faces, even at public universities such as Southern Illinois University or the University of Michigan.[29] Even more dramatically, *Life* reported in early 1957 that Sherman Wu, son of former Taiwan governor K. C. Wu, had been forced to resign from Psi Upsilon fraternity at Northwestern University when eight other pledges dropped out in protest of Psi Upsilon pledging an Asian. Wu was shown in one photo dejectedly leaving Psi Upsilon at Northwestern and, in another photo, smiling and shaking hands with members of Kappa Sigma Alpha—at Olivet College—even though he would remain in school at Northwestern.[30]

In that ten-page late 1970 *Life* article on co-ed dorms, fifty-one students and administrators were pictured in nineteen photographs. Although an almost equal number of men and women were pictured, only two blacks were, and no other ethnic minorities were mentioned or visible. Oberlin College, though a particularly liberal liberal-arts college, was still seen as an almost all-white preserve. The one exception was the shadowy photo, almost a silhouette, of two blacks, with the cutline:

> Freshman Gloria Jackson sings while her classmate Joe May plays the piano in the student lounge at Afro House. The girls in Afro House decided not to have co-ed living quarters because the place was too small. But with 24-hour visiting privileges, the men are always there anyhow.[31]

An early 1996 *Time* article, going so far as using the phrase, "undoing diversity," told the story of the U.S. circuit court of appeals' ruling that the University of Texas law school could not use different admissions standards for minority students than it did for white students. Pictured were nine minority prospects at Texas (whether or not they were law school applicants is not noted) and Cheryl Hopwood, the plaintiff in the case—*Hopwood* v. *State of Texas*. The story—that colleges were still a battleground over race—was sympathetic to Hopwood, as was the federal circuit court panel.[32]

Although college officials admitted that they were not necessarily ready logistically for the large enrollment increase expected in the early 1960s, at least some were greeting it for another reason: they expected that increased applications would drive up the quality of students, so that they could be more demanding in the classroom. An early 1957 *Time* article asserted, "In the classrooms the professors can insist on high achievement levels and dismiss the loafer...The time has come when the college student must produce...How the educators love this," as a headmaster of a private preparatory school was quoted. From the other end of the system, the chancellor of the Oregon state system of higher education added, "It seems to me that if the weight of numbers of students threatens college instructional quality, then it is our clear obligation to control the numbers." In the same article, though, other administrators were quoted as admitting "well-rounded" students, not necessarily the brightest students.[33]

An early 1954 *Life* article, written by a professor, was pro-intellectual, as it conveyed a professor's enthusiasm at teaching students who were eager to learn. The article made a demanding undergraduate environment (at Columbia College of Columbia University), appear to be a win-win situation; the faculty and students also obtained much out of the experience and are said to know it. Conversely, the article suggested that Columbia was an unusual place in a simpler time, something not easily attained in the more complex present.[34]

"The No-Nonsense Kids" was what *Time* called college students in late 1957, when the magazine's education section was devoted to the contemporary mood on campus. *Time* indicated that the mood varies from campus to campus and, then, that "No campus is without its atrocity story of intellectual deadness" (*Time* proceeded to note several). Although *Time* tried to give credit where credit is due, the "no non-sense [sic]" students still were said to be only half-serious about academics. The number of student concerts and plays had increased dramatically, and students were flocking to music appreciation classes—the reason for which was implied later in a discussion of the emphasis on high grades for graduate school applications. Three photographs reinforced this arts, not scholarly, theme. One was "Actress Agnes Moorehead & Wisconsin Students: Amid intellectual calm, increasing intensity." (*Time* did not explain how one might be intellectually calm and intense at the same time.) The second was: "University of Kansas Language Students Listening to Mozart & Bach: After the goldfish swallower, a new kind of individualism." (Again, *Time* didn't explain how going to a Mozart or Bach concert constituted individualism—or why it could or should.) The third photo, a mugshot of J. D. Salinger, noted, "A new voice, but no new idols" despite the story's claim that Salinger "has something approaching universal appeal."

In addition to the arts theme of the photographs, numerous sources in the story showed the international paranoia, cultural conformity, and intellectual complacency of the period. Columbia University Prof. Lionel Trilling said that undergraduates were not committed to anything, and Smith College Prof. Daniel Aaron said the intellectual calm was due to what *Time* called the "rising level and increasing intensity of the average campus' intellectual demands." However, the overall context suggested that perceived employment demands, rather than campus intellectual demands, were to blame, as *Time* paraphrased the professor as saying that college students had "too much ground" to cover for his/her future.[35]

A 1968 book, *Campus 1980*, predicted that colleges would be liberal arts utopias by 1980, implying by contrast that in 1968 they were not. The book's "pro-intellectual" editor, Stanford higher education professor Lewis B. Mayhew, wrote that "Students will fashion their own curriculum, teach each other, study on their own up to a third of the time, and quit school, return or transfer at will." *Time* summarized Mayhew's beliefs as "the 1980 curriculum will accent the liberal arts, de-emphasize purely fact-oriented classes," and deal with "'the big, perplexing questions of mankind.'" Moreover, Mayhew predicted (as *Time* wrote), "Technical and vocational training will be discarded from the undergraduate curriculum; corporate employers will supply that in a modern version of the apprentice system," and that "all educators will come to recognize that a balanced, liberal arts college education can be absorbed by and [be] helpful to almost everyone, provided that the pressures of grading and lock-step progress are eased."[36] If Mayhew and his co-authors explained why these changes would occur, *Time* did not report such explanations. *Time*, by devoting more than a third of a page to Mayhew's book and not citing any facts or experts to the contrary, seemed to endorse Mayhew's vision. However, *Time* also did not offer evidence for why it would occur. As it turned out, Mayhew was correct in predicting increases in international and older students, but he was wrong about most everything else, particularly in his belief that "technical and vocational training will be discarded." The largest increases in enrollment since 1968 have been precisely in those areas if broadly defined.

Evidence for Support of Right-Wing Populism

For Hofstadter, Rigney, and others, the best evidence of the populist anti-elitism and anti-intellectualism was the popularity of political figures such as the Rev. Charles Coughlin during the 1930s, Sen. Joe McCarthy during the 1950s, and George Wallace and Spiro Agnew during the 1960s and early 1970s. No media reports about higher education were found, among those analyzed, in which McCarthy or Wallace were supported, endorsed or normalized, and coverage of Agnew seemed tied to his position and outspokenness more than any other consideration. However, right-wing populism has been and still is manifested in many other ways. One is criticism of intellectuals and the highly educated that come from the right end of the political spectrum. Another is popular support of intellectuals or the highly educated who are considered by the general public to be "right-wing." Yet another is criticism of intellectuals and higher education grounded in religious conservatives (see religious anti-rationalism section above). Evidence for all three was found in the magazines.

Harvard President Conant, in his lengthy policy statements about higher education in that 1948 issue of *Ladies' Home Journal*, explicitly concluded that the United States should not educate any more "doctors, lawyers, engineers, scientists, [or] college professors" than jobs available to them, and explained that Americans who are well educated are essentially overeducated and a threat to democracy because of it:

> May not advanced specialized education make a man a desperately unhappy citizen and hence an unstable member of the body politic? It is a rare individual who is not deeply frustrated if he has spent years in acquiring certain skills and knowledge and then finds society unable to find a place for him to function according to his expectations; and from frustrated individuals with long education and considerable intelligence society has much to fear.

Conant said those frustrated individuals—"professionally trained but unemployed 'intellectual proletariat'"—become "leaders of anti-democratic movements" (such as Nazism) on both the left and right. At this point he discussed at length community colleges and junior colleges,[37] presumably on the basis that the "intellectual proletariat" must be subdued by vocational education rather than threaten democracy with their frightening bachelor's degrees.

S. I. Hayakawa, later a U.S. senator from California, and then-governor of California Ronald Reagan also became right-wing populist figures, for their tough stances against student protests. Part and parcel of Hayakawa's position was that too many students who didn't belong there had been admitted to college. In 1968, *Reader's Digest*, condensing an article from *The Wall Street Journal*, quoted a statement by Hayakawa (then president of San Francisco State College): "From about the age of 15 on, our young people, whether or not they have a bent for intellectual life, are pushed and prodded by parents and teachers—and even more by community expectation—to go to college. Once there, the men stay to protect their draft deferments." He added that "the bored student[s]" are "social dynamite." Hayakawa recommended expelling them and claimed that he would do so were it not for faculty resistance. In contrast, he said, other students were taking college seriously as "preparation for becoming a teacher, a lawyer, an engineer, a scientist, a poet, a businessman."[38]

In addition to doctrinal tests, one way in which the populist right wing has taken the measure of the country's morality has been to assess citizens' factual knowledge about religion. In 1948, a *Time* article headlined simply, "Illiterates," excerpted a *Religious Education* article about sophomores (at an unnamed college) who had just completed a semester-long survey of religion class. The journal article's author complained that of fifty students (almost all from religious homes), only eight or nine were "religious literates" and then summarized students' factually incorrect beliefs about key aspects of the Bible.[39] *Time* left the professor's remarks to stand on their own, the implication being that the students, their parents, clergy, or earlier teachers were at fault for their ignorance. *Time*'s reporting did not answer the question implicit in its uncritical coverage of college expansion of how such expansion would solve such professors' problems. *Time* repeated this same theme two and a half years later, this time under "Religious Illiterates," when it quoted parts of a *Christian Century* article written by a professor who had studied 2,000 students at three colleges. Of eighty-three typical students, R. Frederick West reported, only four knew all Ten Commandments, only nine knew "even approximately" what Jesus emphasized as the two most important, and only thirteen could name the four Gospels. The professor said teaching religion to postwar college students "must begin from scratch."[40] Ironically, today's conservative leaders often try to paint postwar America as having had a devout middle-class of sophisticated Christians.

In 1987, Allan Bloom published his *The Closing of the American Mind* to wide acclaim, particularly among right-wing populists and Bloom's fellow elitists (see chapters one and two). "A most uncommon scold," was the headline of *Time*'s three-page story in late 1988—in the form of an edited, transcribed interview. Although the interviewer, William McWhirter, asked Bloom several tough questions (including asking Bloom to respond directly to several pointed criticisms), the professor appeared to be reasonable and the overall portrayal of him was favorable. Accused of having written an "anti-democratic" book, Bloom responded that his book's points were proven "in spades" by the "violence and passion" of its critics. He scoffed at being called "elitist" or "sexist" ("all the great political terms") by bogus "intellectuals." In the interview, Bloom essentially called students anti-intellectual and blamed universities for not even trying to battle the anti-intellectualism of their incoming students. He explained that students were not reading "seriously" because universities did not challenge students' "belief that they can't learn important things from books. They believe books are just ideologies, mythologies or political tools of different parties." Bloom believed that the "peaks of learning" needed to offer "some shining goal in the distance"—and that such a goal would also answer demands for multicultural curricula because it would be "very attractive" to students with "very diverse backgrounds." Here he was reminiscent of Gramsci's claim that liberal arts served all students while professional and technical programs were divisive.

Bloom clearly opposed anti-elitism because humans, to identify their "leaders," do and must have a "capacity to recognize rank order, or decent people, or moral people, or intelligent and wiser people." (On this point, Bloom was like William Henry in his *In Defense of Elitism*.) The "central perspective of education," he said, was "inspiring one to human perfection," and otherwise "it would be very boring to be man." Bloom didn't address those Americans who are content with boredom. He was particularly critical of feminist scholarship, but not African-American studies or interests, because the latter was not "challeng[ing] the basic curriculum," while the former was "arguing that there has been an entire misinterpretation or an evil interpretation throughout history."

Students simply wanted to avoid theoretical and political battles, Bloom believed, and their anti-intellectualism was "new" (rather than inherent in the culture as per Hofstadter). Its results, he observed, were students who were simply less "interested" in say, "the purpose of life," than in talking about "rights" and being generally "angry" — a "new kind of thought control" preventing any "serious discussion." Black students especially, Bloom claimed, were separating themselves from others on campus, not taking theoretical courses (perhaps because they "distrust the value of humanities"). McWhirter asked the University of Chicago professor for an "ideal of Bloom's campus," in other words an intellectual or pro-intellectual campus, rather than an anti-intellectual one, and Bloom explained, "The universities are practically all that we have left of our intellectual life... [W]e stake everything on the universities." One way to save the universities, he suggested, was to assign students books, about subjects in which they are interested, in necessarily interdisciplinary courses (note that Bloom was on Chicago's interdisciplinary Committee on Social Thought):

> These would be the places where the physicists have to think about Kant and Hegel, not just Einstein; where the social scientists consider what is a good society as well as polls and survey results; where a political scientist asks whether he can justify giving advice to tyrants as well as democrats.

Contrary to claims that his book was at least partially motivated by 1960s student protests at Cornell, when he taught there, Bloom said, "I felt a certain kind of release when these very powerful and intense things happened." His only complaint, he claimed, was that "black power" made its debut at Cornell under a "weak president" who could not defend his "bourgeois" institution and who admitted too many black students unprepared for a college such as Cornell. However, the key point about *Time*'s devoting three pages to Bloom the year after his book was published was that no news event drove *Time*'s coverage. Instead, *Time* helped Bloom by promoting his ideas as influential for shaping the debate in the late 1980s about higher education.[41]

Opposition to drug use generally, but particularly among high school and college students, has been a perennial issue of populist right-wing elements on the American scene, from anti-marijuana efforts in the 1930s, to anti-crack initiatives in the 1980s, to anti-all drugs efforts continuing today. Drug use by high school and college students has become a staple topic of journalism about education in the United States, although only one such story was included in the sample examined here. A stereotypical drug scare story, with an anonymous author, was published early in 1968 by *Reader's Digest:* It argued that smoking marijuana does lead to harder drugs, and that students' common beliefs about drugs were untrue. He estimated that 20 percent of Yale undergraduates were smoking marijuana.[42] Rather than being a well-reasoned article supported by medical or crime data, however, this article was a one-sided polemic.

Whether the image of students as "spoiled rich kids" was more of a right-wing populist stereotype or left-wing populist stereotype was unclear, but in any case such complaints reflected American populism. One article in which it is found was a 1984 *Time* piece about students' fears about a nuclear holocaust. The first two paragraphs covered a vote by Brown University students (1,044 to 687) asking the university administration to buy cyanide pills that students could take in the event of nuclear war. Brown's administration refused, and *Time* quoted an unnamed "blue collar worker in Lynn, Mass." who commented, "These spoiled rich kids. Everyone else is going to suffer a slow death, and they want a quick way out." The remainder of the one-third page article was about Harvard child psychiatrist Robert Coles's empirical finding that only children of "affluent parents" were worried about nuclear holocaust: "The children in the ghetto are worried about the next meal, about where they will find work."[43]

Evidence For and Against Support of Right-Wing Populism

No evidence was found that these magazines' content directly or indirectly opposed the right-wing populist manifestation of American anti-intellectualism. However, one common characteristic of much higher education coverage in which the current status of higher education has been criticized is that so many of the critics either were quoted or paraphrased as admitting that they belonged to a small dissenting group, or magazine coverage portrayed them this way anyway.

A good example of this is *Time* magazine's favorable coverage in late 1949 of Isaiah Berlin, a philosophy professor at Oxford University and former First Secretary of the British Embassy in Washington ("his brilliant reports on U.S. thinking and doing made him Winston Churchill's most penetrating official observer of wartime America"). The article was composed primarily of lengthy quotes from Berlin's blistering critique of the U.S. culture and economy's effects on its higher education. It is a good example of what Foucault would call the quoting of official, credentialed sources and what Habermas would call the employment of "formal opinions." *Time*'s editors paraphrased Berlin as having diagnosed the "sinister cause" of academic "congestion and confusion": Students and professors who had survived "war service" or other traumatic experiences were "painfully aware of the social and economic miseries of their society." This, in turn, led such people, "[l]ike the youthful Kropotkin" (a Russian scientist and anarchist/communist activist who denounced his noble title of "prince"; he died in 1921) to "wonder[] whether it can be right for him to continue to absorb himself in the study of, let us say, the early Greek epic at Harvard, while the poor of south Boston go hungry and unshod." In short, *Time* said Berlin observed, "scholars and intellectuals find they can no longer believe in their scholarly or intellectual pursuits for their own sake." Berlin was quoted as having concluded, based on history, that "Once a community automatically begins to consider disinterested curiosity as being something idle, time-wasting, self-indulgent and, therefore, immoral, it is in a very bad way." Neither great art, nor great science, are possible, Berlin pointed out, if their creators have an "eye on the social consequences."[44] So while he was opposed to the anti-intellectualism of U.S. scholars and intellectuals, Berlin also became an expert source for the observation that anti-intellectualism among U.S. scholars is rampant. Such anti-intellectualism therefore was seen as dominant, difficult to resist, and even socially undesirable to resist even if one could.

An article in *Life* many years later (1972) offered a different take on left-wing populism: the idea that college graduates can and even should pursue blue-collar, not white collar, jobs upon graduation. It was the story of Harvard graduates either temporarily or permanently working in jobs for which they may have been overqualified: truck driver, glassblower, auto mechanic, bartender, carpenter, moving man, humane officer, and house painter. The article painted an elitist picture of the Harvard student, even while suggesting at least some Harvard students seemed average. It broke down the notion that college-educated Americans were unwilling or unable to take blue-collar jobs, while at the same time hinting that Harvard graduates could leave them at any minute and suggesting that Harvard grads were helped in landing the blue-collar job of their choice (an advantage that not all blue-collar workers enjoy). According to the article's first page, Harvard graduates had left behind their "bittersweet academic agony" and were looking forward to "no more cramming for exams until dawn washed the elms of the Yard, no more term papers, no more lectures, no more quizzes that expose the unprepared as nakedly as an X ray." The article did not say whether all college educations were "academic agonies," and Harvard's was simply "bittersweet," or whether only elite schools inflicted "agony" on their students. In any case, the article's lead was based on old elitist myths: "You always used to be able to tell a Harvard man—but as the pictures here suggest, it's getting more difficult. The old joke was that you couldn't tell them much. You still can't"—here because they have chosen to pursue blue collar work rather than going to graduate school or "starting careers in the executive corridors of business and industry." *Life* went on to call college graduates who would work with their hands "intellectually disaffected" and part of a "whole growing spectrum of young Americans who simply cannot make up their minds what they want to do—or be." However, the article made it clear that Harvard graduates, if not all college graduates, had numerous options, as "Many donned the blue collar only while awaiting openings in crowded medical and law schools or the white-collar job market." *Life* reassured readers that Harvard was not about to offer "shop courses," but ventured that students' decisions suggested that colleges and universities could "encourage travel or work" between high school and college and that the employers offer internships instead of demanding that graduates make "long-term commitments."

Life provided plenty of detail about individual Harvard graduates so that anti-intellectualism could appear concrete rather than abstract. Joel Scott Coble was described as fleeing the "bloodless world of teleology and epistemology and the analytic formulas of the likes of Ludwig Wittgenstein" for the "driver's seat of a 10-wheel dumper" owned by a California construction firm. Coble had found philosophy "detached" from real-world problems: "It's lying and it's bull." He's additionally quoted as saying that he smartly avoided the "mistake" of going to law school: "Why do I want this false bull—fame,

glamour, the *appearance* of knowledge, like my Harvard diploma?"
What he really wanted, *Life* showed, was "to understand what the hell
is going on"—something one apparently couldn't do on a university
campus. Similarly, new glassblower Jamie Maslach decided at Harvard
that he liked cooking better than studying. Judy Norsigian enjoyed
fixing cars so had decided to become a doctor to fix people. Four
bartending graduates planned to go to medical school, law school, ar-
chitecture school, and run a restaurant, respectively. Joel Nichols
would become an architect instead of an artist for a secure income.
Humane officer Jim Muscato found, in *Life*'s words, that "close textual analysis just isn't nearly as interesting as a woebegone mutt in
need of help or a newborn Nilgai antelope he met while checking on
animal care at the zoo." Finally, housepainter Dave Johnson decided,
in *Life*'s words, that there "seemed few other ways to use his degree"
other than going to graduate school, which he didn't want to do.[45]

Evidence Against Support of Left-Wing Populism

Rigney might suggest that opposition to left-wing populism is the
counterweight to left-wing populism, but another possibility is its
apostates: persons who at one point were left-wing populists and later
recant their previous positions. Such was the case with Joan Didion, in
her mid-1970 *Life* editorial, "A generation not for barricades." It
pointed to college as a landmark time in young Americans' lives; she
wrote about thinking back to attending Berkeley in the early 1950s,
why students then did not protest, and why she did not protest in 1970
either. Almost nihilistic in tone, the editorial's main point seems to
have been in its middle, where she wrote that her so-called "silent
generation" wasn't silent because of the 1950s' "official optimism"
or its "official repression"; rather, the "exhilaration" of "social action" was just another "escap[e]" from the "dread" of how
"meaningless...man's fate" is. Because 1950s Berkeley students accepted that both the world and the university were "imperfect," their
"discourse [was] less than spirited, and debate nonexistent...the
mood...mild but chronic 'depression.'" Didion in 1970 was still resigned, not going to the "barricade" because it would make no difference (if it did, she said, it would be a "happy ending"). She
pointed out that of students she knew at Berkeley, only one had "dis-

covered an ideology" and become famous, while a "few" others committed suicide. One who failed at the latter, Didion noted, "in a recovery which seemed in many ways a more advanced derangement, came home and joined the Bank of America's three-year executive-training program. Most of us live less theatrically..."[46] Publishing her editorial, *Life* held out the possibility that, although one may be a left-wing populist (or some other variety of anti-intellectual) when one is young, one may reverse one's views later; of course it also means the opposite.

Evidence for the Devaluation of Book Learning and Standards

Along with support and defense of "common people's interests," discussed above, the devaluation of book learning, high academic standards in jeopardy and the neglected development of the most gifted students is the other primary constellation of phenomena that compose populist anti-elitism. Gramsci, as discussed in the previous chapter, would attribute much of this to "intellectuals" and "masses" being "far apart," and to the public's assumption that intellectuals often are hostile to pluralism and the loss of tradition. Habermas, Hofstadter, Rigney, and Katchadourian and Boli, as explained, attributed these phenomena to an incorrect conclusion that intellectuals are "unproductive" (Habermas would add that intellectuals are not given due credit for furthering democracy) in a late capitalist economy.

Some references to intellectual students are vague generalizations, which have their own kind of impact as they appear to reflect "common wisdom." For example, in mid-1964, *Life* started an editorial with this:

> It seems like just the other day that everybody was down on college students for being such greasy grinds. No politics. No demonstrations. No adventure. Nothing but books, books, books and maybe an argument about which corporation gives you the best retirement benefits. Well, *that* phase is over, for better or worse. Mostly better. . . .[47]

However, this subtle devaluing of intellectualism on campus was mild compared with other instances. What is striking about U.S. magazine coverage of higher education was how often intellectuals were not ignored, but portrayed as a cause and effect of stereotypes constructed in clearly negative ways. That late 1970 *Life* article about coed dormitories, which called intellectual Oberlin students lonely with cold parents, was not the only article of its type.[48]

Another story did nothing but suggest how difficult, how unusual, and even how unpleasant it can be to be highly intelligent. The average Caltech student had an IQ of 140, gifted students at Caltech volunteered to take a non-credit physics course from Richard Feynman (who would win the 1965 Nobel Prize in physics), and highly intellectual students might be allowed to skip college and go directly to graduate school, reported *Time* in early 1956 with "Exceptionally Exceptional." Late in the article, it was pointed out that only two universities train school teachers to "handle...exceptionally bright students," whereas twenty universities train teachers about the "exceptionally handicapped." Further, a Caltech professor was quoted as saying, "There's a stigma attached to being called a brain. The athletic department is much more successful than we are at singling out its exceptional students."[49] In other words, America had spoken, and it not only valued athletics more than academics, but stigmatized intelligence, with Caltech and MIT as voices in the wilderness.

A late 1964 *Life* article was just as melancholy about intellectuals as its headline suggested, "Gifted Boy Finds His Way: Barry Wichmann's Escape from Mediocrity." The headline may have made it sound as though Wichmann (from Rockwell City, Iowa) was once mediocre and was now gifted, but the story revealed that Wichmann always was gifted, and it was the anti-intellectualism of his primary and secondary school teachers and curricula that caused him to turn in a mediocre school performance. *Life* had covered Wichmann before, in 1958, in a story on the "tragic failure of the American school system to provide challenges to gifted children." Then, he had an IQ of 162 and was "bored and inattentive" after being "Lumped in with average students." *Life* claimed in 1964 that "massive concern" for bright students since 1958 had led to "standards stiffening for everybody, the brilliant minds...coddled and courted the way that potentially great football players have been for decades." Thus, *Life* showed a world in which educators had realized the errors of their ways in ignoring smart students and in six years had made a change in schools that would be roughly equivalent to making a U-turn with an eighteen-wheeler in a narrow alley.

The breadth and depth of U.S. anti-intellectualism was detailed in this article, clarifying how difficult this cultural phenomenon would have been to change. First, Wichmann himself had not responded well to his parents' efforts to keep him intellectually stimulated. Second, after the 1958 article, Wichmann's own teachers would ridicule him and repeatedly question his intelligence in class. His parents accepted a scholarship for him from Culver Military Academy in South Bend, Indiana, but its regimentation made his life even worse. Wichmann completed his sophomore, junior, and senior years at a public high school in Winchester, Virginia, where his problems with algebra resulted in his dropping that course for journalism. The article concluded with Wichmann as a happy freshman at the new branch of St. John's College in Santa Fe.[50] (The College's curriculum consists entirely of students reading books and then discussing them with their professors.)

Overall, *Life* constructed an image of middle America (there's nowhere more middle in America than Rockwell City, Iowa) as almost hopelessly anti-intellectual, and kids such as Barry Wichmann as weird curiosities. However, it also implied that the entire U.S. culture was anti-intellectual: starting out in anti-intellectual Rockwell City, life was worse for him in South Bend and only slightly better in Winchester. The only place he could get away from it all was at St. John's, a small and unique (not normal) school. The report gave no indication of what Wichmann might do when he finished college, arguably implying that there was no obvious role or function in the United States for highly intelligent citizens such as Wichmann. Finally, guilt over neglect of the gifted was assuaged by the information that "brilliant minds" were finally being "coddled and courted." *Life* relieved readers by noting that the nation's Barry Wichmanns were not drawing on too many resources: almost parenthetically, the article noted "standards stiffening for everybody." In the light of this article, that claim seems, and must have seemed, difficult to believe, and the article's more vivid message was that no one would want to be like Barry Wichmann.

By 1976, most of the articles in U.S. magazines indexed in the *Reader's Guide to Periodical Literature* under "College Graduates" related solely or primarily to jobs. Naturally, a March 1976 *Nation's Business* article was titled, "What Recruiters Watch for in College Graduates" (majors in "business, engineering, computer science, or the physical sciences," with humanities and social sciences way down the list). An early 1976 *Time* article was bluntly headlined, "Slim Pickings for the Class of '76," and an article late that year, "Dear Candidates: Watch Out," consisted of excerpts of a letter from Wellesley College President Barbara W. Newell to presidential candidates Jimmy Carter and Gerald Ford about college students of the day. The March article portrayed anti-intellectual attitudes about college education as most prevalent and reasonable. The article indicated that based on a then-forthcoming book (*The Overeducated American*, by Harvard economist Richard B. Freeman), the number of Americans obtaining college degrees each year started exceeding the number of professional, technical, managerial, and administrative jobs available in 1965, and the oversupply of college graduates would be getting worse. *Time* summarized employer attitudes toward Ph.D.s thusly: "[C]orporations often regard Ph.D.s as otherworldly"—as if it were possible in an increasingly complex economy to be overeducated. The article noted graduates who already have bachelor's degrees going back for second, more "practical" degrees, and liberal arts colleges generally trying to offer more "practical" courses.[51]

The magazine coverage not only slapped intellectual students with negative stereotypes or emphasized characteristics that could be considered negative, but the magazines also repeatedly offered the insight that one no longer needed to be an elite student to be admitted to an elite college. For example, a mid-1957 *Reader's Digest* article told prospective college students and their parents that although 700,000 students attend college, prospective applicants need not "get panicky" nor "fear that only the outstandingly brilliant students will make the grade." On the contrary, "The fact is that even outstanding institutions do not want their campuses predominantly populated by bookworms and near-geniuses. Their goal is a well-rounded student community." It went on to detail how applicants can instead give evidence of "industry," "integrity," "initiative," "enthusiasm," "concern for others" and, finally, "intellectual curiosity" (only the latter has any exclusive connection with learning). In the "enthusiasm" section, Harvard Admissions Dean Wilbur J. Bender said, "We get more and more doubtful about the nose-to-the-grindstone boy. I'd rather have a C student who is bursting with energy"—bursting with energy apparently to do anything but study! Students were then advised that they could gain extra points with their applications if they: "Don't scorn good marks," "Form regular study habits—the sooner the better," "Get useful experience through jobs," and "Have hobbies—and make them meaningful." That anti-intellectualism was widespread and socially acceptable was communicated by sentences such as this, "Many high-potential youngsters destroy their chances by falling for the 'anti-brains' snobbism of irresponsible schoolmates."[52]

Many articles, in addition to noting that admissions criteria were broader than simply academic achievement or academic promise, went on to describe the entire admissions process as something of a crapshoot, with admissions officers making decisions that were subjective almost to the point of being arbitrary. Quoting statistics and admissions committee members and others, reciting details of several individual students' situations, Time in mid-1960 painted a picture of colleges overwhelmed with highly qualified applicants and, at the same time, unwilling to take only the most qualified. The result, reported the magazine, both in the article's words and spread as a photo cutline under mugshots of four applicants, was that "The decisions often seemed downright whimsical." Dartmouth's admissions director was quoted as admitting, "We say in the net we think this boy is a better boy for Dartmouth (to hell with numbers) and we take that boy." Near the article's end, Time paraphrased college "officials" opposed to "strictly academic criteria" and an "overemphasis on tests" and were understanding of "besieged admissions men...due to depend more and more on subjective criteria." The magazine's editors had no objection "unless the Ivy League colleges expand" (unlikely), or until the nation creates more good colleges that also enjoy Ivy League prestige" (apparently also unlikely).[53] The New York Times editorialized about this Time article, saying that college admission should be based entirely on objective measures. However, its editorial was denounced by the New York Times'' own elderly publisher, Arthur Hays Sulzberger, using a known pen name.[54]

Admissions controversies also were covered by Time in another mid-1960, issue, although the story's headline conveyed the entire point: "something has to give."[55] A Time article late that year, "Luck & Pluck," quoted Yale and Dartmouth officials wishing for a computer program that could take all characteristics of all students into consideration for admissions.[56] "The Search for Something Else" was the headline of an article in a mid-1968 Time about college admissions committees seeking applicants who had "a wild sense of humor, a weird hobby, or almost anything else that sets a student off from the ordinary." *Time*'s writers then went on to detail a student who was admitted by the University of Pennsylvania despite a "generally undistinguished academic record," and one who entered Columbia despite "below-average grades." A Princeton admissions official confessed that the last eighty-nine spots had been filled by "whimsy and brutality," and Yale took a student who was unsure that he even wanted to go to college.[57] "New Ways into College," in *Time* in mid-1972, was about the wacky examples of their work that applicants were sending to admissions departments at Yale and Bowdoin, although Bennington, Harvard, and Hampshire also were mentioned. Yale, for example, rejected applicants who had mailed in a hand-stitched pillowcase, an apple cake and a "sexy black negligee handmade of appliqued silk. At Bowdoin, President Roger Howell took a bite of cookie made by one aspirant and grunted, 'She'd better be good in class because she's not in the kitchen.' She wasn't, and was not admitted." Another applicant had seen a tear in a Bowdoin official's pants and had sent him an embroidered linen patch. In all of this coverage, *Time* suggested that concentrating on academics in college admissions was no better than other criteria and may be worse, and that colleges were doing what they could; more importantly, it suggested that students should not count on intellectual promise or high academic achievement as the best way to get into the college of their choice.[58] *Life*'s coverage was similar: recall from above its 1960 article on that fall's freshmen: it was reported that Duke had "a goodly number of spots for athletes," Harvard had a "Student body apt to be overbalanced with the very bright — needs tempering with the average," Pennsylvania "in admissions seems to consider average student," and so on.[59]

Much magazine coverage particularly devalued book learning for women students, especially during the 1940s, 1950s, and 1960s. To the question posed in its mid-1957 headline, "Is College Education Wasted on Women?" the magazine essentially answered, "Yes, but it could be different." The teaser on the article's first page read, "Many college girls don't want what a higher education is supposed to offer, survey revealed. Here with some peppery comments from our readers." The eye was immediately drawn to handwritten comments surrounding the first two pages of the article, all signed with initials, all supposedly direct quotes from reader mail. One claimed that it "take[s] as much intelligence, education and all-round wisdom to raise a family as to have a successful career" and that any notion otherwise is "just silly." Another claimed that women in earlier years had time for "intellectual pursuits" (and presumably took advantage of this opportunity!) because of the availability of "capable helpers" (domestic employees) in the "old days," but that such workers no longer were available. On the second page, a reader wrote, "A distinguished analyst says 'men are basically hostile to the intelligent woman,' and 'Men cannot stand competition from women'" but that the real problem in U.S. society was ignorant men. Another wrote, "Let's face it. Most females between 18 and 25 are out to get a chap."

Such quotes formed a parameter, both ideologically and visually, around the article's words, and convey how bleak U.S. society was for smart women (and women in general). Elsewhere, it was asserted that some "women students...go through four years of college without being appreciably influenced by their academic work." Many women attended college because they could afford to, to avoid any "social handicap," to make friends, to meet "eligible" young men, and to learn "how to get along with others." Certainly, they were not going, it was written, because of any "thirst for knowledge" (later, the article alleged that even women among the "intellectual elite" may not have "scholarly interests or get much out of college"). Besides, "What else, indeed, are we to do with an 18-year-old girl who is not needed at home, and who is not yet ready for marriage?" Because American culture is one "in which merely being intellectual does not cut much ice," the article continued, at the very least the desirable "benefits" of college should be "less expensive."

The article's male author gave credit to colleges for at least attempting to interest students in the "satisfactions of learning." But he then argued that professors' efforts were no use against students' anti-intellectual culture; after making a case for student culture's power, Sanford explained that students believe college should be "taken seriously...not too seriously. Frivolity is discouraged," but "outstanding" work is only "tolerated" and not "applauded." Student culture discouraged those who thought too much or talked too much, as such students were viewed as "too ambitious"; "moderation" in both "behavior and accomplishment" was hegemonic. (The only benefit was that students also supposedly policed any individuals who were "too indifferent.")

Further, intellectual female students comprised one of only two groups that were "exceptions" to a general rule of dating a lot while a freshman (to establish a presence on campus) and a senior (to actively find a marriage partner), and less so as a sophomore and junior. Sanford believed that the women "superior scholars" tended to be either engaged or "deeply in love, but do not feel they must sacrifice their own individualities or their aims for a career if they wish to marry." Later, however, the article justified women's thinking that life has only two paths, work or marriage, and that they were mutually exclusive. Among other reasons, "they [women] suspect—not without foundation—that there is no real place in our society for the liberally educated person who is not identified with some accomplishment or activity." Then, though, the writer circled back to defending college. He blamed the Cold War for forcing women to feel more traditional, and "Thus is that we have an upsurge of the attitude that one must not appear too bright or too competent, lest this threaten one's ability to take traditional feminine roles."[60]

"College, Who Needs It?" published in 1972 in *Time*, was one of the more dramatic examples of anti-intellectualism among those examined. It was based on many young Americans' attitude, said the Educational Testing Service's Richard Peterson, that "a college education is not needed for what they consider the good life. More and more, they feel that they can live satisfactorily without a college degree." The message was that one did not need to have a job that required a college degree to be happy; the article did not point out that going to college involves more than just preparing for certain jobs. The article reported that "Enrollment figures seem to indicate that to attract students, colleges should consider ways to accommodate stopouts, special programs for minority students, more vocational training and new interdisciplinary curriculums [sic]." It then detailed the new ecology-oriented curriculum at the University of Wisconsin at Green Bay, Ferris State College in Michigan offering associate's degrees in auto repair and body mechanics, and Evergreen State College in Washington with its "no grades, no departmental requirements."[61]

Four years later, *Reader's Digest* used an almost identical headline, "College—Who Needs It?" to publish a condensed version of a story, "Who needs college?" from an early 1976 issue of *Newsweek*. It told of a Phi Beta Kappa graduate from the University of Colorado who was a restaurant manager, and a Columbia University Ph.D. in

English who was a welder. However, these were just hooks to get readers into the story, where they were told that parents were worrying about the cost of education and the relevance of curricula to a constructive life. Anti-intellectual concerns solely about the link between education and jobs may lead, the article speculated, to this: "For the first time in American history, large numbers of young people may deliberately choose to be less well educated than their parents." The article then paraphrased and quoted Caroline Bird's book, *The Case Against College*: "Only a minority enjoy study for its own sake. 'They should get no more public subsidy for this amusement than those who like to ski,' she insists." Harold L. Hodgkinson, director of the National Institute of Education, pointed out, "We must separate the college-degree-granting function from the occupational-licensing function."[62]

By 1978, some colleges (Harvard as reported) started going in the other direction from "courses to turn you on," as its dean of arts and sciences, Henry Rosovsky, turned in a thirty-six–page proposal for a core curriculum. Government professor Michael Walzer, in favor of the plan, was quoted in an early 1978 issue of *Time* as complaining, "We can't function as a nutritionist who tells his patients that they are very intelligent and that there's a supermarket around the corner." Opponent Orlando Patterson, a sociology professor, retorted, "Arriving at some fixed notion of what constitutes an educated person—in this day and age, it just won't wash. It moves away from a view that learning to think for oneself is the key to a modern education." No student was quoted. They were represented by only the *Harvard Crimson* newspaper, which editorialized that "the core will not solve one of Harvard's fundamental problems, the dearth of close association between students and faculty members." *Time* reported that the core curriculum was expected to pass.

Intriguing in this story was that the proposed core curriculum wasn't exactly restrictive; apparently without the core curriculum policy, Harvard had almost no requirements or even guidelines. The editorial cartoon that accompanied *Time*'s story (along with a mug-shot of Rosovsky) overreacted: one older man says to another older man, "I like what this young fella Rosovsky says about this core curriculum, by God! Only after studying subjects in which one has absolutely no interest can one claim to be an educated man."[63] This cartoon satirized and reflected U.S. anti-intellectualism extremely well.

In the 1970s, an issue mentioned in many magazine articles was "stopping out"— students taking time off from college and then returning. The message of a mid-1978 *Time* article, "When in Doubt, 'Stop Out': More and more students are hitting the road instead of the books," was ambiguous even though the headline may not have been. Students discussed here were not quitting college, nor did they doubt the value of a college degree *per se*, but had expressed the need for a break during college and often compare and contrast college with the "real world." In any case, the article made it clear from its lead that neither *Time*'s editors nor many people on college campuses think of campuses as being real: "Harvard's daily, the *Crimson*, publishes a news digest titled, 'The Real World.' Traditionally, that was a place undergraduates had to wait many years to see firsthand. But now more and more students, finding that it is a long way from kindergarten to graduate school, are 'stopping out,' as educators put it." The article highlighted Stanford senior Doug Patt, who at twenty-eight had "stopped out" twice, and other students who had "stopped out" of Rice, Johns Hopkins, Princeton, and Yale. Only one of the students discussed was a woman, and it was not clear if any were minorities, although Princeton student Steven Hayishi might be either Japanese or Japanese American. Students were happy they "stopped out" and, although they came back to college, *Time* quoted several negative comments about education. Patt needed to get out of Stanford to "see how life is out there in the streets" and to learn how to handle money, while Yale student Oliver Miller said that while working for Jimmy Carter's presidential campaign he received an "incredible education, the kind I don't think you could ever get from a textbook." Yale student Paul Albritton added, "You go for so many years in a classroom with theoretical models being placed in front of you. Getting out and working, getting your hands dirty, gives you a much better idea of what you are studying for."[64]

College students (and high school students) have held "mock" or "model" political party conventions throughout the twentieth century, and mass market magazines occasionally have covered them, probably with the idea that these stories "add color" to election year coverage overall. Such mock political conventions increased dramatically in number in 1964, and *Time* that May published a round-up type of story with a fact or two each about conventions at several colleges: Washington and Lee, Oberlin, Vanderbilt, Claremont, Wellesley,

Morgan State, Brooklyn, City College of New York, and Ohio University. These stories constructed contradictory images of students. On the one hand, they portrayed students seriously discussing (even debating) politics for hours, after having expended effort to research politicians, real delegates, and issues. On the other hand, at Vanderbilt students spent only twenty minutes choosing a vice presidential candidate. At Wellesley, Rockefeller supporters told campus police that a riot was about to erupt, causing police to break up the convention. At Ohio, "delegates rode motorcycles through the gymnasium, [and] watched coeds do a striptease."[65] With the latter fact, *Time* ended the article, framing college students' political activity as not serious, because college students ultimately were rather nutty. Likewise, in 1972, *Time* covered Washington & Lee University's mock Democratic convention. The article gave students credit for "correctly" nominating the out-of-power party's eventual candidate ten out of the last fourteen presidential election years, but then highlighted students' irreverence. George Wallace's mock delegates referred to themselves as "redneck power." The West Virginia delegation had introduced itself by claiming Jerry West, Don Knotts, and Soupy Sales as native sons. Students listened to then-Georgia Gov. Jimmy Carter speak with "remarkably convincing mock boredom."[66]

Finally, at least one 1984 *Reader's Digest* article, reprinted from the Spring 1983 *Wilson Quarterly*, simply laughed at the results of anti-intellectualism in the nation's schools: "College Kids Say the Darnedest Things: Mrs. Malaprop is alive and well in today's halls of ivy," consisting of a series of supposedly verbatim quotes from students' papers on European history. Every sentence was a student "blooper." *Reader's Digest* reported that had assembled the piece "possibly as an act of vengeance," but it was published without comment,[67] as if its point were more to provide humor than any real comment on students' inability or unwillingness to learn history.

Evidence Against the Devaluation of
Book Learning and Standards

Evidence from the examined text suggests or supports intellectualism in the general public or on college campuses, or is explicitly resistant to anti-intellectualism, was scattered across the time period being examined, with no discernible trends or other patterns in the coverage.

For example, in that mid-1957 *Reader's Digest* article about college admissions, one criterion for college admission was "intellectual curiosity": "a questing mind: 'the capacity to get steamed up over some subject'…'interest in books and ideas, in the meaning of life and its values'…'a youngster whose antennae are out.'" The article also claimed that colleges were looking for a student's "'ability to come up with ideas,'" and "'growability,'" documented by "Horizon-expanding interests and hobbies" or "seriously developed creative talents in music, drama, writing, and the other arts."[68] This definition is consistent with those of Hofstadter, Katchadourian and Boli, and others. However, note that "intellectual curiosity" was only one, apparently a minimal one, of a variety of otherwise non- or perhaps even anti-intellectual criteria.

Out of place with coverage just a few years earlier and a few years later was *Life*'s late 1957 article, "Sad News from the Campus: Nobody Loves the Football Hero Now; The Triple-Threat Star of Yesterday Has Become a Faceless Employee, Unknown, Unwanted and Unsung." Spread over seven pages (including five editorial cartoons and five photographs), the article was based on the single and simple theme that college football players weren't getting as much respect (or as many dates) as they once did, and that undergraduates' enthusiasm at football games was way down. However, the article presented something of a mixed message: On the one hand, it presented reasonable-sounding arguments from students and professors about football players. They were perceived as paid employees of the university, the growth in size of football teams having made it more difficult for an individual player to become a well-known and much-loved hero. Many college women found football players to be men too unrefined to date. It was easier to cheer for the university band than the team. All of this might suggest a rather "pro-intellectual" slant to the article.

However, *Life*'s dedication of seven pages to the story, which made only one major point repetitively, also conveyed that this new state of affairs was a crisis. The lengthy headline, beginning with "sad news" and juxtaposing words such as "hero" and "triple-threat star" with "unknown, unwanted and unsung" also made it look as though undergraduates no longer so interested in college football had overreacted and done the football players a grave injustice. *Life* called the traditional football player the "extraordinary man," "idol," the cause of the "outrageous frenzy," and an "object of...adulation." Then *Life* described 1957 football players as "ostraci[zed]," "ridicule[d]," and referred to by students as "animal types" and "apes," their dorm as "The Zoo" or "The Ape House." (University of Alabama sorority women were said to be very cautious about dating a football player, not because he may not be very intelligent or interesting, but because "He has to prove that he's a nice guy more than the ordinary student does.") The magazine attributed the lack of interest to "cynicism," which hardly made the anti-football fad seem defensible.[69]

With so much of the rhetoric about higher education through the 1950s and 1960s being anti-intellectual in one way or another, it was not until the 1970s that a real assessment of the previous two or three decades apparently was considered timely (important) by the news media. For example, that early 1976 *Time* article, "Slim Pickings for the Class of '76," primarily addressed job prospects for that year's graduates. It could have concentrated on only that issue and left it at that. However, the article went on to oppose U.S. anti-intellectualism, although the phenomenon was not labeled as such. For instance, the article concluded that "The vocational bent in higher education has obvious pitfalls," and quoted a Harvard official who pointed out that individual fields can quickly become "hot" or not, meaning that students matching majors to jobs are playing "Russian roulette." Berkeley's career planning director, Herbert Salinger, was quoted as asking, "'Should we turn someone off to a field that really interests him' because job prospects are slim?" *Time* believed that "many educators" agreed with the Organization for Economic Cooperation and Development's James R. Gass, who said higher education should help students "adapt themselves to a variety of jobs." (*Time* then pointed out federal estimates that the "typical American changes his job seven times during his lifetime, and his career three times.") Finally, Harvard's career services director, Francis Fisher, emphasized liberal arts as a "necessary resource in a civilized society," adding that "we must break the assumption that the purpose of education is to prepare for work."[70] Likewise, in that *Reader's Digest* article with the same headline as an earlier *Time* article, "College—Who Needs It?" it was noted that many educators were "deeply disturbed by the capitulation to careerism" and preferred that higher education "nourish a host of intangible virtues that cannot be measured by economic criteria. And liberal arts students, the educators insist, are far better prepared by the breadth of their knowledge and the flexibility of their schooling to undertake" numerous job changes over a lifetime.[71]

At the end of that decade, *Time* published in early 1980, "Milk vs. Cream? Acute discovery from 1928," about the writer of a reading and vocabulary test in 1928, Alvin C. Eurich (seventy-seven years old in 1980). He administered it to a group of University of Minnesota students just as he had done fifty years earlier to find out how 1970s students would fare. Minnesota students' vocabulary scores declined from an average of 60 percent correct in 1928 to 50 percent in 1978, and the reading comprehension scores declined from nearly half the students scoring 20 percent on a speed-reading exam to only 19 percent of students scoring at least 20 percent in 1978. Eurich noted that in 1928, only 12 percent of students started college versus 45.5 percent in 1978. Even though University of Minnesota had "open admissions" for Minnesota high school graduates in both years, a Minnesota higher education administrator said that, "In this study, we're comparing 1978 milk to 1928 cream."[72]

Other "pro-intellectual" material in the magazines was scattered:

* Columbia University President Grayson Kirk told *Reader's Digest* readers in mid-1960 that, "College Shouldn't Take Four Years" (reprinted from a *Saturday Evening Post* from earlier that year). Suggesting that students attend college year-round, he explained that its "strongest recommendation" was "promot[ing] better student attitudes toward the serious business of acquiring an education. There is a vast psychological difference between breezing through college in four years and buckling down to three years of hard work." Kirk explained that "rigorous intellectual competition" will result in "better study habits" than the then-current schedule, in which students were "distracted constantly by vacations and campus capers." The 1960 schedule was not unlike today's, except that many universities have since switched to a semester system from a quarter system.[73]

* That late 1960 *Time* article on "little known" but "good" colleges suggested the reverse: that high school seniors—and persons already in college—should do what they could to get a good education. It highlighted fifty high-quality, but obscure private liberal

arts colleges (such as Coe, Shimer, and Simpson) and mentioned employment prospects only when noting numbers of graduates who earned doctorates, went to medical school, or—in the case of Ohio's College of Wooster—ended up themselves as college presidents.[74] It was (and is) an unusual article for *Time* (and for mass market magazines generally), taking for granted the idea of young people seeking out a high quality education and not being obviously concerned about employability.

* In mid-1960, *Time* gave *A Teacher Speaks*, a book by former Boston Latin School master Philip Marson, two-thirds of a page coverage (including a photo) in which he complained that Harvard College's entrance requirements were at an all-time low—and that this had had a "disastrous" (*Time*'s characterization of Marson's opinion) effect on all U.S. secondary schools. The article also reminded readers of his comment in 1958, when he resigned from Boston Latin, that "The American school system, from first grade through college, has become a huge kindergarten." In his book, he complained about curve-grading, essays not being required in either school or national standardized exams, and subjective college admissions standards.[75]

* "The Many Commencements of Callie Trent," a lead article in *Reader's Digest* in mid-1964, concerned a West Virginia woman who saw her husband go back to college for his senior year at age forty, and then eventually saw all six of her children graduate from college. It was a story of perseverance and self-discipline, and of a family committed to education in more ways than one: Her husband was a school principal, as were two of her sons. Another son and one of her daughters were school teachers, while the other daughter was becoming a music teacher; only the oldest son went in a different direction, becoming an oral surgeon.[76] (Arguably, however, this article was as much or more about "family" than it was about education.)

* *Time*'s coverage of the then new Comprehensive College Tests (now called College Level Examination Program [CLEP]) in 1964 gave some credence to the idea that what a college student learned (or already knows) in college was more important than how many hours he or she sits in class. The article concluded with a comment by an Educational Testing Service (which developed CCT) official: "Europeans measure knowledge in terms of what the student

knows. This will offer a new flexibility for the student who can demonstrate that he has knowledge by giving him credit regardless of how he got it."[77]

* Also in 1964, *Time* emphasized that a new guide to college (*Comparative Guide to American Colleges*, by James Cass and Max Birnbaum) details the academic environment of colleges, and thus underscores the importance of taking intellectual climate into consideration. The book "describes the academic environment at each college so that applicants will not learn too late whether a school is intellectually lazy, rigorous, or so tough that the dropout rate is alarmingly high. Cass and Birnbaum examined such matters as the number of full professors in a department to judge its real strength, rated the faculty by the quality of schools where they got advanced degrees, discovered solid and improving regional colleges that are anxious to acquire a national student body."[78]

* In 1970, a noted former editor of *Harper's* wrote in *Reader's Digest* that his ideal college would have no dorms (students could live in "motels, boardinghouses, brothels or communes"), no sports teams, no sit-ins, no faculty governance because professors tend to be poor administrators, and no tenure. He described his ideal college's admission policy as "elitist" but only because freshmen would be required to "already know what they want to do with their lives," and also would have to prove their "ability to write a page of coherent, correctly spelled English prose." There would be no exams, no grades and no diplomas, only a "Certificate of Competence." In short, other than requiring freshmen to already know what they want to do with their lives, and issuing a Certificate of Competence, Fischer proposed a pro-intellectual, or at least an anti–anti-intellectual university. However, headlined "Cheers for Old Curmudgeon! A noted commentator conjures up the college of his choice," the story was framed as fanciful and contrary, thus effectively undermining with humor any serious message.[79]

* As noted above, in late 1970, *Time* made a point of including in an article on admissions policies at the City University of New York that Chancellor Albert H. Bowker was aware that "outstanding students" might be put off by CUNY's expansion. So he "redoubled recruiting efforts and succeeded in attracting the

same proportion of academic whiz kids" as usual.[80]

* The recommendations of former University of California President Clark Kerr and the other members of the Carnegie Commission on Higher Education were highlighted by *Time* in late 1968 with the headline, "Expensive, Expansive Equality" and, under a photograph of Kerr, the line, "The need is now"—referring to improving education in the United States. The article reported the Commission's request that the federal government increase its annual spending on higher education by $10 billion, and its suggestion that hundreds of new colleges be started.[81]

* In 1988, *Reader's Digest* underscored the accepted importance of higher education in the United States with a twenty-four–page section in its July issue, "*Reader's Digest* College Guide." The first section heading was "Academic Record" in its first major section, "Planning ahead." Sections that followed, "Finding the Right College," and "Winning Admission," also concentrated on educational and intellectual aspects of attending college. However, the section continued *Reader's Digest*'s habit of emphasizing prestigious schools.

* Finally, *Time*'s coverage of the 1968 book, *Campus 1980* (discussed above) also was a good example of content not supporting the devaluing of book learning and standards, for the same reasons that it also did not advocate "common people's interests"; again, highlighted were individualized majors, lifetime learning, and explicit conversion of "technical and vocational training" in favor of a modern apprentice system.[82]

Evidence For and Against Beliefs That Intellectuals Are Snobs

Despite Rigney's theorization that typical Americans consider intellectuals to be snobs, no direct evidence of this was found in the sample. In other words, no examined material specifically stated or implied that intellectuals belong to inaccessible cultural or intellectual organizations, that their consumption tastes are refined and elite, or that they look down at non-intellectuals. However, occasionally in references to professors trying to "market" their courses to students, it is hinted that scholars were attempting to counteract imagery of snobbishness. For instance, as mentioned above, a late 1972 *Time* article,

"Courses to Turn You On," reported that professors, particularly in disciplines unpopular among students, were responding to student fickleness by promoting their courses.[83]

No evidence was found of magazine stories' constructing defenses of the notion of intellectuals as snobs, nor denying the notion outright. Nor was evidence found for Rigney's contention that today's intellectual class is, in effect, both emancipatory and elitist.

The Self-Defeating Process of Democratizing Higher Education

The victory for advocates of "common people's" interests, most notably more vocationally oriented education (not to mention the entire apparatus of career planning and placement services, internship coordinators, practicum programs, so-called "service learning," and so forth), lowered admission standards, lowered graduation standards, and less rigorous courses, did not happen quickly or easily in the United States. In the mid- to late twentieth century, professors whose careers spanned forty, thirty, or even only twenty years in particular could easily observe changes and choose to fight them. The demands of science and technology, particularly the space program, medicine, agriculture, and manufacturing, were a reminder that the "pure" or "theoretical" research conducted at universities was often as important, if not more important, than "applied" research of immediate value to corporations and politicians. Overall, those ostensibly given license to oppose change were primarily older academics and journalists, or speaking about elite institutions, but these figures often seemed to be quoted for journalistic balance, or in deference to their positions; ultimately, what they said was marginalized one way or another. This was especially true about Allan Bloom, whose book was a bestseller, but whose ideas were either opposed or ignored, and then essentially forgotten.

Despite the fact that the anti-elitist movement usually had economic motivations and economic results, the process—which more accurately would have been called "expansion," "massification" or "popularization"—was given the label "democratization," a word that in and of itself discourages scrutiny or objection; even those complaining about lowered standards were portrayed as out-of-date, out-of-touch, and worse. If college education often was tied to employment by students, their parents, legislators, and others as early as the 1950s, that conflation was complete by the 1970s. The processes involved in obtaining a higher education were openly and clearly cynical: articles told students and their parents how to beat the odds in obtaining admissions (and when, in a sense, one could not or did not need to beat the odds), and students and parents often seemed more concerned about a college's prestige (and how that might translate into employment or marriage) than its quality. The middle class became increasingly determined to send their children to college regardless of what their children would gain from it, whether the teenagers wanted to go to college, or how much it cost; clearly the motivation, rarely if ever, was education for education's sake. Throughout, especially in the 1940s, 1950s, and 1960s, daughters—who often were pressured to make college expenses supposedly pay off by finding a husband in addition to, or instead of, preparing for a career—were presented with career choices that usually were still explicitly and implicitly limited.

Ironically, as more and more students went to college primarily to get a good job, the chances of that decreased because the percentage of Americans graduating from college grew more quickly than the percentage of jobs requiring a college degree; today the number of Americans with a college degree significantly exceeds the number of jobs that require one. However, the needs and opportunities in the United States in the areas of arts, sciences, government, journalism, retail politics, and the overall American culture and American society— even the complexity of day-to-day life for the average citizen—suggest that more citizens, not fewer, should be learning, and not only a finite amount for a degree, but learning more and over a longer period of time. Unfortunately, American anti-intellectualism makes the idea of even necessary, let alone optional, lifelong learning a tough sell.

Chapter 6
Unreflective Instrumentalism, Hedonism, Sexism, and Age Discrimination

Impatience with theories, ideas—the entire practice and process of abstract thought—is perhaps the most common manifestation of anti-intellectualism throughout American popular culture and average Americans' day-to-day lives. Therefore, it should be no surprise when that attitude is found even in magazine coverage of higher education —the one institution in which Americans have expected (not to say preferred) and perhaps even tolerated this core requirement of intellectual activity. Based on the always relatively low, often nominally low, circulation figures of every truly intellectual magazine in the United States, one need not ask whether the majority of the American public still—if ever—demanded idea-driven mass media, nostalgia for *Partisan Review* notwithstanding. An obviously closely related result of anti-intellectualism is pressure for vocationalism in the humanities and social sciences curricula of universities—pressure whose handiwork seemed almost complete by the late 1990s as many second- and third-tier public universities counted business, education, agriculture, engineering, computer science, and journalism students by the hundreds (or thousands) and philosophy majors by the handful. That such a trend effectively does, or could, reduce major state universities to the purposes of community college and technical institutes did not seem to concern its proponents.

However, other components of anti-intellectualism also were easy to locate: there were no signs of students (or professors for that matter, at least not in the articles studied) who questioned the ethics of professions or late *laissez-faire* capitalism. A consumerist mentality toward higher education developed, made obvious by the "shopping" for a college of parents and students, as well as by the shaping of both the substance and marketing of campuses to their "customers'" needs.

Finally, this book concludes, even with its relatively limited sample of examined articles, that U.S. anti-intellectualism is even more pervasive than how Rigney or Hofstadter wrote about it. Rigney was onto something with his term "unreflective hedonism" to connote orientation toward pleasure (one is reminded of Neil Postman's book title, *Amusing Ourselves to Death*) and away from challenging thought. In part, this may understandably reflect the fact that Americans have the material success and comfort to pursue pleasure, and something of the classic free rider problem: Why do I, as Citizen A, have to contemplate X when surely someone else will do that for me?

Articles studied for this book, though, also revealed anti-intellectualism that never was justifiable, and should have even become less understandable as time went on: anti-intellectualism as a cause and/or effect of sexism (repeatedly implied but not fully explored by Hofstadter), anti-intellectualism as a cause and/or effect of age discrimination (against the young!) and intellectuals viewed as unpatriotic (a concern of Said, Hage, and others).

Evidence For or Against the Suppression of Ethics Questions

Throughout the entire period, with the exception of a few articles in the late 1960s, magazine reports constructed students as being overwhelmingly interested in supporting and becoming part of the status quo rather than challenging it. In particular, students in such fields as business, journalism, and the sciences were never seen portrayed as questioning the performance or goals of their chosen professions and industries. Therefore, it would seem safe to conclude that the sample of articles demonstrates the suppression of such questions. News media workers could have posed those issues to their readers, and/or ask their sources about them and then report sources' responses, but they did not.

Beyond student protests of science and technology employed to prosecute the Vietnam War, no evidence was found in this sample of magazine workers or their news sources questioning the ends of scientific, professional, and vocational education; this lack of evidence suggests Rigney is correct.

Evidence for Impatience with Theory and Ideas

As in the words of Isaiah Berlin, quoted more than fifty years ago by *Time*, U.S. college students were consistently portrayed as especially interested in facts for the sake of facts, but not theory, and this (as Hofstadter and Rigney point out) is a major hallmark of U.S. anti-intellectualism. Berlin said "more serious" college students "would throw themselves upon the recommended pabulum [assigned readings] and would try to absorb it in a very frenzied fashion. They read rapidly, desperately, and far too much." That would be bad enough, Berlin said, but as they valued only facts, such students often developed a "fearful intellectual congestion from which many of them will probably suffer for the rest of their lives"[1]

Similarly, students of the late 1940s were said to have a "practical workaday approach to world problems."[2] Princeton President Robert F. Goheen gave 1957's college students credit for understanding themselves, but the only reference he made to their intellectual view of the world, other than a "combination almost of cynicism and idealism," was that "they reach for secure answers where they find them"—a distinctly anti-intellectual approach.[3] An unnamed Harvard professor in 1957 told *Time* that students worked hard not because they were truly interested in learning, but because they wanted to get into graduate school. Students told *Time* that having to compete against so many other college graduates for jobs was the major (anti-intellectual) reason for attending graduate school. *Time* concluded that campuses no longer had "goldfish swallower[s]," but neither did they still have the "dilettante and the knowledge-for-knowledge's-sake boy. Today's student has little patience with mere intellectual flash...Nor...obscurantism. 'The college student,' says Editor Howard Seemen of the University of Minnesota's *Minnesota Daily*, 'wants something he can put his hands on. The double meaning is not popular.'"[4] The "knowledge-for-knowledge's-sake" person was, of course, a colloquial way of defining an intellectual, and here, *Time* continued its long-time habit of not responding, nor quoting opposing sources, to an opinion as a way of endorsing it—and thus anti-intellectualism.

One mid-1950s article went so far as to suggest that for the entrepreneurially minded student, attending college was not only useless, but even counterproductive unless one were careful. About a student who made successful real estate investments while still in college, the article's primary "angle" was that the student also earned a "near-failing D...in a course on real estate." The cutline under the photograph read: "Student Falk & Bride/Thirty Gs and a D."[5]

Articles about students "stopping out" of college, discussed above, also prompted questions about why students went to college, why they stayed in college and how they chose majors. In articles such as one in *Life* in 1972, "The Big Year Off: More and more students are spending time between high school and college to learn about themselves," it was explained that, "The plan [stopping out] is an excellent Rx for those entering college without goals, those who start asking, 'Why am I here?' and then drop out."[6] No examples were given of students for whom "stopping out" was not a solution to problems.

The debate in the 1940s and 1950s between students who wanted only "facts" and professors who wanted to teach "theory" metamorphosed, in the late 1960s, into a debate between students and their parents for "relevance" versus faculty who wanted to continue teaching the traditional curriculum, or a modified traditional curriculum. The issue was the same: Anti-intellectual Americans were impatient with what they viewed as impractical courses, utopian professors, and theoretical texts. The major mass market magazines took up the word "relevant" (or "relevance") and began using it as a shorthand term assuming that readers would understand what it referred to in higher education stories. For instance, one unsigned essay in *Time* in 1968, included a section titled, "Wanted: Relevance & Involvement"—which referred to both demands for more "practical" courses and also black students' demands/needs and anti-racism.[7]

In another 1968 *Time* article, students still wanted more "practical" classes, including "black-culture." UCLA student Brian Weiss had not been interested in many "social concerns or intellectual interests" growing up, and he joined the *Daily Bruin* student newspaper staff mainly to make friends. However, he met a husband-wife anthropology team he called "sharp, biting, absolutely brilliant," and was planning to obtain a Ph.D. at the University of New Mexico. It was reported that Harvard student Hyndman studied Chinese, but it was unclear why. Robert Reich, later President Bill Clinton's Secretary of Labor, represented Dartmouth and was depicted as an intellectual theoretically analyzing politics and protests while planning to go into law or teaching. Berkeley's Brian Patrick McGuire was quoted as saying that ending up with the highest GPA in the College of Letters and Science "was not worth it" (he reportedly made no friends in four years!), but McGuire concluded philosophically, "Students must wake up and realize that what they want is not to tear down the universities—but to embrace each other." African American Vernon Ford at Northwestern said an "upper-middle-class conservative school isn't immune to bigotry. For the black man, there's no utopia"; he planned to teach in a "ghetto" while earning a master's degree in sociology.

The sole woman interviewed, Liz Stevens at Wheaton College, was tutoring blacks, planning to become a social worker reconciling slums and suburbs, and noted, "A lot of white suburban society is sick." The sole student whom *Time* constructed as an intellectual was described last: Columbia's David Shapiro, Phi Beta Kappa, son of a Newark physician. *Time* reported, "he played violin under Leopold Stokowski at sixteen, had his first book of poems (*January*) published as a college freshman; he has written a play, a short novel, and an opera, this spring he won the university's prestigious Kellett fellowship for graduate study." What does Shapiro say? "Most of the intellectuals in this country have abdicated their critical role or are being sentimentalists. Robert Lowell may march on the Pentagon, but then he goes off to tea parties. This is sentimentalism."

What *Time* editors thought of the activists was not only implied; numerous parenthetical comments provided continuity, highlighting the students' ignorance or misinterpretation of history, their speaking "sometimes naively and too glibly...They also ignore the reality that undergraduates throughout history have always had ideals." The students criticized the anti-intellectualism of much suburban middle-class living, but then *Time* commented, "Condemnation of their elders occasionally comes too easily for the young today" (as if young people have not always criticized their elders).[8]

Controversies over the "relevance" of curricula were not the only manifestation of anti-intellectualism in the late 1960s. The student and other protests of the 1960s were simultaneously intellectual (in the sense that intellectuals have a responsibility to challenge the status quo, and college students were in a privileged place to do so) and anti-intellectual (in the sense that they believed that universities had the capacity to effect social change and were not doing so, that belief due at least in part to the perception that universities were not interested in doing anything practical or immediate). The news media generally preferred to construct these students as anti-intellectual. Other than the 1960 *Life* editorial mentioned above, no evidence was found that media welcomed students' questioning of the status quo. *Life*, while publishing more and larger photographs of student protests than did *Time*, put the by this time typical *Life* spin on activism and protests, e.g., students as wacky young people and happy endings. In its story about 1970 graduation ceremonies, *Life* paraphrased Harvard President Nathan M. Pusey as indicating the class of "'70 had not been playing games but living 'the real thing' during four years that were 'among the most tormented that have ever beset institutions of higher learning.'" Note Pusey's implication that for earlier generations of students, college had not been a "real thing." *Life* then went on to show that students were still protesting—and noted a computer printout of campuses "in protest [is]...10 feet long"—but they were harmless and by implication, ineffective. After all, students nationwide turned their commencement ceremonies into "mocking parody. Caps and gowns were often abandoned and money for renting them donated to help pro-peace politicians or war orphans." *Life* also showed students as whimsical or clownish: photographs depicted students wearing peace symbols on their caps or gowns (and one "pro-Administration senior" wearing a flag on his), other students eating bananas to protest an honorary degree being given to the U.S. ambassador to Guatemala, Brandeis students performing a pantomime routine on the graduation dais, a mock funeral before the Brown graduation, and empty chairs at Tufts—where all but twenty-five students skipped the ceremony.[9] Finally, in late 1970, one *Time* journalist attempted to assess the effects of the student movement on public attitudes toward higher education. In the article, the anti-intellectual Gregory W. Wierzynski wrote that activism forced a reassessment of the "old absurdities of trivial research and needless Ph.D.s."[10]

In coverage of college students involved in political campaigns, they were portrayed as anti-intellectually impatient with higher education, but also not to be taken seriously in the political world. For example, two *Time* subheads, "Clean for Gene" and "New Stevensonians" referred to Eugene McCarthy campaigners shaving and largely giving up drugs and alcohol, and a rough idea of their politics. The article described various sacrifices students had made to work on the McCarthy campaign, and what they might do if he didn't win (burn draft cards, flee the country). Even so, it was the headline that cast doubt on the legitimacy of the whole effort: "Crusade of the Ballot Children." Such language was not used anywhere in the story, and the word "children" suggested that college students working in politics are too young to be taken seriously and/or too young to know what they are doing.[11] The "ballot children" labeling was echoed two years later in another *Time* headline, "How Goes the Second Children's Crusade?"[12]

In 1970, *Time* juxtaposed statements about the overall mood on campuses (and particularly student protests), between San Francisco State College President Hayakawa, representing an anti-intellectual view, and Yale President Kingman Brewster Jr., representing an intellectual view. Hayakawa was quoted as saying "there is something very pernicious about liberal arts education," because many liberal arts students: believed themselves "educated to rule," developed an "aristocratic, elitist bent," and soon enough would develop a "profound contempt for democracy" and "contempt for middle-class values." He went on to make the same charges against the U.S. news media. Brewster, in contrast, said students and other Americans all had come to realize that the country's problems could not be solved quickly, and that solving them at all would depend on resolving two issues. The first was "whether or not the younger generation feels that the critic, the skeptic, and the heretic are still welcome, even honored and respected in the United States" and the second was whether American young people thought "channels of communication, persuasion and change are truly open."[13] Brewster was also lauded for having "earned high marks for transforming Yale from an elitist institution for the conventional education of affluent prep school graduates into an innovative coeducational campus...and he gets credit for doing it without lowering graduation standards in the process."[14]

Vice President Spiro Agnew, before being himself discredited and resigning, also gave speeches in which he asserted that protesting college students were anti-intellectual, among other sins. *Time* even pointed out that Agnew would agree with Brewster on several points, including the Yale president's statement that "reason must be honored above the clash of crude and noisy enthusiasms and antipathies." Agnew was quoted as portraying colleges as "susceptible to capture and destruction by the radical or criminal left," and therefore it was no "[s]mall wonder, then, that each year a new group of impressionable consumers falls victim to the totalitarian ptomaine dispensed by those who disparage our system..." Students, Agnew argued, thought "radicals" were "architects of a brave, new compassionate world," when in reality they were for radical, violent change with help from "'rock' music, 'acid' and 'pot.'" He also accused students of compelling administrators and faculty to compromise their integrity: "When peace comes through appeasement and capitulation—that sellout is intellectual treason." By contrast, the students were not credited with doing anything intellectual at all.[15] Other, similar, 1970 articles about student political activity include "Youthful Volunteers," "Uneasy Return to Campus," "The Politics of the Cop-Out," "The Aggressive Moderates," "A Student Campaign to Get Peace Started," and "Kent State: Another View."[16]

Evidence Against Impatience with Theory and Ideas

Brown University President Henry M. Wriston, an outspoken, decisive leader, in 1963 proposed to revitalize U.S. universities with a traditional curriculum, but taught in a more lively way. Reporting that Wriston believed college had become "dull" and "often soporific" (*Time*'s words, not Wriston's), it quoted the president as saying, "most textbooks are hardly worth reading. If they are not barren of ideas, they are impoverished in that respect." What was the solution proposed by Wriston and a group of professors who had been meeting on the issue since 1946? "No regular lectures or textbooks," but instead reading "some of the great classics and the best of scholarly commentaries...analyzing, not...memorizing," including Voltaire in French, Cervantes in Spanish, Dante in Italian. In one of the most "pro-intellectual" articles found among those analyzed for this book, this half-page piece concluded with Wriston's assurance that the cost of cutting professors' teaching loads was not too high, because, "The great mistake in American education from kindergarten through graduate school...has been an underestimation of the capacity of students...The minds of freshmen need to be awakened [to] a new adventure."[17]

A second article, in 1976, that expressed or covered support for theoretical learning was primarily, even solely, concerning jobs. In it, anti-intellectualism is summarized as follows: "'As Americans, we really prize a degree, but I'm not sure we prize an education,' muses Georgetown Dean Royden B. Davis, S.J."[18]

Evidence of Pressure for Vocationalism in the Humanities and Social Sciences

The magazines examined, particularly *Time*, used as a perennial story topic the question of how much college graduates were making after ten or fifteen years, how much money new college graduates were being offered, what jobs new college graduates were suited for, and so on, constructing a clear message that college education is to be linked primarily—if not solely—with jobs and salaries. This was not a new development; magazines had been publishing such stories since before 1944. Examples found within this book's parameters included:

* For the class of 1948 and their successors, *Life* assured them that going to college was only about getting the best possible job when one finished. Devoting six pages, including seventeen photographs, to Cornell University's class of 1948, *Life* that year displayed college students sitting or standing around and talking about nothing but "jobs and the immediate future." Despite educators' complaints that "students seem more concerned with getting jobs than getting an education," *Life* clearly sided with students, implying that even the brightest students were settling into

jobs rather than graduate school, and writing as if a student "after quick success, like Jim Ford" was making a significantly different decision than those "like Doug Foote ...after good training, security and a solid chance to make their own way."

Foote (labeled by *Life* as a "careerist") and his new career were featured first on an anti-intellectual two-page spread, and the magazine's writers assured readers that he would have a starting salary of $275 per month because of, or despite, the fact that "His golf score, in the low 80s, was somewhat higher than his scholastic average." The article remarked, "He likes American business; American business ap-pears to like him; and they both know they have a big stake in each other."

The one woman included in the story, Sylvia Kilbourne, was president of the Women's Student Government Association, but was predictably described by *Life* thusly: "An earnest girl, Sylvia faces her future squarely. 'Coed seniors talk about big jobs and careers,' she says, 'But in the back of their minds they really think about marriage.'"

Bud Bartholow, "a sought-after engineer," was described as the most intellectual of the group, and yet not idealistic either. He was pictured and described last. The article bragged that he would have a starting salary of $300 per month at Riegel Paper Co., but also raised the question of whether his technical/scientific life had been worth it: "He has been taking chemical engineering, the toughest course in Cornell. While the other students are having beer parties and picnics on the lake shore Bud has to stay in his room cramming or in the laboratory fussing with beakers and re-ports." The only student described in the article who was not solely interested in money and/or marriage was Lindsey Grant, labeled by *Life* as "a self-denying idealist." A student of China and Chinese, he was depicted as too idealistic. Grant had turned down oil companies and $3,000-per-year offers to work in bank branches in China and was graduating from college at twenty-one despite two years in the Navy. Finally, Grant had a "Negro" roommate (law student Sam Pierce, chosen thirty-three years later to be Ronald Reagan's Secretary of Housing and Urban Development).[19]

* The "Education" page of a 1948 issue of *Time* reported the results of the magazine's own survey of 9,064 college graduates of all ages. Leading the story with the question, "What does college do for you?" *Time*'s writers announced first that the American college graduate was forty-nine times as likely as the nongraduate to be listed in *Who's Who in America*. Second, he or she was fifteen times more likely to earn $10,000 per year (15.1 percent of college graduates versus 1 percent of nongraduates) and graduates who had good grades were making only $49 more per year than those with lower grades. Finally, it was reported that 70 percent of college graduates thought that their college coursework was helping them "'a lot' in their present occupation." Notably, 83.5 percent claimed they would attend the same college all over again, and only 2.1 percent said they wouldn't go to college if they could decide again. About a quarter of the graduates said they should have chosen another major, and 60 percent said a college education should include more "specific vocational training." However, as a sign of how American culture surely has changed since 1948, physicians were the happiest profession—with only 9.1 percent of them expressing any regrets.[20]

* More than a page of a 1952 *Time* was given over to highlights of a national survey published in book form as *They Went to College*: college graduates on average were making more than twice what nongraduates were making, with physicians making the most (at least $7,500) and "teachers and preachers" the least: $3,584. Career choice mattered, but grades: "hardly enough . . . to inspire anyone to burn the midnight oil." The difference in income between A students versus C and D students overall was not substantial, with one exception: "In the learned (and low-paying) professions, the Phi Beta Kappa's advantage is greatest: he is twice as likely to be making over $5,000 as his C or D counterpart. In business, his advantage dwindles to almost nothing."

Further, 31 percent of female college graduates stayed unmarried, as compared with 13 percent of all U.S. women. *Time* commented, "Since it [the survey] deals with statistics alone, the real worth of U.S. higher education is left unassessed. A college education obviously pays off in dollars and cents. Whether it pays off in various other ways, the figures cannot say."[21]

* A similar article was published in *Time* in 1952 on Yale's class of 1936. The lead fact? That 830 grads were earning a total of $9 million a year working ($10,843 each), plus $6 million more from

investments ($7,229 each).[22]
* Fifteen Southern states banding together to form the Southern Regional Education Board, through which students in a state that did not have a certain graduate school would be directed to a state that did (along with some financial assistance from their own state legislatures) was given attention by *Time* in 1952.[23]
* In 1956, the emphasis in a *Reader's Digest* article reprinted from *Fortune* was how much starting salaries had increased since 1947, and the number of college graduates major corporations planned to hire.[24]
* That fall, the president of Earlham College, D. Elton Trueblood, claimed—also in *Reader's Digest*—that he had wanted to teach at small, private colleges because their students were more elite and generally more intellectual. He then publicized what a fraternity member at his own university said (with the caveat that he did not believe it to be the prevalent opinion among students): "I'll tell you what interests me. I want to get out of this place with a degree and get a high-paying job. That's what I care about."[25]
* The value of college was painted as questionable at best by a 1956 *Time* article. More jobs were then available at daily and weekly newspapers than journalism school students who wanted to take them—meaning a journalism degree was a sure bet for getting a job. In other words, the primary reason for attending college was to get a job. The article also reported that public relations workers were offered higher salaries, reinforcing the idea that a college education was achieved only for the purpose of obtaining the highest paying job; also suggested was the question of why a person would attend college at all if starting salaries in a field such as newspaper journalism were so low.[26]
* A 1957 *Ladies' Home Journal* article, bluntly headlined, "Is College Education Wasted on Women?" tied college education to the possibility of women meeting their future husbands and getting jobs. It then discouraged women from attending college by noting, "Figures from the Bureau of Labor Statistics confirm our own observations that a smaller and smaller proportion of college girls today want to prepare themselves for professional work..."[27]
* *Time*'s story on *The Academic Revolution*, a 1968 book by David Riesman and Christopher Jencks, was headlined, "The Power of Professors," but *Time* quoted the authors largely as linking stu-

dents' future jobs with universities' teaching and research. They applauded 1960s admissions, which were based more on merit than ever before, but anti-intellectually suggested that college research, as well as teaching, should "answer[] real questions or solv[e] important problems." Moreover, the authors were quoted as admitting that, "The majority of those who enter college are plainly more concerned with accumulating credits and acquiring licenses than with learning any particular skill while enrolled..."[28]

* The article, "The System Really Isn't Working," was a call by a literature professor at a liberal arts college, Antioch, for a radical change toward practical education. He wrote that the curriculum should be oriented toward "politics, religion, sex, personal ethics, family relationships" because these were the "areas of experience that matter as one prepares for citizenship, parenthood, or any other role outside the school." It applauded learning foreign languages without bothering with the grammar, and "groups of students and faculty [who] move in to combine service with learning in such ways that the acquisition of knowledge is inseparable from its active use." He went on, "Relevance, as our students have taught us, is the key word."[29]

* In 1968, *Time* devoted most of two pages to the links between film school and becoming a successful professional director. In so doing, college students were shown as partially professionals, partially artists, partially intellectuals. New York University and Northwestern University were featured to represent the social elites but, because of the subject, efforts at the University of Southern California, UCLA, and even the University of Iowa also were detailed. *Time* concluded that "[Marshall] McLuhan-age educators, moreover, welcome this form of creative endeavor. Some foresee the day when film training will be an accepted and universal part of education." However, the magazine also implied that almost all of the students were not very serious or creative: too many UCLA students had parodied Bonnie and Clyde, "not...any of the students are embryonic [Russian director Sergei] Eisensteins," and "campus movies are something of an acquired taste" because "the bulk of them are simply the exuberant and untalented posturings of youth." *Time* called a film by George Lucas, then twenty-three, "portentous" in theme and technically excellent, and noted that a UCLA grad from the previous year, Francis Ford

Coppola, had had "instant success." However, it predicted "instant obscurity" for filmmakers such as "Marty Scorsese," then twenty-five, who had won first place at a student festival in 1965 and had gone on to make a movie "flawed and immature in plot and structure...[with] almost no commercial possibilities." In the end, the article expressed little confidence in young filmmakers and suggested that U.S. movies would improve only if "audiences demand better things of it." For *Time*, this didn't include "Marty Scorsese."[30]

* In the 1972 *Reader's Digest* article, "Facts to Know in Picking a College," author Loren Pope stated that Myth 5 about higher education was that "You should choose your college on the quality of its department in your major field," and instead advised student not to rush into "vocational training."[31]

* The magazines of the 1970s were continuing their tradition of publishing articles nearly every year on that year's job prospects for college graduates.

* In that 1972 *Life* article, "Harvard grads go blue collar," Ivy League alumni were portrayed as glad to take, temporarily or not, blue-collar jobs so they could leave behind their "bittersweet academic agony" and enjoy "no more cramming for exams until dawn washed the elms of the Yard, no more term papers, no more lectures, no more quizzes that expose the unprepared as nakedly as an X ray." Recall from chapter 5, for example, the particularly anti-intellectual description of Joel Scott Coble as fleeing the "bloodless world of teleology and epistemology and the analytic formulas of the likes of Ludwig Wittgenstein." He said of philosophy, "It's lying and it's bull," and he was glad he did not make the "mistake" of going to law school. Other Harvard graduates had similar motivations and complaints.[32]

* Carl T. Rowan and David M. Mazie, in a 1972 *Reader's Digest* article "A College Education; Exciting New Ways to Get One: Some colleges now let you design your own exams, some have no campuses or classrooms at all. Whether they work out or not—and some may not—they're certainly not irrelevant or dull," condensed from the *Kiwanis Magazine*, assumed that "For most young people, 'going to college'...[results in] after four years, a degree which provides credentials for a job."[33]

* Students can afford to be intellectuals only when times are good

was the idea of the article, "Bear Market in Sheepskins," under the section head "Young Executives" in a 1970 *Time*. One result that the magazine highlighted with a subhead is "Down with Egg-heads"; a Newark College of Engineering placement director was paraphrased as saying that "the vague, egghead type is being left out."[34]

* The 1972 *Time* article "College, Who Needs It?"—already discussed above—quoted the ETS's Richard Peterson as saying that "a college education is not needed for what they consider the good life. More and more, they feel that they can live satisfactorily without a college degree." The message was that one does not need to have a job that requires a college degree to be happy; the text did not point out that going to college involves more than just preparing one for certain jobs.[35]

* A 1976 *Reader's Digest* article with the similar headline, "College—Who Needs It?" (condensed from an April *Newsweek*) suggested that it is a tragedy when a Phi Beta Kappa graduate from the University of Colorado ends up a restaurant manager; in addition, a Columbia University Ph.D. in English had ended up as a welder. Implied was the idea that if these graduates failed to get jobs in their fields (never mind the question of whether jobs potentially existed for them before their higher education, let alone after), their educations were a waste.[36]

* The 1984 *Time* article, "Taking a Course in Go-Getting: Students hustle as company recruiters return to campus," appeared in the magazine's "Education" section, but—strangely—the story had nothing to do with education. It concerned the hot job market for 1984 graduates and, other than passing references to the majors of hotly sought-after students (accounting, for one), the story had nothing to do with learning or knowledge either. This was also true of *Time*'s 1988 article, "In Demand: The Class of '88," which concentrated mostly on what jobs students want (management consulting and teaching were in; investment banking was out since the stock market crash of 1987), how hard students were working to get them, and that more students were going to graduate school. Almost absent was what students majored in, what they learned, their philosophies of learning, what they knew or believed or thought about.[37]

* In 1988, *Time* also reported in 1988 ("Hail and Beware, Fresh-

men: Some hard choices ahead for the class of '92"), that "Sophomore Mark Rodgers, at the University of Michigan, believed at one point that his parents might cut him off financially if he majored in English. 'My parents were pressuring me to be an economics major,' he says. 'The idea is to have marketable skills when you get out of school. It's job, job, job.'" *Time* didn't give any indication that it should be any other way, attributing the attitude simply to students' being more realistic about the world.[38]

* *Time*'s 1992, article, "Campus of The Future," went even further. Although giving token attention, noted above, to the University of New Hampshire president's insistence that universities need to maintain their independence, most of the article concerned colleges' vocationalism—greeting the prediction that the trend would intensify. Quotes such as "To justify their existence as servants of society, all schools will come under pressure to be less theoretical and more practical in preparing students for careers," and, "Inside what was once the ivory tower, there is a growing interest in new kinds of alliances with business," suggested that these are positive trends. In the article, the best that traditional, intellectual scholars could hope for was that the humanities, sciences, and social sciences would be linked with professional and technical courses, also Foucault's last prospect for battling anti-intellectual universities.[39]

Evidence Against Pressure for Vocationalism in the Humanities and Social Sciences

Almost no evidence was found of liberal education being defended on its own merits without regard to career concerns, and such articles tended to date from the early part of the period studied. In a 1956 *Time*, under the headline, "Missing: The Common Core" (the de-emphasized third of four stories in the "Education" section), the magazine "turned the tables" on college officials complaining about high school graduates by quoting Columbia University's law school dean's complaints about college graduates. The dean, William Warren, said that only 49 percent of his students took a course in American political history after their freshman year, only 30 percent a course in English history, and 20 percent each took no course in American government, economics, or English composition.[40] This comment was not put into any context and, therefore, stood as a critique of the plight of liberal education.

"Set the Student Free" was the headline on a 1957 *Time* article about colleges allowing students to skip classes or skip from high school to sophomore standing, and requiring undergraduates to conduct their own original research. The article's lead asked, "Are today's students too tightly chained to the textbook and the lecture, too little prodded into original work?"[41] But the article waxed ambiguous through the inclusion of unexplained detail.

Evidence For and Against Advocacy of
Less Autonomy in Education

Although many magazines have covered the increasing influence of corporations and government agencies on university research, most such articles were not within the parameters of the sample of articles studied for this book. But a 1960 *Time* article, "Surging into the '60s"—about the projected future of higher education and a new book, *Financing Higher Education, 1960–70*—included a mug shot of Ford Foundation economist Philip H. Coombs and indicated growing pressure on institutions of higher education to be managed more like businesses.[42] *Time*'s editors did not indicate that they minded.

One example was found of a source specifically advocating the autonomy of universities in the face of increased pressure from government and business. The president of the University of New Hampshire, Dale Nitzschke, was quoted more than halfway through a 1992 *Time* article about the future of higher education as saying, "We don't enjoy a separation anymore between the university and the political system. It is critical that we don't become pawns of the government, the legislature or business and industry. If we lose our autonomy, we've lost the ball game." Nitzschke was the only source for this point of view in the article, and therefore his opinion was not given much importance, did not appear to be popular.[43]

Beyond Hofstadter: Unreflective Hedonism and
the Flight from Reflective Thought

Isaiah Berlin, in that 1949 *Time* article, also picked up on what Rigney calls the U.S. culture's movement toward unreflective hedonism. Berlin, an ironic name given the then recent Berlin airlift, complained that "naïve, sincere and touching morality" had resulted in a common worldview that people exist to help each other and that "frictionless contentment" is the ideal. "Disinterested study has no place" in such a scheme, he said, because it means no "bothersome questions as [about] the nature of the universe and man's place in it." Berlin didn't apologize for the fact that such questions are unanswerable and in any case are "painful, [and] give rise to anxieties and maladjustments." Modern society has devoted more energy than ever to the "protection" of people from the "intellectual and moral burden of facing problems that may be too deep or too complex"—avoiding a "painfully difficult task of looking for light."[44]

Although evidence was found in this sample for supporting the liberal arts or science, no evidence was found that specifically advocates reflective thought as an important activity for intellectuals or typical citizens in a modern democracy.

Beyond Rigney

One aspect of U.S. anti-intellectualism that emerges in this book, and that was noted by Hofstadter but not by Rigney, is that anti-intellectual sentiment is at least partially gender related: women—at least women college students and perhaps women college professors—have been, all other things equal, more "intellectual" than their male counterparts; Katchadourian and Boli (1985) also provided evidence to support this. However, Rigney, Katchadourian, and Boli did not mention that considerable evidence suggests that anti-intellectualism has been at least partially sexist, and perhaps that sexism has been at least partially anti-intellectual.

Starting early in the period studied, for example, *Time* in 1944 reported that "girls" were attending college in "record-breaking numbers," although it did not specify a total national figure. Barnard College Dean Virginia E. Gildersleeve, in saying, "The Government has the boys. Families have college money for the girls," implied that if so many college-aged men had not been on military duty, many fewer women would have enrolled. In other words, for women, attending college was a lark, something done only if money were available and men did not need it. The magazine reported that women were editing student publications at Iowa State College and Knox College; at the latter the "petticoat rule" (control by women) continued for a second year. *Time* noted that "More of them were working in laboratories than ever before. They were guiding more tracing pens over engineers' drawing boards," but these statements were attached to no number or source, and thus one cannot even be sure that *Time* writers witnessed what they wrote.[45]

In 1957, college-educated women were described as causing problems in Catholic parishes largely because of their higher education. A relatively brief *Time* article that year depicted educated Catholic women as frustrated with the church because no church jobs with any status were open to women, and because educated Catholic women would invariably compare a typical parish priest unfavorably with a priest on or near a college campus. The article concluded by paraphrasing a Jesuit leader's assertions that "new" Catholic women—even, or perhaps especially, well-educated ones—should do "anything that needs to be done... whether she thinks it interesting and important for her or not." This would include working in Catholic youth and social organizations, visiting the elderly and ill, managing a parish library, and babysitting.[46] However, the article obviously showed that Catholic parishes were not modern at all, and that such so-called "new women" were welcome back only if they still acted like "old" women; the anti-intellectual message was that college education was wasted on, even a negative for, Catholic women.

The 1957 *Life* story, "Sound of Girlish Voices Strikes a New Note at Muhlenberg," showed colleges in transition in terms of gender. Women had just been admitted to Muhlenberg College (Allentown, Pennsylvania), the last of thirty Lutheran liberal arts colleges in the United States to go coed. On the one hand, the story showed that women had not gotten very far, as colleges were still going coed in 1957 and, on the other hand, the fact that it was the last of the Lutheran colleges to make the move perhaps meant that women had "finally arrived." This mixed message was also present in the story's thirteen photographs, which primarily showed women being initiated, hazed, and disciplined by upperclassmen. The fact that the women students were being treated the same as the men showed growing equality for women—after all, they were not exempted on the basis that it would be "unladylike" or that they were incapable of handling it. Nevertheless, nearly every photograph showed men in a dominant position both in terms of where men are located in the photos (sometimes above, sometimes below, but always supervising women and staring at them). In four of the photographs, women were clearly shown as smiling in response to the attention of the men, and in one photograph, a woman was portrayed in the equally stereotypical pose of wiping away "tears after relentless heckling."[47] No photographs showed male freshmen being hazed; women were depicted as invading men's territory, and men were controlling the situation, with *Life* reproducing the sexist imagery.

The 1957 *Ladies' Home Journal* article, "Is College Education Wasted on Women?" (already discussed above), was yet another example of sexist anti-intellectualism. Comments supposedly from readers included one that claimed it "take[s] as much intelligence, education and all-round wisdom to raise a family as to have a successful career" and that any notion otherwise is "just silly." Another claimed that women in earlier years had time for "intellectual pursuits" (and presumably took advantage of this opportunity) because of the availability of "capable helpers" (domestic employees) in the "old days," but that such workers no longer were available. On the second page, a reader wrote that "A distinguished analyst says 'men are basically hostile to the intelligent woman,' and 'Men cannot stand competition from women'" but that the real problem in U.S. society was ignorant men. And yet another wrote, "Let's face it. Most females between 18 and 25 are out to get a chap." Later in the story, it justified a woman's thinking that life has only two paths, work or marriage, and that they were mutually exclusive. Among other reasons, "they suspect—not without foundation—that there is no real place in our society for the liberally educated person who is not identified with some accomplishment or activity."[48]

By the early 1960s, the division between men and women in higher education was visually and verbally beginning to fade in magazine reports. A late 1960 *Life* article, "Freshman Class: 1960; Flood of grown-up war babies finds colleges unready—and *Life* looks ahead with guide for applicants," started with a photograph of hundreds of University of Michigan students on campus for orientation. Although the crowd comprised largely men, women were pictured as distributed throughout the auditorium. But as Krista E. White detailed in her 1996 master's thesis, other photographs portrayed women in traditional roles. Six women were shown in a home-like environment in a Southern Illinois University (SIU) dormitory, and two other women were displayed studying together on a bed they share at one of SIU's "family-style unit" trailers. Another female student at Southern Illinois was shown walking between two groups of men sitting on a sidewalk, and all the men had their eyes only on her. At Cornell, a college with a primarily male student body, only male campus guides for new students were pictured. On the next two pages were three photographs of Berkshire College (a new two-year institution in Pittsfield, Massachusetts), where an unnamed female "trim librarian" was pictured in a mostly empty room that will be the college's library. Another woman, Arlene Leavitt, was shown sitting on one of many chairs, *sans* desks, in the typing room. The largest of three photos, showing about fifty of the school's first 125 students, indicated that the overwhelming majority of students at the college were men; however, the overall message was that women were relegated to teaching at second-rate schools, but college students still were mostly men.[49]

The only article that specifically advocated strong academic and intellectual development for women was a late 1956 *Life* article that constructed college and intellect as natural for women. Including eleven photographs of female students, with mostly female professors, at a Pennsylvania college ("Bryn Mawr, tough training ground for women's minds"), the article insisted that, "Today a third of all American college students are women, and college has become almost as much a part of a woman's life as of a man's." Women were pictured in a physics lab, chemistry lab (twice), and an American history course; attending a conference with a history professor; talking with novelist Elizabeth Bowen; working on composition homework and studying unspecified materials (twice). However, the article also suggested that Bryn Mawr College was an unusual place: "the intellectual process has been kept pure, undiluted by any vocational or domestic-science courses," a high percentage of graduates obtain advanced degrees, and only 80 percent of alumnae ever have married. The story, through both words and photos, gently suggested alternatives to all of this: One student was shown "studying on a date" with a University of Pennsylvania graduate student, and two photo cutlines focused on what clothes students were required, or preferred, to wear.[50] Most importantly, however, this article about Bryn Mawr was buried deep in a 172-page "special issue on the American woman," which began with the photo spread "the American girl at her beautiful best."

Comments by Berlin, again in that key 1949 *Time* article, offer evidence of Said's complaint that intellectuals are sometimes treated as unpatriotic by their countrymen. Berlin recalled advising his "more socially conscious" Harvard students that "intellectual curiosity" is not a "sin or even frivolity," even though it may be pursued "merely" out of interest; he also recalled perceiving those students as deciding that he was advocating a "'European' point of view—at best something exotic and over-refined, at worst cynical and slightly sinister."[51]

One point Rigney missed is that, apparently, one way in which Americans can be constructed as non-intellectual or anti-intellectual is to describe them as children or as child-like. For instance, despite the fact that almost all of them are over eighteen years of age, college students also were typically referred to by the magazines as "boys" and "girls"; this was less true only in the late 1940s, when many ex-GIs in college were twenty-four years old, twenty-six, or even older. The word "kids" used to describe college students seems to have made its debut in the mid-1950s, and was used in headlines such as the 1957 label, "The No-Nonsense Kids." Ironically, photos with that story showed students listening to actress Agnes Moorehead and a Mozart and Bach concert; a photograph of the author J.D. Salinger also was included to illustrate Salinger's students' near-"universal" interest in his "picture of the tortured process of growing up." In 1968, as noted above, students active in political campaigns were literally referred to in press coverage as "children."

Media Cultivation of Consumerist Attitudes about Higher Education

If students and their parents were at all idealistic about higher education before reading mass media articles about it—one or both parents were happily highly educated, perhaps the family had a tradition of educational excellence or even an intellectual home life, and so on—the continual bombardment of typical Americans easily could have disabused them of such notions over a period of years. One need only imagine a typical American family during the studied period subscribing to one or two newspapers, several magazines, listening to the radio, and watching television. At least from many major magazines, if not most or all other mass media (and there's no reason to think that mass market magazines are more anti-intellectual than other media, and good historical and economic reasons why magazines may be less anti-intellectual than network television), they would have been subjected to a continuous steam of articles, week after week, month after month, about college students—culturally, socially, politically, intellectually, and psychologically—discussed and described primarily like children, only slightly older. The part of the portrayal that one did not associate with children—choosing compatible degree majors and jobs, applying for jobs, and so on—was about money, money, and more money. In most ways, colleges and universities couldn't have engaged in more self-destructive public relations if they had tried to, and political and economic elites who sought docile college students, docile college graduates, and silent or discredited intellectuals, certainly were not about to object.

Chapter 7
Anti-Intellectualism, the Mass Media, and Society

The study of anti-intellectualism in American society has to date neglected the role of the mass media in maintaining the hegemony of an anti-intellectual American culture. However, Hofstadter's 1963 thesis has remained unchallenged, and the notion that the U.S. social formation is hostile to intellectualism has been generally accepted. Rigney called attention to previous scholars' neglect of the mass media's role but did not investigate that area himself.

This book provides additional evidence in support of Hofstadter's arguments. The evidence also supports the three prongs of Rigney's theory of American anti-intellectualism and his hypothesis that the mass media are partially responsible for maintaining and promoting that anti-intellectualism. As the previous three chapters document, the primary textual strategy of anti-intellectualism predominates, thus supporting hegemonic anti-intellectualism.

Among the manifestations of religious anti-rationalism, extensive evidence was found that supports or reflects interest in the utilization of formal education for social and affective development and a resulting de-intellectualizing of college curricula. Substantial evidence was found for opposition to the questioning of authority, and opposition to and/or fear of reason and relativism and their outcomes. Because of the parameters of this book's sample of magazine articles, no evidence was found explicitly opposing science.

Among manifestations of populist anti-elitism, extensive evidence was found for the devaluation of "book learning" and high academic standards, with evidence to the contrary not always clearly and credibly valuing "book learning" or high academic standards. Substantial evidence was found for magazine content advocating "common people's" interests; evidence ostensibly to the contrary often held up expensive, private—apparently elite—liberal arts colleges as role models, but often undermined the "pro-intellectual" message. Some evidence was found for magazines giving coverage and credibility to both left-wing and right-wing populist attacks on intellectuals and/or higher education and, occasionally, an article suggested that intellectuals are snobs not to be emulated by "democratic" Americans. No evidence was found supporting or refuting Rigney's hypothesis that the United States hosts a new class of intellectuals that are simultaneously emancipatory and elitist.

Among manifestations of unreflective instrumentalism, substantial evidence supported narrow vocationalism, with very little evidence to the contrary. Substantial evidence was found for impatience with "impracticality," theory, and utopianism with very little contrary evidence. Minimal evidence was found for the advocacy of less autonomous educational institutions, and no contrary evidence was found.

Hofstadter implied that U.S. anti-intellectualism is at least partially related to sexism, and although Rigney's theory omits gender, evidence here confirmed Hofstadter's observations. Hage and Hofstadter both tied anti-intellectualism partially to hostility toward homosexual and effeminate men, and the evidence assembled for this book included no evidence to the contrary. Finally, certainly age discrimination (directed at the young, not at the elderly) and possibly racism also appeared to be linked in the text to anti-intellectualism, although neither Hofstadter nor Rigney explored these possibilities.

This book makes a contribution to the sociology of knowledge literature by testing Rigney's theory and providing evidence that supports each and every aspect of it. It makes a contribution to the scholarly literature on the intellectual history of the United States by serving as a supplement to work by Curti, Commager, Hofstadter, Fink, and others. More specifically, this book suggests, like Hage's study and Caudill's book, that the mass media's role(s) in the country's intellectual history has been grossly underestimated and understudied.

This book makes a contribution to research on U.S. higher education by analyzing a sample of higher education coverage by popular magazines over a relatively long time span and by suggesting that the mass media's roles in the history of higher education has been similarly underestimated and understudied. It also indirectly provides new evidence supporting Katchadourian and Boli's theorization of intellectualism and careerism among college students. Further, this book makes a contribution to U.S. scholars' cultural studies literature and critical education literature through its documentation of anti-intellectualism as a pervasive and long-term attitude or philosophy in U.S. mass media.

This book contributes to scholarly literature on mass communication through additional evidence and conclusions about how the media cover higher education, and suggests an area of research only implied by Hage or Caudill: media coverage of intellectuals as a class. It is one of only a handful of works, along with those by Hage and Caudill, that could be described as an intellectual history of the U.S. mass media. However, perhaps the greatest contribution of this book is that it begins to consider the terms in which the media exist in a society antagonistic to intellectuals/ism. Using textual evidence, this book provides evidence of how the media function as one ideological apparatus among others (education, religion, business, politics, and so forth). The choice of national magazines as the source of evidence is also a significant contribution because, to date, magazine content rarely has been treated across titles as a single text. Here is an appropriate place to elaborate on these two contributions as well as others and look ahead.

The media are of profound importance in the ongoing cultural work of solidifying the hegemony of today's particular phase of local and global capitalism. In some sense, the media are at the center of cultural studies because cultural studies tend to be organized in a circular model in which various moments within the circuit can be singled out for study but also where none is privileged as more important than others. The mass media, as a business, as content, as both personal and mass information/entertainment/advertising phenomena, and in their other roles, provide a kind of exemplar of the social formation as it has existed in the post–World War II era. Thus, clearly, the media are a nucleus for any other social phenomenon; none exists without the media. Although this book examines only one topic of media coverage (news about higher education and, in particular, coverage of students or graduates) in five popular magazines, the evidence is sufficient to support Rigney's three types of anti-intellectualism: religious anti-rationalism, populist anti-elitism, and unreflective instrumentalism. All three were sustained and promoted through content in several ways: story concepts, the strategic use of visuals, thematic approach (e.g., "angle" of the story or news peg), textual arguments and support chosen (e.g., sources quoted, omissions, and so forth) and others as noted in the previous chapters.

The choice of five popular magazines helped discern the tendency of antagonism toward intellectualism in different types of magazines across an important time period. The immediate postwar period has been called the beginning of a significantly different era, and the latter half of the twentieth century has been characterized by rapid technological change. Although the media themselves have been revolutionized by technology, consumer magazines have been a consistently popular form.

Higher education has been covered in varying ways in each of the magazines examined; since each is, or practically is, a general interest magazine directed at somewhat different audiences, together they provide both a broad picture and some particular eccentricities. However, across the lot, the anti-intellectual rhetoric is consistent.

It is not altogether surprising to find that the mass media tend to reflect and promote a hegemonic social value. Critical theory teaches that even widely different institutions function within social formations to help perpetuate and solidify the status quo. Even so, the media in the U.S. are unique in the sense that they have another role. As part of the corporate structure, the mass media function like other institutions. However, in their normative role as a "Fourth Estate," news media have the opportunity, arguably the obligation, to maintain and encourage certain values and institutions, especially democracy and democratic governments, through routine news coverage, investigative reporting, editorials, etc.—much of which exposes and criticizes deviance and even gets goals and standards. News media ostensibly play a role in maintaining diversity in public discourse and, to the extent that one exists, furnishing a public sphere by serving as a public forum to at least a limited extent. As the scholars and theorists discussed earlier all agree, the successful implementation of democracy depends on news media that are independent, active, and simultaneously analytical of events and issues while also accessible to the general public, to citizens. Therefore, there was also reason to expect that the news media might also provide space for contradiction or resistance to the anti-intellectual norm.

Time and *Life* were the two magazines with the heaviest coverage of higher education. What emerged from these two was an understanding of higher education and of students and graduates that was both particular and very limited. *Time*'s practice of packaging news into sections meant that higher education topics tended to be covered only under the "Education" banner. That has lifted those stories out of the most news-oriented sections and relegated them into a news ghetto that suggests that education has not been a political (or other first-rank) topic. The reliance on officials at mostly small, elite colleges and universities as sources further characterized higher education as unessential in the functioning of American democracy and American capitalism and, therefore, peripheral. Intellectuals and "intellectualism" have both tended to be characterized as deviant explicitly and implicitly, thus further distancing them.

Life's coverage was of course much more visual. *Time*'s graphics tended to be limited to uncreative representations, often "mugshots" of officials. *Life* used photographs, other graphics and white space, complimented by shorter verbal material (sometimes only a headline), to convey the story. Higher education, as described by *Life*, signified lighthearted fun. Even during the period of student activism, students were infantilized, portrayed as exceptional, neither childish nor adult, but existing in a rarified world apart. Thus, whether the story concerned pranks (as in the earlier time period) or protests (late 1960s onward) students were always too rash, too idealistic, too violent, too apathetic, too promiscuous, too "high," and so forth, and therefore not to be treated seriously.

The evidence assembled for this book included extensive examples of magazine reporting that emphasized social and affective development among college students almost to the exclusion of other topics. The sheer number of stories about student fun, dating, sex lives, and getting married (along with stories about "better" jobs and careers) sent an overriding message: college is fun while "real life" is work. This segmentation into neat and exclusive categories was consistent in all of the magazines. The media's messages thus adopt the role of conveying both the purpose and the limits of higher education as well as drawing a picture of later life that excludes fun and perhaps education.

Life used the term "intellectual" rarely and then usually to label a student with a difficult major and high grades; thus, as in *Time*, an intellectual, even where one exists, becomes a curiosity, someone to be gazed at, objectified, perhaps marveled at, but certainly as a phenomenon with little relation to average members of society.

Reader's Digest articles tended to be structured around the sensible financial consideration: cost of college admission; *Ladies' Home Journal* asked "should women?" questions (e.g., "Should women go to college?" or "Should women look for husbands in college?" and the like). *Nation's Business* contained too few articles to even speculate on a particular pattern, but their stories did not read as strikingly different from these others.

The previous three chapters were arranged in terms of Rigney's types of anti-intellectualism and clearly some of his types have been better supported than others by the evidence reported here. Overall, though, no articles contradicted his typology, and it is possible that other evidence might provide stronger support where this evidence fell short. However, based on these findings, it does appear that Rigney's theory may need fine-tuning, perhaps by suggesting the ranking of types of anti-intellectualism likely to occur in various institutions and settings.

Populist anti-elitism and unreflective instrumentalism, two of Rigney's types of anti-intellectualism, were clearly supported by this evidence, while there was less support (although no contradiction) of his religious anti-rationalism, especially the purely religion-related aspects. (This may be because American news media generally have substantially undercovered religion.) The evidence also suggested several manifestations of anti-intellectualism that deserve to be considered as types: issues of gender, age, race/ethnicity, and sexual orientation were not accounted for by Rigney's theory, yet enough material was in the magazine articles to suggest that these variables may be a significant aspect of, if not crucial for, constructing anti-intellectualism.

Throughout the entire period studied, 1944–1998, college students were portrayed as white, middle class, male, and heterosexual. Exceptions were always noted but rarely appeared. When they appeared it was often as abstractions, such as numbers or percentages of minority students. Hofstadter implied many times that gender partially drives anti-intellectualism, although he did not pursue the topic further. The messages about women were more anti-intellectual than those about men, despite the findings that women students are more driven by intellectual pursuits (Katchadourian and Boli). Further, the great majority of sources cited as educators or experts were men. Hage's 1956 study found evidence that intellectualism tended to be associated with effeminacy or homosexual men. Articles analyzed for this book included no evidence that intellectuals are stereotyped as gay men, but neither did any evidence contradict Hage; certainly no intellectual men were stereotyped as especially masculine.

In short, these findings suggest that the mass media work along with other institutions to maintain the anti-intellectual social formation of American society, routinely marginalizing intellectuals and intellectualism, and not providing significant space for resistance to that overriding social basis. Thus far, researchers have offered little expectation that this characteristic of American culture can be checked or changed. Critical theory suggests that hegemonic structures are often all but invisible since their success masks their contradictions and hypocrisies, and even phenomena that are counter-hegemonic. It seems striking that the noted sociologist Daniel Bell suggested that the revival of religion could or would be a potential force to restrain the excesses of *laissez-faire* capitalism, a suggestion that all but conceded anti-intellectualism as a permanent force.

However, despite the findings presented in this book, the mass media may still play a role in offering a place for at least a diminution of the active hostility toward intellectuals and intellectualism. With the contradictory missions of corporate goals and Fourth Estate responsibilities, the media may provide an opening where messages will expose some contradictions that other institutions would inevitably attempt to bury.

As is clear from reading the historical work of Hofstadter or Jacoby, Bloom's polemic, or the theoretical writings of Rigney and

Goar, it is extremely unlikely that the United States will spontaneously start becoming less anti-intellectual.[1] Indeed, Gramsci's theories and the available evidence together suggest that U.S. anti-intellectualism is hegemonic, and can be resisted only by mass social movements. In the United States today, such an occurrence also would be extremely unlikely. Foucault might suggest that the hegemony of anti-intellectualism be resisted only through individual decisions at each and every person's site(s) in the culture and society. However, in a country in which scholars have located anti-intellectualism in politics, business, education, evangelical Protestant religions, the military, judges' chambers, popular fiction, and, according to Hage and this book, the news media, widespread decisions by individuals to resist anti-intellectualism again seem extremely unlikely.

As Gramsci, Habermas, Dewey, and others have pointed out, only the educational system and the mass media are capable of transforming modern societies in positive ways; government, corporations, labor unions, religious groups, voluntary associations, and other institutions are controlled by elites who generally are unable and/or unwilling to initiate or facilitate movements that both affect the entire culture and benefit the general public. The futility of depending on modern democratic government to improve American society is particularly dramatic: the United States never achieved Jefferson's ideal of a country of participatory citizens well informed on a wide variety of important public issues. (Today, even the general public realizes big business's far disproportionate influence in Washington, D.C., and campaign finance and lobbying laws are seen as *prima facie* ineffective or at least easily circumvented.) Nor is it easy to identify any class or group that has a vested interest in change, because most powerful groups can maintain support for their position with minimal input from the public. The news media, both as powerful institutions and in reaction to their particular public, simply move their resources to increased coverage of sports, business, arts, and/or entertainment.

Suggestions

This book's findings suggest the need for reexamining not only the roles of the media but our expectations for the educational process and the roles of journalists. Many researchers[2] believe that traditional print media (newspapers, magazines, books) in particular need to become more intellectual simply to survive. Print media have so many competitors that they need to concentrate on what they do best, i.e., presenting large quantities of information and often complex ideas, in depth, on an ongoing basis. One way in which print news media contending with anti-intellectualism can differentiate themselves from anti-intellectual mass media is increasingly to publish ideas and information from intellectuals that is not otherwise available to the public.[3] As *American Journalism Review* Editor Rem Rieder[4] has pointed out, the print media's attempt to compete with broadcast media for timeliness on breaking news, motion, color, graphics, and so forth, is a losing battle. I agree with his implication that print media, to stay in business, need to accept lower profit margins operating in their own market niche rather than go out of business attempting to achieve high profit margins in other media's market niche(s). Print news media should, even must, use intellectual means (publishing extensive information and ideas, from a wide variety of viewpoints, on a wide variety of topics; employing intelligent, highly educated, creative workers) to accomplish the unreflective instrumentalist (i.e., anti-intellectual) goal of staying in business, which in turn discourages anti-intellectualism through the continued influence of intellectual media. An old saw about journalism education has the professor asking his student, "What is the first responsibility of the press?," to which the student replies, "To print the truth." The professor responds, "No, the first responsibility of the press is to make a profit, so that it can afford to print the truth." What we are witnessing today is media executives who believe that they can make higher profits both in the short-run and long-run by not printing the entire truth (which is not to say that they deliberately publish untruths). However, they are mistaken, because print news media that do not serve a unique and important purpose—in their case, printing comprehensive, accurate and fair stories that cumulatively approach the truth—become bankrupt, first in their content and eventually on their financial statements, if they futilely try to become more like television.

Journalism education also needs to move away from its burgeoning partnerships with media corporations, which have resulted in journalism education increasingly co-opted into the hegemonic power structure, and revitalize its curriculum with a critical (Fourth Estate) orientation. As Hanno Hardt[5] has argued, journalism and mass communication educators have a responsibility and an opportunity to resist anti-intellectualism among their students and, I would argue, among college students generally. Instead of teaching introduction to mass media courses that emphasize the technology, political, and macroeconomic history of mass media (including their success as corporations in capitalist economies), they should also or instead teach courses on the philosophy of journalism and the responsibilities of the mass media to democracy. Critical thinking needs to be an integral part of every journalism and mass communication course. Media management and economics courses should be oriented toward empowering future media workers to change media management practices for the benefit of readers/viewers and employees, not only advertisers and stockholders. Reporting and editing courses should put a much higher emphasis on publishing enough facts and ideas so as to paint a picture of truth, rather than simply reporting the "news" — which currently often includes unchallenged statements by lying politicians and business executives. All journalism and mass communication courses need to place a higher emphasis on ethics, not only considerations in particular dilemmas, but the question of why mass communication professionals need to implement systems of ethics to fulfill their democratic responsibilities in the face of capitalistic pressures. Finally, journalism and mass communication programs need to be opened up to non-majors (as has been done at the University of Missouri at Columbia) so that all college students have the opportunity to take courses such as media analysis and criticism, media and public opinion, politics and the mass media, history of mass media, and ethics (journalism, advertising, and public relations).

Journalism and mass communication professors and researchers need to participate, perhaps in partnership with working journalists in their communities, in matters of public affairs to in essence become public intellectuals. One university, Florida Atlantic University, has recognized the need to help develop such citizens by offering the country's first Ph.D. program (in comparative studies) oriented toward the development of public intellectuals, but this arguably seems to be most appropriately taken on by journalism educators. Raymie McKerrow, an Ohio University speech communication professor, recently campaigned during his term as president of the National Communication Association for a new scholarly journal concerned with communication and public intellectuals; at this writing, his effort has yet to bear fruit. McKerrow's successor as NCA President, James L. Applegate, also called for communication professors to be "public intellectuals" (although his emphasis on "engagement," "action," and "partnerships" with corporations, government agencies, and others suggests that he is at least as interested in professors obtaining research grants and consulting contracts as he in them voluntarily and independently thrusting themselves into the public sphere). I have worked in the Association for Education in Journalism and Mass Communication, another professors' organization, to introduce to journalism professors and journalists a more pure and traditional concept of public intellectuals, but also so far with little if any impact. However, the effort must be made.

Future Research

This book defines the borders of a new cultural study within the field of mass communication. The core concepts of American anti-intellectualism, media, and education direct attention to several points for future research. One model for such a project exists in the European study of similar issues as exemplified by two issues (one in 1982, the other in 1995) of *Media, Culture & Society* devoted to intellectuals and the mass media. Other suggestions for approaches to the topic are: how the media cover intellectuals; how media other than those studied for this book cover higher education; intellectuals' role as media workers and sources (Richard A. Posner's book has not by any means exhausted this subject); and the roles of U.S. mass media vis-à-vis anti-intellectualism in U.S. culture, among others.

Research that either replicates this project or changes parts while retaining other parts (e.g., examining different media or different types of messages) can be anticipated, such as examining anti-intellectualism in coverage of other primary and secondary education, anti-intellectualism in coverage of education by other mass media (newspapers, television, radio, film, the World Wide Web, and so forth) or responses to regular content, either letters to the editor (and other reader feedback) or guest columns and editorials. Such responses might suggest whether the collective text of mass media is flexible and how it either co-opts or promotes resistance to anti-intellectualism, if there is any. Since the literature suggested that public relations plays a role in how news reports higher education, it might be productive to re-examine evidence for textual indications of the originators of story concepts. Even more important, the textual relationship, both graphically and verbally, between news content and magazine advertising, also should be investigated.

However, perhaps the most exciting possibilities lie in two areas. First, arguably the most important questions emerge from the current situation of globalizing media. If the United States' media are structured by American anti-intellectualism, and since American (or at least United States–based) media predominate worldwide, will American anti-intellectualism be exported wholesale? (Certainly American economics research and free market political rhetoric, each of which fuel unreflective instrumentalism, has been increasingly influential since the Reagan-Thatcher partnership period, and U.S. ideological domination of the World Bank and the International Monetary Fund). Alison Wolf's 2002 British book, *Does education matter? Myths about education and economic growth*, complains:

> Contemporary writers *may* pay a sentence or two of lip-service to the other objectives of education before passing on to their real concern of economic growth. Our recent forebears, living in significantly poorer times, were occupied above all with the cultural, moral and intellectual purposes of education. We impoverish ourselves by our indifference to those...
>
> The 1997 Dearing Report was the last major review of UK university policy, and its effects are only now working through the system. In its first pages it offers a ritual obeisance to the notion that education 'contributes to the whole quality of life,' but then proceeds to ignore this for the remaining 466 pages of the main report...Do we really believe that economic relevance is the only justification for the university? (pp. 254-5)

Certainly since Sept. 11, 2001, Americans have learned, or at least been reminded, of American media's impact on the rest of the world, especially how violent, stupid, and ethnocentric U.S. media content impacts other peoples' opinions of the United States. A second area of research is suggested by the du Gay *et al.* "circuit of culture" model. This project examined media content, but other areas such as corporate organization, workplace practices, and media audiences could be explored under the overarching umbrella of examining the role of the media in American anti-intellectualism. Said, Chomsky, Sholle, and Carey have each raised questions about the roles of intellectuals and the functions of anti-intellectualism. McChesney and

Hanno Hardt have sounded clarion calls for journalism educators to join with working journalists as public intellectuals. All of these scholars have acknowledged the centrality of the mass media.

In sum, the future for research in this area and the contribution of this project coalesce around the same process: linking one of the most powerful apparatuses of the postwar era to one of the key dimensions of American society, i.e., anti-intellectualism and questioning the apparent partnership of mass audience news media with that anti-intellectualism. As the United States' mass media, increasingly integrated vertically and horizontally, spread messages globally, this topic is of concern both at home and abroad.

Appendix
Sources of Evidence and
Methods of Inquiry

One of the first examples of a textual analysis emerged from British cultural studies researchers. Although now many researchers have conducted media studies using textual analysis, *Paper Voices: The Popular Press and Social Change, 1935–1965*, by A.C.H. Smith, with Elizabeth Immirzi and Trevor Blackwell, remains a definitive explication of the method and is a methodological exemplar for this book.

That book's Introduction, written by Stuart Hall, articulates its structure and, in some ways, this book's research method with the alteration of only a few words in each paragraph of Hall's explanation. *Paper Voices'* authors chose the "'popular' rather than the 'quality' press as the main focus," chose popular periodicals that had a "circulation spread through the social pyramid," chose a relatively lengthy time period for study ("Second World War to the mid-1960s" in its case), chose qualitative research methods ("literary-critical, linguistic and stylistic methods" in *Paper Voices*), and decided to "count and quantify where, and *only* where, it seemed relevant and economic to do so" (emphasis in original).[1]

Paper Voices' authors ultimately ask "why-the-content-is-like-that"; "adopted the practice of giving as much of the evidence in its own terms as we could manage"; recognized that both the "technical and social organization" and the "readers who buy" are important; and treated print mass media as a "structure of meanings, rather than as a channel for the transmission and reception of news. Our study, therefore, treated newspapers as *texts*" (emphasis in the original). This book analyzes verbal and visual content in several magazines together, as O'Sullivan would specify, as a text "that has a physical existence of its own, independent of its sender or receiver, and thus composed of representational codes"; mass media content generally is considered to have "preferred"—usually "closed" readings—but texts studied for this book are sometimes more "open" than they might at first appear.[2]

For *Paper Voices'* authors, studying texts also meant recognizing not only how one print medium differs from another visually and organizationally, but that each publication, "within...generally available rhetorics" will "make[] a selection of rhetorics appropriate to its *persona*"—and that each print mass medium has its own "*persona* or personality." Finally, the *Paper Voices* scholars asserted that "the separation between two kinds of research into newspapers—that which focuses on the social processes by which newspapers are produced, and that which focuses on newspapers as symbolic artefacts...are *not* two opposing types of research, but essentially complementary" (emphasis in original). This book is embedded in a discussion of the strengths and weaknesses of two different methods, e.g., the more conventional (and often quantitative) content analysis, and textual analysis.[3]

Although *Paper Voices* is a landmark in cultural studies, the reader cannot discern exactly how the *Paper Voices* researchers selected specific articles to analyze and discuss. It seems obvious from the content and organization of their book that they did not analyze every article, directly or indirectly related to social change, published in two daily newspapers during the course of thirty years. Instead, the *Paper Voices* authors addressed some articles at length, merely mentioned others, and did not even mention yet others. Indeed, in a section in which they are explaining their use of "literary, stylistic and linguistic analysis," the authors emphasize that such a method "uses the preliminary reading to select *representative examples* which can be more intensively analysed" (emphasis added); but they do not give a definition of "representative" nor explain how that definition was operationalized. If, by "representative," these researchers mean "typical" or "average," the reader must take the authors' judgment on faith, while probably suspecting that unusual or atypical articles were the more remarkable. At the very least, then, a book such as this one, or any other study, using *Paper Voices* as a model should clarify the process by which articles are selected for analysis.

The *Paper Voices* researchers informally asked, when reading and writing about articles, the following questions:

> [W]hen dealing with so complex a process as historical and social change, what already available stock of meanings was brought to bear by the newspaper so as to make that process intelligible to its readers? Are there core-values in a newspaper which provide its staff and its readers with a coherent, if not consistent, scheme of interpretation? Do these meanings change over time? And, if so, in response to what events?
>
> Using "affluence" as our way of cutting into the material, then, what picture of social change in the period emerged from our study of the two newspapers? How did the press interpret and define social change? What competing models of society were mediated by the press?
>
> [What are] not the direct and explicit political or social appeals the newspapers made, but the structures of meanings and the configurations of feeling on which this public rhetoric is based[?]...[What is the] image of the readers the newspaper was taking for granted when it assumed it could write in that way about politics and society[?]...[W]hat image of society supported the particular treatment given to any set of topics[?]...[H]ow [did] such assumptions come to be formed—in response to what historical and social circumstances: and how, through time, they were changed or adapted[?][4]

This set of questions forms the near-equivalent of a content analysis coding sheet. To be more precise, this set of questions foregrounds how each part of the text as a whole was separated, analyzed, and re-integrated.

Evidence of media participation in abetting or resisting U.S. anti-intellectualism could have been sought in different milieus: journalism training during formal education, other journalism training, media gate-keeping decisions, media corporation policies, media recruiting and hiring practices, and others. In this case, media content was chosen because content is the most readily accessible site for examining anti-intellectual phenomena. Second, content by itself provides not only verbal and visual evidence, but also hints at production processes and practices (including gate-keeping) and audience consumption.

Searching for evidence of anti-intellectualism in mass media coverage presents a complex task. Few print media articles use the term "anti-intellectual" or "anti-intellectualism." This book operationalizes words such as "intellectual," "intellectualism," "anti-intellectual," and "anti-intellectualism" in two ways: first as words that may be located within the text, and second—much more often—as synonyms for, descriptions of, or categories of other words, sentences, paragraphs or entire articles.

Because the amount of news coverage and other portrayals of intellectuals both inside and outside higher education, non-intellectuals inside higher education, and higher education generally has been voluminous, the time period under consideration must be limited, a method of content selection must be developed, and the criteria for conducting an analysis of text and visual content must be formulated.

Sources of Evidence and Selection of the Time Period

The period 1944–1998 was selected for this book because of the significant and rapid growth and changes in higher education since the G.I. Bill, as explained in most detail in the Introduction but also generally throughout the book. Print mass media were chosen as the site of inquiry for several reasons:

* Print media articles are typically longer in length and therefore include a greater breadth and depth of coverage.
* During most (perhaps all) of this period, print media covered a larger number and variety of stories than did broadcast news media.
* A greater amount of and wider variety of print mass media exists in libraries and archives than other media (important as an access issue both for researchers and audiences).
* During the first part of the period in question, television was still emerging and radio was undergoing a major transformation due to the advent of television, while print remained popular through-

out.
* Print mass media are indexed more consistently and thoroughly.
* Print mass media enjoyed a reputation as the dominant and most credible mass medium during most of the period.
* Finally, the primary professional and scholarly backgrounds and interests of its author, Dane S. Claussen, were and are in print media.

Among print mass media, national popular magazines were chosen precisely because they were national: their content is consistent with a large national audience and their editors presumably keep a national audience in mind while managing their content. Feedback in the form of readers' responses and advertising sales also is national. Some national magazines also boasted staffs with diverse backgrounds. Moreover, most of the advantages for this book's arguments that print media claim over other media are even more substantial for magazines than for newspapers.

The Readers' Guide to Periodical Literature historically has indexed magazines that either had the largest circulations and/or were considered the most influential. Because higher education was growing so quickly and changing in many ways during the twentieth century, it becomes highly likely that the largest circulation magazines may have had the most influence on public conceptions of higher education and closely related topics, which poses advantages in presenting evidence and arguments in this book.

For example, Scannell (1966), in his triangulated study of what leaders and typical citizens in two South Dakota cities (Aberdeen and Huron) read about higher education, what they knew and thought about higher education, and what publications they read, presents scholars and the magazine industry with a probably representative picture of which magazines typical Americans regularly read—or at least saw.[5]

A second reason to examine national magazines was that, although they sometimes display discernible regional biases in terms of content, their claim to a national audience suggests the possibility of national influence. Third, the *Readers' Guide*, and all of the periodicals it indexed, were widely available for consultation in public libraries, school libraries, newsstands and other locations, as well as by personal subscription. Fourth, the *Readers' Guide* is a current barometer of the national magazine industry, because it indexes large-circulation new magazines as they establish themselves in the national marketplace. Finally, the analysis of magazine coverage of higher education in previous historical studies has been neither systematic nor comprehensive. To the contrary, articles cited are often those found in small circulation publications and/or written by now famous figures such as Walter Lippmann.

During the fifty-five–year period under study, the *Readers' Guide to Periodical Literature* indexed thousands of articles related to higher education. Therefore it was necessary to examine selected magazines' coverage. This book drew its evidence from four magazines, but not the same four throughout the entire period. *Reader's Digest*, *Ladies' Home Journal*, and *Time*, all published from prior to 1944 to the present, were sources of evidence throughout. *Life* was used as a source of evidence until December 1972, when Henry Luce's original *Life* ceased publication. In January 1973, *Life* was replaced as the fourth source of evidence by *Nation's Business*. The rationale for each selected magazine follows.

Reader's Digest was chosen in part because it was the largest circulation magazine in the United States during the entire period being analyzed. Although *Reader's Digest* did not have an audited circulation until the late 1950s, earlier publishers' claims are widely accepted; in 1948, for instance, *Reader's Digest* claimed a paid circulation of more than 8 million, and the next largest circulation was *Life's* 5.4 million (*Information Please Almanac*, 1949). When Audit Bureau of Circulations released its Dec. 31, 1957, report, one of the first few years that *Reader's Digest* was audited, ABC reported a paid circulation of 11.3 million for the U.S. edition and 800,000 more for Canada's English language edition.

Second, *Reader's Digest* reprints articles from other magazines, thus giving further circulation to articles that already have been published. It has been a quintessential general interest magazine with a relatively diverse readership. *Reader's Digest* did not accept advertising until 1955, and thus has been freer of potential and real pressures from advertisers than other mass market magazines. Finally, *Reader's Digest* has been studied before by mass communication scholars; most studies are content analyses of the magazine's articles or advertising.[6]

Ladies' Home Journal was chosen because it was one of the seven largest magazines by circulation throughout the period and because it has been the largest circulation magazine aimed at women readers for almost the entire period of study. In 1946, *Ladies' Home Journal* had a larger circulation (more than 4.1 million) than any magazine in the United States, except for *Reader's Digest* (*Information Please Almanac*, 1947). By 1948, *Ladies' Home Journal* (with 4.5 million circulation) had been bumped out of the second position by both *Life* and the "Fawcett Comics Group." Throughout the 1944–1998 period, *Ladies' Home Journal* moved up and down the lists of best-selling magazines. However, from its commanding position in 1946, it was not until 1960 that *Ladies' Home Journal* (6,550,415) was just barely topped by *McCall's* (6,560,452), and it wasn't until 1963 when it also was surpassed by *Family Circle*. In 1995, *Ladies' Home Journal* (circ. 5.0 million) was still in fourth place among women's magazines. *Ladies' Home Journal* always has been a leading, if not always the largest, women's magazine in the United States. *Ladies' Home Journal* also has been consistently indexed by *Reader's Guide* (not true for all of the women's magazines). Finally, *Ladies' Home Journal* has been studied before by mass communication scholars.[7]

Time was chosen because it has been a large circulation magazine throughout the period. Although early in the period, for example, in 1946, the United States boasted nineteen magazines with larger circulations than *Time* (which at the time had 1.3 million), *Time*'s relative stature grew, although its circulation numbers varied. *Time* has always had a larger circulation than its two primary competitors, *Newsweek* and *U.S. News & World Report;* in many years, *Time*'s circulation has been slightly higher or slightly lower than those of its two competitors combined. *Time* was chosen in part because of its relatively diverse readership and its news magazine niche positions it as a general interest magazine. Finally, *Time*'s departmentalized format both allowed and forced it to regularly cover education once that subject was established as a beat on the staff and as a department in the magazine.[8] Finally, *Time* also has been widely studied by mass communication scholars, mostly through content analyses.[9]

Life was chosen because it was one of the largest magazines by circulation for more than half the period. In 1946, *Life* was third behind only *Reader's Digest* and *Ladies' Home Journal*. Throughout the 1950s, *Life* was third behind only *Reader's Digest* and then also *TV Guide*. In the 1960s, *Life* also was overtaken by *Look* and then *McCall's* and finally *Family Circle*, but even at the end of 1971, only one year before it closed, *Life* was still the ninth largest U.S. magazine by circulation, exceeded only by *Reader's Digest, TV Guide, National Geographic*, and five women's magazines (including *Ladies' Home Journal*).

Further, *Life* was chosen because it had a relatively diverse readership; it was even more of a general interest, mass circulation magazine in nature than either *Time* or *Ladies' Home Journal*; and because of its emphasis on photography, which has been somewhat less prominent in *Time* and dramatically less so in the other magazines selected. The selection of *Life* also could be justified in part on the basis of its status as a cultural institution, even icon, in U.S. culture; when the original *Life* closed, the U.S. public missed it so much that the magazine was reincarnated first for special issues and then as a long-running monthly that lasted until beyond the end of the period covered by this book. Even though *Time* and *Life* were each owned by Henry Luce's Time-Life company, they both were included here because of their significant yet differing roles in American journalism and popular culture. They typically did not cover the same stories, their writing styles were different, and of course *Life* was much less political.

Life historian Dora Jane Hamblin called the magazine's photographers, whose product was the lifeblood of the product, "God the Photographer," and explained that

> ...the photographer epitomized the casual arrogance which permeated the entire staff. *Life* was the most important magazine in the world...And because it was built on pictures, the lordliest of all its lordly crew was the photographer. Photographers managed to persuade a staggering number of persons that this was true.[10]

Kozol, who also has written extensively about *Life*, reported that when, in 1936, Henry Luce, founder of *Time* and *Fortune*, was preparing to launch *Life*, "the editors conceived of *Life* as a magazine directed at Midwestern, middle-class, white Americans who held conventional ideas about domestic roles." Luce's own mission statement for *Life* reflected this, including perpetuating sexist views of women: "To see life; to see the world...[to see] the women that men love and many children; to see and take pleasure in seeing..."[11]

Anderson (1958) studied the reasons why various magazines ceased publication between 1926 and 1956, and concluded that *Time,*

Life, Reader's Digest, and other magazines were more appropriate for twentieth-century U.S. culture than many of those that went out of business (of course financial or sales mismanagement also play large roles in many shutdowns). Anderson believed that many forces were at work:

> *Time, Life, Look,* and *Reader's Digest,* as well as that of their imitators, typified the "new look" in periodical journalism. They were a clear result of the national mood—one of speed and complexity, changing and increased interests. The public demand for brevity and the consequent saving of reading time was met by the new publications...

Life has been previously studied by mass communication scholars, again primarily through content analyses,[12] and was singled out in Jacques Barzan's book, *The House of Intellect* (1959), as *not intellectual*—despite his report that "In army camps during the last war [World War II] *Life* was considered a highbrow magazine by the majority, for whom the principal reading matter apart from newspapers was the so-called comic books."

Nation's Business was selected for study in part because of its historically leading role among business magazines in the United States and was selected in part because refocusing this book from a magazine such as *Life* to one such as *Nation's Business* in the early 1970s is a rough reflection of changes that were occurring both in the magazine industry and among the general public: more interest in business and less on community, family, and so forth. In the 1970s, the combined circulations of magazines such as *Forbes*, *Fortune*, *Business Week*, and *Nation's Business* jumped dramatically. *Money*, started in 1972, had a circulation of more than 446,000 by mid-1974; five years later (mid-1979), it had a circulation of more than 845,000; and five years after that (mid-1984), more than 1.5 million. By mid-1995, its circulation was almost 2 million; as the official magazine of the U.S. Chamber of Commerce, *Nation's Business*'s circulation was more than 863,000, having just been surpassed by *Business Week* but still comfortably ahead of *Forbes* and *Fortune*. Although apparently no scholarly articles have been written by mass communication researchers solely or even primarily about *Nation's Business* (or any major business magazine), research has been conducted about various aspects of business magazine journalism, particularly its overall financial health, public credibility or development of the business magazine industry.[13]

Criteria for Selecting Specific Content

Coverage examined for this book was selected according to criteria determined following an initial reading of selected articles throughout the period. This book's author analyzed all articles that fit all of the following criteria:

* Published in *Reader's Digest, Ladies' Home Journal, Time* or the original *Life* (ceased publication Dec. 31, 1972), and *Nation's Business* since January 1, 1973;
* Indexed in *Reader's Guide to Periodical Literature*, under selected headings[14] that included articles about the nexuses of higher education, intellectuals, intellectualism, and anti-intellectualism in U.S. culture.
* Published during the following years: Magazines from every fourth year were chosen starting with the G.I. Bill year of 1944, to obtain a systematic sample over the fifty-five–year period. In addition, other years were chosen for analysis because of highly significant news events related to higher education during those years: 1944 (G.I. Bill), 1948, 1952, 1954 (*Brown v. Board of Education*), 1956 (President's Committee on Education Beyond High School), 1957 (Sputnik), 1960, 1964 (Free Speech Movement at Berkeley is traditional launch point for student protests), 1968, 1970 (Kent State and Jackson State shootings; President's Commission on Campus Unrest), 1972, 1976, 1978 (*Bakke* v. *University of California*), 1980, 1984, 1988 (continued coverage of *The Closing of the American Mind*), 1992, and 1996. Ultimately, hundreds of articles, published during eighteen different years were analyzed.
  Aspects of each article that are of potential interest include:
  1) Article content
     a) Topic
     b) Type of story (news, feature, personality profile, photo essay, etc.)
     c) Sources quoted
     d) Possible sources not quoted
     e) Number of sources

    f) Structure of story, discourse/rhetoric, latent biases, and so forth

2) The article's placement in the magazine—particularly if a higher education story is a cover story, or if higher education coverage is emphasized or de-emphasized by its placement.
3) Headline content and size
4) Length of story
5) Photographs/illustrations and their content
6) Photograph cutline content
7) Other elements other than illustrations, main headline, and body text: subheads, jumpheads, pulled quotes, and so forth.

Because this book concerns ideological construction within the social formation and not news performance (or media criticism), the articles were not scrutinized for their satisfaction of professional criteria of U.S. journalism, such as fairness, accuracy, completeness, timeliness, geographical proximity, and so on, although these characteristics have sometimes been stated or implied in this book's discussions.

Organization of the Evidence

This book's evidence—that is the various aspects of the magazine articles examined—has been presented in a manner that mirrors Daniel Rigney's theory of U.S. anti-intellectualism, i.e., evidence was organized first by the three typologies of his U.S. anti-intellectualism theory (religious anti-rationalism, populist anti-elitism, and unreflective instrumentalism) and then, within each typology, based on whether it supported and/or did not support his descriptions of the most significant manifestations of those typologies' in American culture.

    In addition to analyzing what the magazines covered, this book also makes efforts to assess what was omitted when such omissions are theoretically important and can be asserted with some confidence. This book also sometimes states, but more often implied, how topics covered could have been different (for instance, anytime a story has only one source, and particularly an obviously biased source, more sources would most likely have made for a more complete story), what forces influenced the coverage other than the sociology and professional competence of news workers (of course this research primarily seeks clues of anti-intellectualism in U.S. culture), and what kind of social formation the media coverage reflects and/or constructs over a sustained period of time.

The guide sheet used to help perform both "macro," and "micro," analyses on each of the articles from the five magazines, which gathered "data points" consistent with the modified version of Smith *et al.*'s *Paper Voices* method, was as follows:

Questions to Assist in Collection of Data Points

1. What assumptions does the article make about its topic(s)?
2. How does the text construct its audience?
3. Does the article use the term(s) *intellectual(s), intellectualism, anti-intellectual(s)* and/or *anti-intellectualism* in the text? If so, in what context, with what apparent definition and to what apparent effect? In the case of intellectual and anti-intellectual individuals, is such labeling done by the magazine or by a cited source? Whose interests in society are reflected by how these terms are used? Are intellectuals and/or the media resisting American anti-intellectualism, through criticizing, avoiding or otherwise distancing themselves from attitudes and phenomena that appear to be reflecting religious anti-rationalism, populist anti-elitism, and unreflective instrumentalism?
4. Is there a pattern in how a publication uses the terms *intellectual(s), intellectualism, anti-intellectual(s)*, and/or *anti-intellectualism* in various articles? If a change occurs in the pattern, can possible reasons for the change be discerned? Whose interests in society are reflected by these patterns and changes in those patterns? Are individual intellectuals and/or the media resisting American anti-intellectualism?
5. What competing models of intellectuals, intellectualism, higher education, intellectual discourse, etc., are mediated by the magazines, particularly in how college students and college graduates are portrayed? Is any "disconnect" between what college students want and/or need (to be educated citizens and/or to be employable workers) to obtain from a college education, versus what they do obtain, discernible?

6. What is the topic(s) of the article? Specifically with regard to the Rigney theory and Hofstadter history of U.S. anti-intellectualism, how does the article directly and/or indirectly construct:

a) the intellect, which refers to the "critical, creative, and contemplative side of mind," which "examines, ponders, wonders, theorizes, criticizes, imagines" (Hofstadter)

b) anti-intellectualism, which generally means "resentment and suspicion of the life of the mind and of those who are considered to represent it; and a disposition constantly to minimize the value of that life" (Hofstadter); and/or anti-intellectualism specifically, which means:

i) one type of anti-rationalism: the belief that "rational intellect is passionless and cold" (Rigney). An example of such anti-rationalism in media coverage of U.S. higher education would be favorable portrayals and/or a lack of negative portrayals of "'deintellectualized curricula' that place a higher value on the social and affective development of students than on the cultivation of their capacities for thought" (Rigney). An example of this anti-rationalism in the social construction of intellectuals is that they are passionless and cold persons.

ii) a second type of anti-rationalism, usually motivated by religion (in the United States, often evangelical Protestantism): the "fear that intellectual discourse endangers the foundations of absolute belief—i.e., that reason promotes relativism by calling absolute truths into doubt" (Rigney). An example of this type of anti-rationalism in media coverage of U.S. higher education is the "fundamentalist conception of schooling as indoctrination in epistemological and moral absolutes" (Rigney). An example of this type of anti-rationalism in the social construction of intellectuals is that they are dangerous because "Left free, there is nothing it [intellect] will not reconsider, analyze, throw into question" (Hofstadter).

iii) populist anti-elitism: "mistrust of claims to superior knowledge or wisdom on the part of an educated elite, especially when such claims are suspected to be instruments in the service of class privilege." This phenomenon is found "primarily in indigenous populist movements and in populist elements within political parties that purport to represent the interests of the 'common people' against the self-serving machinations of more advantaged classes" (Rigney). An example of populist anti-elitism in media coverage of U.S. higher education would be favorable portrayals and/or a lack of negative portrayals of "de-value[d] book learning, jeopardize[d] high academic standards, and neglecte[d]...development of the most gifted students" (Rigney). An example of anti-elitism in the social construction of intellectuals is seen in the fact that "the phrase 'ivory tower' has become an almost universal term of contempt" (Rigney).

iv) unreflective instrumentalism: the "devaluation of forms of thought that do not promise relatively immediate practical payoffs," including but not limited to "impatience with ideas that are deemed impractical or utopian but also a disdain for purely theoretical inquiry as a valuable activity in its own right" (Rigney). Unreflective instrumentalism often entails suppressing questions about the ends of, and ethics surrounding, solving "practical" problems" and is found "primarily in the economic institutions of American capitalism" (Rigney). An example of unreflective instrumentalism in media coverage of U.S. higher education would be favorable portrayals and/or a lack of negative portrayals of "narrow vocationalism, discouraged purely theoretical work, and devalued...intrinsic rewards of learning" (Rigney). An example of unreflective instrumentalism in the social construction of intellectuals is seen again in the fact that "the phrase 'ivory tower' has become an almost universal term of contempt" (Rigney).

v) unreflective hedonism: the "flight from the hard and often painful work of reflective thought" (Rigney). Rigney's informal and half-hearted contribution to Hofstadter's work, unreflective hedonism is essentially another name for "Huxley's vision of a brave new world, a trivialized culture that creates an almost limitless appetite for amusement and diversion. News and education are now essentially popular forms of entertainment, competing with situation comedies and video games for the fun-consumer's shortened span of attention" (Rigney). An example of unreflective hedonism in media coverage of U.S. higher education would be favorable portrayals and/or a lack of negative portrayals of institutions, programs, or professors who emphasized whether students are amused or diverted than whether they were thinking and learning; in other words, are the "consumers" or "customers" having "fun"? An example of unreflective hedonism in the social construction of intellectuals would be portrayals of them as "boring," or in some way the opposite of "fun."

Finally, whose interests are reflected by how subjects are constructed and by which topics are omitted?

7. Does evidence emerge, for instance, that intellectuals and/or college students are expected, to have certain knowledge—general or technical—but not obtain so much knowledge or become politicized—so that intelligence and education threaten the status quo? Whose interests are served by various expectations or the lack of same? In other words, are persons, groups, institutions, ideas, or practices linked with certain ideologies or corporations? Who judges whether expectations have been met? What other evidence emerges about processes by which intellectuals, college students, college graduates, intellectualism or anti-intellectualism are constructed and reproduced?

8. What observations can be made about the frequency, amount, position, headline type size, presence (and content) or lack thereof of illustrations, or other physical characteristics of the articles in the sample?

9. What evidence emerges of how intellectuals and/or college graduates are "consumed" in U.S. society? Consumption here has two meanings: the consumption of education/curricula, and the society "consuming" intellectuals (i.e., what does U.S. society do with intellectuals?). This brings up questions such as whether intellectuals and/or college students resist how they are treated by society, the various ways in which they are "consumed," and the possibilities for change.

Notes

Introduction

1. See David O. Levine, *The American college and the culture of aspiration 1915–1940* (Ithaca, N.Y.: Cornell University Press, 1986); Diane Ravitch, *The troubled crusade: American education, 1945–1980* (New York: Basic Books, Inc., Publishers, 1983); and Frederick Rudolph, *The American college & university: A history* (1962; Athens, Ga.: The University of Georgia Press, 1990).
2. Richard M. Freeland, *Academia's golden age: Universities in Massachusetts, 1945–1970* (New York: Oxford University Press, 1992), 74.
3. Ravitch, *Troubled Crusade*, 12.
4. John D. Millett, *Financing higher education in the United States* (New York: Columbia University Press, 1952).
5. Ravitch, *Troubled Crusade*, 184.
6. Ravitch, *Troubled Crusade*, 184. Today it is common for college administrators to respond to questions about higher education's public image by simply pointing to the percentage of Americans in college or paying for college (usually students and/or their parents). This argument avoids this issue of whether so many Americans would attend college if they didn't believe a college degree were necessary for employment, or at least a significant income and occupational prestige.

7. Oscar Handlin and Mary F. Handlin, *The American college and American culture; socialization as a function of higher education* (New York: McGraw-Hill, 1970), 73.
8. Ernest Havemann and Particia S. West, *They went to college* (New York: Harcourt, Brace, 1952), 126–37; Helen Lefkowitz Horowitz, *Campus life: Undergraduate cultures from the end of the eighteenth century to the present* (New York: Alfred A. Knopf, 1987), 18.
9. Angus Campbell and William C. Eckerman, *Public concepts of the values and costs of higher education* (Ann Arbor, Mich.: Survey Research Center, University of Michigan, 1964) and University of Michigan Survey Research Center, *The public image of state and private universities* (Ann Arbor, Mich.: Author, 1964).
10. Susan J. Douglas, *Where the girls are: Growing up female with the mass media* (New York: Random House, 1994), 21–22.
11. Howard R. Bowen, *The costs of higher education* (San Francisco: Jossey-Bass Publishers, 1980).
12. Freeland, *Academia's Golden Age*, 356.
13. Phillip G. Altbach, *University reform: Comparative perspectives for the seventies* (Cambridge, Mass.: Schenkman Publishing Company, 1974), 211.
14. Rudolph, *The American College & University*, 487.
15. David D. Henry, *What priority for education?* (Urbana-Champaign, Ill.: University of Illinois Press, 1961), 76–77.
16. Handlin and Handlin, *The American college and American culture*, 85.
17. Krista E. White, *How the girls really are? Images of college women in* Life *magazine during the 1960s* (unpublished master's thesis, University of Colorado—Boulder, 1996), 14.
18. Campbell and Eckerman, *Public Concepts, Ibid*; University of Michigan Survey Research Center, *The Public Image, Ibid*.
19. Donald F. Scannell, *Mass media use, information, and opinions concerning higher education* (unpublished doctoral dissertation, University of Minnesota, 1966), 155, 158, 156, 164.
20. Horowitz, *Campus Life*, 223; Altbach, *University Reform*, 18.
21. Ravitch, *Troubled Crusade*, 197, 199, 205, 214.
22. Freeland, *Academia's Golden Age*, 114, 115.
23. William R. Hazard, *A study of attitudes and opinions held by 465 Iowans concerning higher education and the State University of Iowa* (Ames, Iowa: SUI Alumnae Research Committee, 1963).
24. Scannell, *Mass Media Use*, 29.
25. Horowitz, *Campus Life*, 20, 245, 248.
26. Horowitz, *Campus Life*, 255, 258–60.
27. Lawrence Mishel and Jared Bernstein, *The state of working America, 1992–93*. Armonk, N.Y.: M.E. Sharp, 1993); Arthur M. Hauptman, *The college tuition spiral* (Washington: American Council on Education, 1990).
28. Horowitz, *Campus Life*, 266.
29. Herant A. Katchadourian and John Boli, *Careerism and intellectualism among college students* (San Francisco: Jossey-Bass Publishers, 1985).
30. Peter T. Ewell, "A matter of integrity: Accountability and the future of self-regulation," *Change 26*, no. 6 (1994): 24–29; and William F. Massy and Andrea K.

Wilger, "Productivity in postsecondary education: a new approach," *Educational Evaluation and Policy Analysis 14* (1992): 361–76.

31. Paul R. Loeb, *Generation at the crossroads: Apathy and action on the American campus* (New Brunswick, N.J.: Rutgers University Press, 1994).

32. Russell Jacoby, *The last intellectuals: American culture in the age of academe* (New York: Noonday, 2000/1987).

Chapter 1: "How Smart Is Too Smart?"

1. David E. Sanger, "Another Bush's Vision Thing," *The New York Times*, 20 January 2002, sec. 4, 3; and Christopher Buckley, "War and Destiny: The White House in Wartime," *Vanity Fair*, February 2002, 78–93.

2. Ron Suskind, "Why Are These Men Laughing?" *Esquire*, January 2003; David Frum, *The right man: The surprise presidency of George W. Bush* (New York: Random House, 2003).

3. One must wonder whether the intellectual Clinton was himself deeply anti-intellectual or only thoroughly political: Benjamin R. Barber's book, *The Truth of Power: Intellectual Affairs in the Clinton White House* (New York: W.W. Norton, 2001), argues that while Clinton enjoyed talking, even arguing with, intellectuals (starting with his Secretary of Labor and old friend, Robert Reich), he took their advice relatively rarely.

      This discussion of presidents' intelligence, fortunately or unfortunately, does not need to address the genius of either Thomas Jefferson (who John F. Kennedy once famously compared to a room of Nobel Prize winners) or Abraham Lincoln, nor that Dr. T. Woodrow Wilson was a history professor and president of Princeton, and prolific author on the history and theory of government.

4. George W. Bush's limitations in terms of his education, expertise, intelligence, and/or public speaking skills are thoroughly discussed in hundreds of newspaper and magazine articles, as well as numerous books: Frank Bruni, *Ambling into history: The unlikely odyssey of George W. Bush* (New York: HarperCollins, 2002); Mark Crispin Miller, *The Bush Dyslexicon: Observations on a National Disorder* (New York: W.W. Norton & Company, 2001); Marley Roberts, *Compassionate Conservatism by Dummys: The Wit and Wisdom of George W. Bush* (San Francisco: Last Gasp, 2000); J.H. Hatfield, *Fortunate Son: George W. Bush and the Making of an American President* (Soft Skull Press, 2001); Jacob Weisberg, ed., George W. Bushisms: *The Slate Book of The Accidental Wit and Wisdom of our 43rd President* (New York: Simon & Schuster, 2001); Jacob Weisberg, ed., *More George W. Bushisms: More of Slate's Accidental Wit and Wisdom of Our 43rd President* (New York: Simon & Schuster, 2002); Paul Begala, *Is Our Children Learning?: The Case Against George W. Bush* (New York: Simon & Schuster, 2000); Molly Ivins and Lou Dubose, *Shrub: The Short but Happy Political Life of George W. Bush* (New York: Vintage Books, 2000), and others. He also is satirized in Kevin Guilfoile, *My First Presidentiary: A Scrapbook by George W. Bush* (New York: Three Rivers Press, 2001).

5. Richard Hofstadter, *Anti-intellectualism in American Life* (New York: Alfred A. Knopf, 1962), 25.
6. Daniel Rigney, "Three kinds of anti-intellectualism: Rethinking Hofstadter," *Sociological Inquiry 61* (1991): 434–51.
7. Rigney, in "Three kinds," added, "If there is an anti-intellectualism of the fourth kind in American culture today, it might be named unreflective hedonism, a flight from the hard and often painful work of reflective thought."
8. See Edward S. Herman and Noam Chomsky, *Manufacturing consent: The political economy of the mass media* (New York: Pantheon, 1988); and Neil Postman, *Amusing ourselves to death: Public discourse in the age of show business* (New York: Viking Penguin, 1985).
9. Timothy Richard Glander, *Origins of Mass Communications Research During the American Cold War: Educational Effects and Contemporary Implications* (Mahweh, N.J.: Lawrence Erlbaum Associates, 2000); Everett M. Rogers, *A History of Communication Study: A Biographical Approach* (New York: Free Press, 1997); Wilbur L. Schramm (Stephen H. Chaffee and Everett M. Rogers, eds.), *The beginnings of communication study in America: A personal memoir* (Thousand Oaks, Calif.: Sage Publications, 1997); Everette E. Dennis and Ellen Wartella (eds.), *American communication research: The remembered history* (Mahwah, N.J.: Erlbaum, 1996); William David Sloan (ed.), *Makers of the Media Mind: Journalism Educators and Their Ideas* (Hillsdale, N.J.: Lawrence Erlbaum Associates, 1990); Elizabeth P. Lester, "Discursive strategies of exclusion: The ideological construction of newsworkers," in *Newsworkers: Towards a history of the rank and file*, eds. Hanno Hardt and Bonnie Brennen (Minneapolis, Minn.: The University of Minnesota Press, 1995); Daniel Lerner and Lyle Nelson, eds., *Communication Research—A Half Century of Appraisal* (Honolulu: The University Press of Hawaii, 1977).
10. John Easton, "Bloom in review," *University of Chicago Magazine* (August 1997), 22–24.
11. In addition to Greenberg's article, Hofstadter has been remembered or analyzed in Arthur M. Schlesinger, Jr., "Richard Hofstadter," in *Pastmasters: Some essays on American historians*, eds. Marcus Cunliffe and Robin W. Winks (New York: Harper & Row, 1969), 278–315; Alfred Kazin, "Richard Hofstadter, 1916–1970," *American Scholar 40* (1971), 399; Lawrence A. Cremin, *Richard Hofstadter (1916–1970)* (N.c.: National Academy of Education, 1972); Stanley M. Elkins and Eric L. McKittrick, eds., *The Hofstadter aegis: A memorial* (New York: Alfred A. Knopf, Inc., 1974); Daniel W. Howe and Peter E. Finn, "Richard Hofstadter: The ironies of an American historian," *Pacific Historical Review 43* (1974): 1–23; Richard Gillam, "Richard Hofstadter, C. Wright Mills, and the 'critical ideal,'" *American Scholar 47* (1977–1978): 69–85; Susan S. Baker, "Out of the engagement; Richard Hofstadter: The genesis of a historian" (unpublished doctoral dissertation, Case Western Reserve University, 1982); Susan S. Baker, *Radical beginnings: Richard Hofstadter and the 1930s* (Westport, Conn.: Greenwood, 1985); Daniel J. Singal, "Beyond consensus: Richard Hofstadter and American historiography," *American Historical Review 89* (1984): 976–1004; Robert M. Collins, "The originality trap: Richard Hofstadter on Populism," *Journal of American History 76* (1989): 151–67; Steven Weiland, "The academic attitude: Richard Hofstadter and the anti-intellectuals,"

Antioch Review 46 (1988): 462–72; and Steven Weiland, *Intellectual craftsmen: Ways and works in American scholarship, 1935–1990* (New Brunswick, N.J.: Transaction Publishers, 1991).

12. Lewis A. Coser, *Men of ideas: A Sociologist's View* (New York: Free Press Paperbacks/Simon & Schuster, 1965); Edward A. Shils, *The intellectuals and the powers and other essays* (Chicago: The University of Chicago Press, 1972); Jacoby, *The Last Intellectuals*; Allan D. Bloom, *The closing of the American mind: How higher education has failed democracy and impoverished the souls of today's students* (New York: Simon and Schuster, 1987); Leon Fink, Stephen T. Leonard, and Donald M. Reid (eds.), *Intellectuals and public life: Between radicalism and reform* (Ithaca, N.Y.: Cornell University Press, 1996); and Leon Fink, *Progressive intellectuals and the dilemmas of democratic commitment* (Cambridge, Mass.: Harvard University Press, 1997).

13. Fink, *Progressive intellectuals.*

14. Richard Gillam, "Richard Hofstadter," 83. The careful reader also must question whether Hofstadter's stated optimism, in his book's introduction and conclusion, about American culture becoming less anti-intellectual was even sincere, given the weight of the evidence in between. In other words, Hofstadter may have felt compelled (by himself and/or by his editors at Alfred A. Knopf) as a writer and teacher to give his readers some sense of hope, regardless of whether he felt such hope was justified.

15. However, Skoble's case is brief and obviously incomplete. Moreover, the book's omission of any reference to Merle Curti, Richard Hofstadter, Daniel Rigney, Allan Bloom, or other historians or sociologists of anti-intellectualism, as well as the authors' only passing references to any key American pragmatists (John Dewey, William James, C.S. Peirce, Max Eastman, and so on)—whose writings have been widely misinterpreted in anti-intellectual ways—make it unclear how knowledgeable Irwin, Conard, and Skoble (whose book was published by Open Court, Chicago, 2001) are on the subject.

16. Noam Chomsky (in Bill Moyers, *A world of ideas: Conversations with thoughtful men and women about American life today and the ideas shaping our future* [New York: Doubleday, 1988] goes even farther than Goar: "The United States is subject to a thought control system so thorough that we are not even permitted to think that our thoughts might be controlled," and "Because it [U.S. society] is so free, the established powers have a constant fear of losing control. They can't even allow the thought that there might be thought control" (Noam Chomsky, speech at Macalester College, St. Paul, Minn., 23 April 1992).

17. See, for example, Daniel Goldin, "Help Wanted: The Head of NASA Forecasts a Bleak Future for American Science," *The Atlantic Monthly*, September 2001, 28.

Chapter 2: American Intellectual History, Anti-Intellectualism, and the Mass Media

1. Merle Curti, *The Growth of American Thought* (New York: Harper & Row, Publishers, 1943), 268.

2. Edward W. Said, *Representations of the Intellectual* [The 1993 Reith Lectures] (New York: Pantheon Books, 1994), 20–21.
3. Henry Steele Commager, *The American Mind: An Interpretation of American Thought and Character Since the 1880's* (New Haven, Conn.: Yale University Press, 1950), 412–13.
4. Harry S. Broudy, "Thought and the Educative Process," *Philosophy Forum 13* (1955): 52; Jacques Barzun, *The House of the Intellect* (New York: Harper Brothers, 1959), 1, 8; George F. Woodworth, "An Analysis of the Concept 'Anti-intellectualism': Implications for the Education of Gifted and Talented Students" (unpublished doctoral dissertation, The University of Connecticut, 1995), 29.
5. Jules Henry, *Culture Against Man* (New York: Alfred A. Knopf, Inc.), 288.
6. Richard Hofstadter, "Democracy and anti-intellectualism in America," *Michigan Alumnus Quarterly Review 59* (8 August 1953), 281–95; Richard Hofstadter, *Anti-intellectualism in American Life* (New York: Alfred A. Knopf, 1963), 281, 283.
7. Hofstadter, *Anti-intellectualism*, 288.
8. Postman's *Amusing ourselves*.
9. Robert D. Cross, "The Historical Development of Anti-intellectualism in American Society: Implications for the Schooling of African Americans," *The Journal of Negro Education 59* (1990): 19–28.
10. Hofstadter, *Anti-intellectualism*, 300–1.
11. *Ibid*, 52.
12. *Ibid*, 305–6, 307.
13. *Ibid*, 320, 344–45. John Patrick Diggins, in his *The Promise of Pragmatism: Modernism and the Crisis of Knowledge and Authority* (Chicago: The University of Chicago Press, 1994) at 315–16 commented:

> Dewey's efforts to prevent teachers from asserting authority are understandable in view of his desire to liberate the child's natural impulses from intimidation and coercion. He did not want to see teachers proselytize, and he rightly criticized the insidious ways of intellectual seduction that pass for education. Yet one may question, as did Richard Hofstadter in Anti-intellectualism in American Life, Dewey's conviction that all education based on authority invariably produces a conformist mentality. Voltaire was taught by Jesuits, Hofstadter noted, and one thinks of other examples in intellectual history when the rebellious mind is a direct product of authoritarian schooling (the sardonic student Thorstein Veblen bewildered his pious teachers when he wrote an essay in defense of cannibalism as the economics of recycling). All true education, it may be added, involves distinguishing between what students are interested in and what may be in their interest to know and learn.

Hofstadter (*Anti-intellectualism*, 361), commenting on so many interpretations and misinterpretations of Dewey, bitterly wrote that he "has been praised, paraphrased, repeated, discussed, apotheosized, even on occasions read."
14. Hofstadter, *Anti-intellectualism*, 342, 345, 346, 350, 352, 356.

15. Hofstadter, "Democracy and Anti-intellectualism in America," and Richard Hofstadter and Walter P. Metzger, *The Development of Academic Freedom in the United States* (New York: Columbia University Press, 1955).

16. Weiland, "The Academic Attitude."

17. See Sam Bluefarb, "Hippies: Another view," *Journal of Popular Culture 2* (1968): 468–80; Paul A. Eschholz and Alfred F. Rosa, "Course names: Another aspect of college slang." *American Speech 45*, 1–2 (1970): 85–90; Fritz Stern, "Reflections on the International Student Movement," *American Scholar 40* (1971), 123–37; and H. Winthrop, "The Anti-intellectualism of Student Radicals," *Colorado Quarterly 20, 2* (1971), 191–204, who complained about "the swill of the mass media" at 200.

18. For a fuller look at this area of H. L. Mencken's writing, see Myrna Nilan Klobuchar, "H. L. Mencken and 'the fabulous foul of the pedagogical aviary,'" (unpublished doctoral dissertation, University of Minnesota, 1991).

19. Jacoby, *The Last Intellectuals*, 16, 132.

20. Jacoby, *The Last Intellectuals* [New Introduction] (New York: Basic Books, 2000), xv–xxii.

21. Perhaps Hofstadter was not mentioned by Bloom because of their political differences; Hofstadter was a Marxist, then a liberal, and eventually a neoconservative, while Bloom was more of a classical conservative.

22. William K. Buckley and James Seaton, *Beyond cheering and bashing: New perspectives on* The closing of the American mind (Bowling Green, Ohio: Bowling Green State University Press, 1992); Lawrence W. Levine, *The opening of the American mind: Canons, culture, and history* (Boston: Beacon Press, 1996); Robert L. Stone, *Essays on* The closing of the American mind (Chicago: Chicago Review Press, 1989); Peter Shaw, *The war against the intellect: Episodes in the decline of discourse* (Iowa City: University of Iowa Press, 1989), especially the final three chapters and the "Epilogue," and others.

23. Lewis B. Mayhew, "Faculty demands and faculty militance," *Journal of Higher Education 40* (1969), 337–50; William Jovanovich, "A tumult of talk," *American Scholar 41* (1972), 40–49; Scott Edwards, "Reich, Roszak and the New Jerusalem," *Midwest Quarterly 13* (1972), 185–98; Lewis S. Feuer, "Student unrest in the United States," *Annals of the American Academy of Political and Social Science 404* (1972), 170–82; Martin Schiff, "Neo-transcendentalism in the New Left Counterculture: A vision of the future looking back," *Comparative Studies in Society and History 15* (1973), 130–42; and Barbara Epstein, "The culture of direct action: Livermore Action Group and the peace movement," *Socialist Review 15* (4–5), 31–61 (1985).

24. John McWhorter, *Losing the Race: Self-Sabotage in Black America,* (New York: Free Press, 2000), 85.

25. The second such dissertation, on which this book is based, was Dane S. Claussen, "Anti-intellectualism as Constructed by American Media: Popular Magazine Coverage of Higher Education" (Henry W. Grady College of Journalism & Mass Communication, The University of Georgia, May 1999).

26. George S. Hage, "Anti-intellectualism in newspaper comment of the elections of 1828 and 1952" (unpublished doctoral dissertation, University of Minnesota, 1956), 35, 36, 79.

27. Santayana wrote of the separation in U.S. culture "between things intellectual, which remain wrapped in the feminine veil, and, as it were, under glass, and the rough business and passions of life" (Handlin and Handlin, *The American college and American culture*, 51), while Merle Curti believed that effeminacy was first associated with intellectualism around the turn of the century, when it was widely believed that primarily women were interested in the arts.

28. George Hage, "Anti-intellectualism in newspaper comment," 169, 170, 171, 173, 229; and David Riesman and Nathan Glazer, "The intellectuals and the discontented classes," in *The New American Right*, ed. Daniel Bell (New York: Criterion Books, 1955), 71.

29. Hofstadter, *Anti-intellectualism*, 300–1.

30. Jeffrey C. Goldfarb, *Civility and Subversion: The Intellectual in Democratic Society* (New York: Cambridge University Press, 1998).

31. Rigney, "Three Kinds of Anti-intellectualism."

32. Gillam, "Richard Hofstadter," 70, 76, 83, 78.

33. Jeffrey Friedman, "On libertarian anti-intellectualism: Rejoinder to Shaw and Anderson & Leal," *Critical Review 8* (1994): 483–92; Barbara J. Culliton, "Science's restive public." *Daedalus 107* (1978): 147–56; Pierre Schlag, "Anti-intellectualism." *Cardozo Law Review 16* (1995): 1111–20; Paul R. Schratz, "The hundred year growing pain: Opposition and opportunity," *Naval War College Review 37* (5): 71–85 (1984). Heidi K. Goar, "Anti-intellectualism as a social control: Reflexivity and conformity" (unpublished master's thesis, Mankato State University, 1992), 28.

34. Goar, *Ibid,* 28.

35. Barnett Singer, "The new anti-intellectualism in America," *Colorado Quarterly 26* (2), 4–18 (1977).

36. Joan W. Scott, "The Campaign against Political Correctness: What's really at stake," *Radical History Review 54* (1992a): 59–79 at 67; Joan W. Scott, "The new university: Beyond political correctness," *Perspectives: Newsletter of the American Historical Association 30* (7), 14–18 (1992b).

37. Harold E. Taussig, *Anti-intellectualism in the public schools: A study of the cultural values underlying Twentieth Century educational practices* (unpublished doctoral dissertation, University of Pennsylvania, 1966); Aimee Howley, Edwina D. Pendarvis, and Craig B. Howley, *Anti-intellectualism in U.S. schools* (Huntington, W.V.: Marshall University, 1990); Aimee Howley, Edwina D. Pendarvis, and Craig B. Howley, "Anti-intellectualism in programs for able students (beware of gifts): an application," *Social Epistemology 1* (1987), 175–81; Craig B. Howley, Aimee Howley, and Edwina D. Pendarvis, *Out of our minds: Anti-intellectualism and talent development in American schooling* (New York: Columbia University Teachers College, 1995); Nicholas Colangelo and Gary A. Davis (eds.), *Handbook of gifted education* (Boston: Allyn and Bacon, 1991); G. F. Woodworth, "An analysis of the concept 'anti-intellectualism'"; and David Isaacson, "Anti-intellectualism in American libraries," *Library Journal 107* (February 1982): 227–32. Those irrelevant to this book include: Vernon Carstensen, "The good old days or the bad old days? History and related muses in the Northwest in the 1930s," *Pacific Northwest Quarterly 68* (1977), no. 3: 105–11; D. Cox, "The Gottschalk-Colvin case: A study in academic purpose and command," *Register of the Kentucky Historical Society 85*

(1987): 46–68; R. Detweiller, "Ben Franklin's 'Dirty Pettifoggers,'" *American Bar Association Journal* 59 (1973): 1165–67; D. Hernandez, "Anti-intellectualism: Tumor in American education." *American Foreign Language Teacher* 1 (3), 17–21 (1971); Alan Tully, "Literacy levels and educational development in rural Pennsylvania 1729–1775," *Pennsylvania History 39* (1972), 301–12; Maureen Ursenbach, "Three women and the life of the mind," *Utah Historical Quarterly 43*, no. 1: 26–40 (1975); Deborah B. van Broekhoven, "Crisis in the life of a literary patriot: Brockden Brown's shift from cosmopolitan to chronicler," *Psychohistory Review 12* (1984), nos. 3–4: 34–44.

38. Paul R. Griffin, *Black founders of Reconstruction Era Methodist colleges: Daniel A. Payne, Joseph C. Price, and Isaac Lane, 1863–1890* (Unpublished doctoral dissertation, Emory University, 1983; John R. Baker, "Fundamentalism as anti-intellectualism," *The Humanist* (March–April 1986): 26–28; S. A. Newman, "Where Southern Baptists stand on anti-intellectualism," *Search 1* (1973): 22–27; S. A. Newman, "Where Southern Baptists stand on anti-intellectualism: 1973–1989," *Perspectives in Religious Studies 20* (1993): 417–30.

39. J. Gerald Kennedy, "Cooper's anti-intellectualism: The comic man of learning." *Studies in American Humor 3*(2): 69–75 (1976); William R. Brown, "Will Rogers: Ironist as persuader." *Speech Monographs 39*(3): 183–92 (1972); Richard Coles, "Instances of modernist anti-intellectualism," in *Modernism Reconsidered*, ed. R. Kiely (Cambridge, Mass.: Harvard University Press, 1983); and Robert Evans, "Hemingway and the pale cast of thought," *American Literature* 38(2): 161–76 (1966).

40. Thomas E. Cronin, "The presidents' man: Henry Steele Commager." *The New York Times Magazine* (3 January 1999): 43.

41. Norman Birnbaum, *The radical renewal: The politics of ideas in modern America* (New York: Pantheon Books, 1988), 51, 76, 103, 134, 185.

42. See, for example, Henry S. Hughes, *The sea change: The migration of social thought, 1930–1965* (New York: Harper & Row, Publishers, 1975); Edwin C. Rozwenc and Thomas Bender, *The making of American society, Volume II since 1865*, 2d ed. (New York: Alfred A. Knopf, 1978); Paul A. Carter, *Another part of the Fifties* (New York: Columbia University Press, 1983); Paul A. Carter, *Revolt against destiny: An intellectual history of the United States* (New York: Columbia University Press, 1989); Douglas Tallack, *Twentieth-century America: The intellectual and cultural context* (London, U.K.: Longman, 1991); Steven Weiland, *Intellectual craftsmen*; Giles Gunn, *Thinking across the American grain: Ideology, intellect, and the new pragmatism* (Chicago: The University of Chicago Press, 1992); John P. Diggins, *The promise of pragmatism: Modernism and the crisis of knowledge and authority* (Chicago: The University of Chicago Press, 1994); Andrew Jamison and Ron Eyerman, *Seeds of the Sixties* (Berkeley, Calif.: University of California Press, 1994); David J. Hoeveler Jr., *The postmodernist turn: American thought and culture in the 1970s* (New York: Twayne Publishers/Simon & Schuster Macmillan, 1996); David A. Hollinger, *Science, Jews, and secular culture: Studies in mid-twentieth-century American intellectual history* (Princeton, N.J.: Princeton University Press, 1996); Fink, *Progressive intellectuals*; and Howard Brick, *Age of contradiction: American thought and culture in the 1960s* (New York: Twayne Publishers/Simon

& Schuster Macmillan, 1998).

43. Hage was a journalism professor, but his dissertation was written in American studies.

44. Edward Caudill, *Darwinism in the Press: The Evolution of an Idea* (Hillsdale, N.J.: Lawrence Erlbaum Associates, 1989), 133–34, 136–37.

45. *Ibid*, 140.

46. Donald L. Shaw, "News bias and the telegraph: A study of historical change," *Journalism Quarterly 44*, no. 1: 3–12, 21 (1967); Michael Schudson, *Discovering the news* (New York: Basic Books, 1978); and Gerald J. Baldesty, "The press and politics in the age of Jackson," *Journalism Monographs* 89 (1984).

47. Caudill, *Darwinism*, 139, 140, 141, 143.

48. Richard A. Posner, *Public Intellectuals: A Study of Decline* (Cambridge, Mass.: Harvard University Press, 2001), 170.

49. *Ibid*, 76.

50. *Ibid*, 26, 33, 44–45.

51. *Ibid*, 43–44, 46, 161–62.

52. *Ibid*, 49, 55, 145–46.

53. *Ibid*, 67.

54. *Ibid*, 81.

55. *Ibid*, 80.

Chapter 3: Media Among Society's Institutions: The "Most Prominent, and Dynamic Part"

1. For an introduction, see Coser, *Men of ideas*; Alvin W. Gouldner, *The future of intellectuals and the rise of the new class*. New York: Seabury Press, 1979); Hofstadter, *Anti-intellectualism*; Jacoby, *The last intellectuals*; Charles Kadushin, *The American intellectual elite* (Boston: Little, Brown & Co., 1974); Everett C. Ladd and Seymour M. Lipset, *The divided academy: Professors and politics* (New York: W.W. Norton and Co., Inc., 1975); and Robert K. Merton, *Social theory and social structure* (New York: Free Press, 1968)

2. Milan Rai, *Chomsky's Politics* (London: Verso, 1995), 22.

3. Noam Chomsky, *Necessary illusions: Thought control in democratic societies* (London: Pluto, 1989), 13–14; Rai, *Chomsky's Politics*, 22.

4. Hanno Hardt, "Among the media: Journalism education in a commercial culture" (remarks to the Qualitative Studies Division, Association for Education in Journalism and Mass Communication Convention, Baltimore, Md., August 1998).

5. David Forgacs and Geoffrey Nowell-Smith (eds.), *Antonio Gramsci: Selections from cultural writings* (Cambridge, Mass.: Harvard University Press, 1985), 405.

6. This retreat has been called a "Gramscian rearguard action," in James Curran, David Morley, and Valerie Walkerdine (eds.), *Cultural studies and communication* (London: Arnold, 1996), 132.

7. Steven Best and Douglas Kellner, *Postmodern theory: Critical interrogations* (New York: The Guilford Press, 1991). Just one example of most media's acceptance of dualisms or dichotomies was clearly pointed out by Randall Sullivan's article in the

Sept. 17, 1998, issue of *Rolling Stone*. He recounted how news media portrayed Kip Kinkel, the Springfield, Oregon, youth who went on a shooting spree at his high school, as an unpopular nutcase, and Kinkel's classmates as "normal" in virtually every way. Instead, Sullivan wrote,

> The sad truth is that Kip was a popular boy, especially with girls, who almost invariably described him as "smart, funny and cute." He had lots of friends and an active social life.

Sullivan also detailed how several other friends of Kinkel had been involved in Kinkel's earlier dangerous and/or sadistic behaviors, and that when Kinkel talked about killing people or blowing things up, other students laughed approvingly. In short, the mass media once again drew a line between "us" (the normal people) and "them" (the crazy people), and marshaled evidence to portray the two groups as dramatically different. Instead, the message Sullivan sent is "There, but for the grace of God, go I." Conversely, an article such as Alice Dreger's "When Medicine Goes Too Far in the Pursuit of Normality," *The New York Times*, July 28, 1998, B10, is rare in general interest, mass circulation publications. It raised questions about the medical imperative to "cure" human intersexuality, that is, people who have "anatomical sexual variations." Foucault and queer theorists would be pleasantly surprised to spot this article in light of standard media fare.

8.   For example, see Chin-Hwa F. Chang, *The notion of power in mass communication research: Foucault and critical communication studies* (unpublished doctoral dissertation, The University of Iowa, 1988)

9.   William Outhwaite, *The Habermas reader* (Cambridge, U.K.: Polity Press, 1996), 37.

10. John D. Peters, "Distrust of representation: Habermas on the public sphere," *Media, Culture and Society 15* (1993): 541–71 at 562. Habermas is not alone in this; see also Thomas C. Leonard, *News for all* (New York: Oxford University Press, 1995).

11. Outhwaite, *Habermas*, 217, 260, 322.

12. See William E. Cain (ed.), *Teaching the conflicts: Gerald Graff, curricular reform, and the culture wars* (New York: Garland Publishing Co., 1994); Leon Fink, *Progressive intellectuals*; Sandra Jackson and Jose Solis (eds.), *Beyond comfort zones in multiculturalism: Confronting the politics of privilege* (Westport, Conn.: Bergin & Garvey, 1995); Peter L. McLaren and James M. Giarelli, *Critical theory and educational research* (Albany, N.Y.: State University of New York Press, 1995); Jack Mezirow and Associates, *Fostering critical reflection in adulthood: A guide to transformative and emancipatory learning* (San Francisco: Jossey-Bass Publishers, 1990); Roger P. Mourad Jr., *Postmodern philosophical critique and the pursuit of knowledge in higher education* (Westport, Conn.: Bergin & Garvey, 1997); Raymond V. Padilla and Miguel Montiel, *Debatable diversity: Critical dialogues on change in American universities* (Lanham, Md.: Rowman and Littlefield Publishers, 1998); Timothy W. Quinnan, *Adult students "at-risk": Cultural bias in higher education* (Westport, Conn.: Bergin & Garvey, 1997); Laura I. Renden, Richard O. Hope and Associates, *Educating a new majority: Transforming America's educational system for diversity* (San Francisco: Jossey-Bass Publishers, 1996); J. Daniel

Schubert, Joan V. Vecchia, and Richard H. Brown, *Higher education in a postmodern era: Ethics, politics, and practices* (Thousand Oaks, Calif.: Sage Periodicals Press, 1995); William G. Tierney (ed.), *Culture and ideology in higher education: Advancing a critical agenda* (New York: Praeger, 1991); William G. Tierney, *Building communities of difference: Higher education in the Twenty-First Century* (Westport, Conn.: Bergin & Garvey, 1993); and Carlos A. Torres and Theodore R. Mitchell, *Sociology of education: Emerging perspectives* (Albany, N.Y.: State University of New York Press, 1998), among others. However, another limitation in this literature is that it often conflates critical theory with postmodernism, despite Gramsci's dying before postmodernism was envisioned, Habermas's opposition to postmodernism, and Foucault's belief that we are not in a postmodern period because it has not begun—if it ever indeed will. Fortunately, the issue of modernism versus postmodernism is not relevant to this book.

13. While a discussion of these groups' historical exclusions may be necessary, this literature tends to omit a major recent change: women now make up the majority of college and university students graduating each year. Further, much of this research assumes that all women and minority group members bring critical perspectives into the classroom, while men and whites never do. Moreover, when this literature refers to intellectuals and intellectualism, it typically is informed by Foucault, Gramsci, and others not writing particularly about the late-twentieth-century United States.

14. Little writing focuses on higher education's role in preserving and promoting democratic politics in the society at large, or on how to shift power within institutions of higher education from administrators to faculty, or from administrators and faculty to students, at least not outside of the interests of minority groups. In fact, what was meant by "democratizing" education among 1990s critical theorists was only a modernized version of what it meant to the Truman Commission: giving members of minority groups only more opportunities to be socialized into, and then work in, the United States' late capitalistic economy. The implicit suggestion was that all that must be done in order to liberate minority groups in the United States was to allow corporate America to replace minority group members' balls-and-chains with golden handcuffs.

15. Fink, *Progressive Intellectuals*, 36.

16. G. Stuart Adam, "Introduction: James Carey's academy," in *James Carey: A critical reader*, eds. Eve S. Munson and Catherine A. Warren (Minneapolis, Minn.: The University of Minnesota Press, 1997), 268–69.

17. Quintin Hoare and Geoffrey N. Smith (eds., trans.), *Selections from the Prison Notebooks of Antonio Gramsci* (London: Lawrence and Wishart, 1971), 350.

18. Antonio Gramsci (R. Bellamy, ed.), *Pre-prison writings* (Cambridge, U.K.: Cambridge University Press, 1994), 9–10; Derek Boothman (ed./trans.), *Antonio Gramsci: Further selections from* The Prison Notebooks (London: Lawrence & Wishart, 1995), 151–52; Hoare and Smith, *Selections*, 40.

19. Tierney, *Culture and Ideology in Higher Education*, 62–63.

20. Robert E. Young, *A Critical Theory of Education: Habermas and Our Children's Future* (New York: Teachers College Press, Columbia University, 1990), 42.

21. Young, *Critical theory*, 55; Best and Kellner, *Postmodern theory*, 235.

22. Young, *Critical theory*, 88, 97; Jürgen Habermas, *Toward a Rational Society* (Boston: Beacon Press, 1970), 2. On the point of what professor should teach, one scholar has complained, "Some professors have suggested to students that only hard work brings academic success, without being candid about the differences in individuals' mental powers. Some educators have obscured the potentially subversive quality of intellectual life" (Horowitz, *Campus life*, 1987), 271.

23. Young, *Critical theory*, 10, 22.

24. Note that Habermas does not reject empirical research methods, only their overextension and unreflexive self-understanding, which in turn result in social science findings withstanding limited predictive power, (often unacknowledged) ideological implications, and implementation in dominating rather than empowering capacities. See Habermas, *Toward a rational society*, 52–53, 55–56, 59, 61; and Young, *Critical theory*, 42.

25. *Ibid*, 59–60, 133.

26. James D. Marshall, *Michel Foucault: Personal autonomy and education* (Boston: Kluwer Academic Publishers, 1996), 153.

27. See Meaghan Morris & Paul Patton (eds.), *Michel Foucault: Power, truth, strategy* (Sidney, Australia: Feral Publications, 1979), 63; and Marshall, *Michel Foucault*, 155.

28. Marshall, *Michel Foucault*, 156 and chapter 5.

29. Said, *Representations*, 3.

30. *Ibid*, 10, 37.

31. Gramsci, *Pre-prison Writings*, 9; Said, *Representations*, 4; and Hoare and Smith, *Selections*, 14–23.

32. Said, *Representations*, 8–9; and Hoare and Smith, *Selections from the Prison Notebooks*, 9.

33. Stanley Aronowitz and Henry A. Giroux, review of *The Closing of the American Mind*, in *Harvard Educational Review 58* (2): 172 (May 1988); and Nancy Warehime, *To be one of us: Cultural conflict, creative democracy, and education* (Albany, N.Y.: State University of New York Press, 1993), 56–64.

34. Young, *Critical theory*, 10; and Jürgen Habermas, *Communication and the evolution of society* (Boston: Beacon Press, 1976), 97.

35. Morris and Patton, *Michel Foucault*; and David C. Hoy (ed.), *Foucault: A critical reader* (Oxford: B. Blackwell, 1986), 249.

36. Karlis Racevskis, *Michel Foucault and the subversion of the intellect* (Ithaca, N.Y.: Cornell University Press, 1983), 135. Foucault identified Charles Darwin as the first "specific intellectual," although he generally thought similarly of all early modern biologists and physicists (Morris & Patton, *Michel Foucault*). Among figures during his own life, Foucault is known to have thought U.S. physicist Robert Oppenheimer was a specific intellectual, as Oppenheimer moved from being a physics professor, to director of the Los Alamos atomic bomb project, to a "sort of commissar of scientific affairs in the U.S." (Said, *Representations*, 10).

37. Said, *Representations*, 8, 13.

38. *Ibid*, 11–14, 22.

39. *Ibid*, 82, 69, 74, 76, 100.

40. *Ibid*, 53, 59, 61.

41. Chomsky, *Necessary Illusions*, 257; Chomsky, *On Power and Ideology*, 51; and Chomsky, *Language and Politics*, 370–71.
42. Nicholas Garnham, "The media and narratives of the intellectual," *Media, Culture & Society 17* (1995): 359–84.
43. Alex S. Edelstein, Youichi Ito, and Hans M. Kepplinger, *Communication & Culture: A Comparative Approach* (New York: Longman, 1989); Said, *Representations*, 26; and Ron Eyerman, Lennart G. Svensson, and Thomas Soderqvist, *Intellectuals, universities, and the state in western modern societies* (Berkeley, Calif.: University of California Press, 1987).
44. Raymond Williams, *Keywords: A Vocabulary of Culture and Society* (New York: Oxford University Press, 1985), 169–71.
45. *Ibid.*
46. Hoare and Smith, *Selections*, 37.
47. Goar, *Anti-intellectualism as a social control*; David Held, *Introduction to critical theory: Horkheimer to Habermas* (Berkeley, Calif.: The University of California Press, 1980), 159; Best and Kellner, *Postmodern theory*, 240; and Young, *Critical theory*, 164.
48. On anti-intellectual ideologies in U.S. social institutions, Goar cited Peter L. Berger, *Invitation to sociology: A humanistic perspective* (Garden City, N.Y.: Doubleday and Co., Inc., 1963); Bloom, *The closing of the American mind*; Noam Chomsky, speech at Macalester College, St. Paul, Minn., April 23, 1992; Hofstadter, *Anti-intellectualism*; Herbert Marcuse, *One-dimensional man* (Boston: Beacon Press, 1964); and C. Wright Mills, *The power elite* (New York: Oxford University Press, 1956). On elites' maintenance of the status quo, she relied on Jürgen Habermas, *Legitimation Crisis* (Boston: Beacon Press, 1975) and Karl Marx, *Capital: A critique of political economy, volume 1* (New York: International Publishers, 1967), among others.
49. Krista E. White, *How the girls really are? Images of college women in* Life *magazine during the 1960s* (unpublished master's thesis, University of Colorado—Boulder, 1996), 14, 27, 29.
50. Scott M. Cutlip and Allen H. Center, *Effective public relations, 3d ed.* (Englewood Cliffs, N.J.: Prentice Hall Inc., 1964), 415.
51. S. K. Stegall, *A Q-methodological coorientation study of college and university public relations directors and newspaper reporters in Missouri* (unpublished master's thesis, University of Missouri–Columbia, 1985); Gaylon E. "Gene" Murray, *Texas education reporters' and university public relations directors' perceptions of public relations, occupations, and news values* (unpublished doctoral dissertation, Texas A&M University, 1991); C.S. Bernstein, *Coverage of education in two metropolitan-area dailies* (unpublished master's thesis, University of Missouri—Columbia, 1982); and D.J. Caldwell, *Education, citizenship, and vocations in the Ladies' Home Journal, 1883–1953* (unpublished master's thesis, The University of Missouri, 1954).
52. Rochelle E. Stanfield, "The Media and Public Perceptions of Tuition Costs," in Gene I. Maeroff, ed., *Imaging education: The media and schools in America* (New York: Teachers College Press, 1998), 144.

53. Richard W. Moll and B. Ann Wright, "What College Selectivity Looks Like to the Public," in Maeroff, *ibid.*

54. Don Hossler, "Everybody Wants to be Number One: The Effects of the Media's College Rankings," in Maeroff, *ibid*, 174.

55. William A. Henry III, *In defense of elitism* (New York: Anchor/Doubleday, 1994), 151.

56. *Ibid*, 154.

57. *Ibid*

58. Bernstein, *Coverage of education*, 1982; Stegall, *A Q-methodological coorientation Study*; Ray E. Laakaniemi, *A content analysis of higher education news related to four Michigan universities* (unpublished master's thesis, Ohio University, 1966), 20, 31, 38, 52, 54; P. H. Binzen, "Less pap for the press," *College and University Journal 1*, 3 (1962): 17–18; and Charles E. Flynn, "The unprofessional professional," *College and University Journal 5*, 2 (1966): 13.

59. Donald F. Scannell, *Mass media use, information, and opinions concerning higher education* (unpublished doctoral dissertation, University of Minnesota, 1996).

60. R. L. Cox, *A variance and factor analysis of readers' preferences for three types of higher education news* (unpublished master's thesis, Oklahoma State University, 1969).

61. Bonnie L. Ross, "Education reporting in *The Los Angeles Times*," *Journalism Quarterly 60* (1983): 348–52 at 352; Roger Yarrington, "Meet the education press," *Currents*, February 1984, 35–40; Roger Yarrington, "J-Schools should encourage higher education writers," *Journalism Educator 39* (4), 11–12 (1985); and A. S. Wells, *A Study of Education Reporting in American Newspapers* (unpublished master's thesis, Boston University, 1986).

62. Ernest C. Hynds, "Survey finds large daily newspapers have improved coverage of education," *Journalism Quarterly 66* (1989), 692–96, 780; Wells, *A Study of Education Reporting*; and William W. Lace, *Opinions of news media members toward public higher education in Texas and predictions of those opinions by college and university public relations directors* (unpublished doctoral dissertation, University of North Texas, 1987).

63. William Chance, *The press and California higher education* (San Jose, Calif.: The California Higher Education Policy Center, 1983); Posner, "Read All About It," especially at 13; Gary R. Ratcliff and Roger L. Williams, "What the numbers tell us: Higher education coverage at seven newspapers," *Currents 20*, 1 (1994): 13–14, Gary R. Ratcliff, *Ivorytowers, watchdogs, and boosters: A comparative case study of how metropolitan newspapers cover public research universities* (unpublished doctoral dissertation, The Pennsylvania State University, 1996), especially at 27; and Philip Walzer, "Selling higher education stories to your editor," *The IRE Journal 18*, January–February 1995, 3–6.

64. Ratcliff, *Ivorytowers, watchdogs, and boosters.*

65. Lynn W. Payne, *Black business students' post-baccalaureate employment expectations: What are they and from where do they originate?* (unpublished doctoral dissertation, The University of Oklahoma, 1998), 12–13, 45–47, 94, 115–16, 118.

66. Harold E. Gibson, *Public relations practices in institutions of higher education for women* (unpublished doctoral dissertation, University of Missouri, 1945); Scott M.

Cutlip, "'Advertising' higher education: The early years of college public relations," *College and University Journal 9* (Fall 1970), 21–28; Scott M. Cutlip, "'Advertising' higher education: The early years of college public relations—part II," *College and University Journal 9*, July 1971: 25–33; Waldo E. Reck, *The changing world of college relations: History and philosophy, 1917–1974* (Washington, D.C.: Council for the Advancement and Support of Higher Education, 1976); Frank A. DeFazio, *The role of public relations as perceived by presidents and public relations officers at private comprehensive universities and colleges* (unpublished doctoral dissertation, Drake University, 1987); Lace, *Opinions of news media members*; Thomas J. Liesz, *An interpretive analysis of factors influencing higher education appropriation and allocation levels in the Pacific Northwest* (unpublished doctoral dissertation, University of Idaho, 1989); Robert A. Bonfiglio, *The history of public relations in American higher education in the twentieth century: From self-interest to national interest* (unpublished doctoral dissertation, Columbia University [Teachers College], 1990); and Albert W. Rowland, *A study of three selected factors in the public relations programs of colleges and universities in the United States* (unpublished doctoral dissertation, Michigan State University, 1955).

67. DeFazio, *The Role of Public Relations*, 45, 47, 53, 54; and Lace, *Opinions of News Media Members*, 171, 173, 176, and elsewhere.

68. Murray, *Texas education reporters' and university public relations directors' perceptions*.

Chapter 4: Religious Anti-Rationalism and Higher Education

1. "Far more than grades; college presidents play up the value of values," *Time 84*, 2 October 1964, 87.

2. K. Thorsen, "Co-ed dorms, an intimate revolution in campus life," *Life 69*, 20 November 1970, 32–41.

3. "Signs of Suicide," *Time 91*, 12 April 1968, 60.

4. Daniel J. Singal, "The other crisis in our schools," *Reader's Digest 140*, April 1992, 111–15.

5. "God & Man at Harvard," *Time 69*, 8 April 1957, 70.

6. M. Hickey, "Students & religion," *Ladies' Home Journal 69*, December 1952, 23.

7. "Missionaries to Moppets: Baylor's student evangelists have own congregations of poor children," *Life 36*, 25 January 1954, 119–20.

8. "God & Man at Princeton," *Time 70*, 7 October 1957, 47.

9. "The Cynical Idealists of '68," *Time 91*, 7 June 1968, 78–83.

10. "Far More than Grades," *ibid.*

11. "Who's Cutting Up on Campus?" *Life 56*, 22 May 1964, 4.

12. "Dawn Patrol: Students under arrest at Stony Brook on drug charges," *Time 91*, 26 January 1968, 74.

13. "The Cynical Idealists of '68," *ibid.*

14. "Signs of suicide," *ibid.*

15. "The Student Phenomenon," *Life 48*, 9 May 1960, 32B.

16. R. O'Brien, "How to Get Through College on Less Money," *Reader's Digest 92*,

February 1968, 97–100.

17. J.L. Barron, "Too much sex on campus," *Reader's Digest 92*, May 1964, 59–62, abbreviated from same in *Ladies' Home Journal 81*, January 1964, 48+.

18. "Boom on Fraternity Row," *Time 51*, 9 February 1948, 75–76.

19. C.W. Morton, "Memoirs of an ex-Greek," *Time 52*, 27 September 1948, 58.

20. "Fraternity Rushing," *Life 41*, 24 September 1956, 141–49.

21. "Freshmen Class: 1960," *Life 49*, 2 October 1960, 94–101.

22. "Fraternity Rushing," *ibid.*

23. This sexism is reminiscent of Rudyard Kipling's line, "And a woman is only a woman, but a good cigar is a smoke."

24. "Females in the Fraternity," *Time 91*, 19 April 1968, 63.

25. "Life Goes to Derby Day at Yale: Annual boat-race weekend brings out some odd attire and odder antics," *Life 24*, 24 May 1948, 152–55.

26. "Fraternity Rushing," *ibid.*

27. "Merry Fraternity Makes Hay," *Life 48*, 7 March 1960, 125–27.

28. "Bed Sheets Bonanza; Toga Party Craze," *Time 112*, 23 October 1978, 88.

29. "Spring Madness: Michigan men raid girls' dorm and the women raid right back," *Life 32*, 7 April 1952, 59–60.

30. "Nebraska Apes Michigan," *Life 32*, 19 May 1952, 105–6.

31. "Girls! Girls! Girls!" *Time 59*, 26 May 1952, 27; "The newest and noisiest college craze—the pantie raid," *Time 59*, 2 June 1952, 22.

32. "Campuses Enjoy a Riotous Spring," *Life 32*, 26 May 1952, 28–31.

33. "Life goes to an Honor Society's Tribal Rites: Redmen at Michigan initiate new braves with noble savagery," *Life 36*, 7 June 1954, 188–94.

34. "Life goes to a foresters ball in Montana," *Life 36*, 1 March 1954, 119–21.

35. "Light turns for Spring fancy," *Life 42*, 15 April 1957, 58–59.

36. "Pact's Happy Pay-off in Bermuda: Four Harvard Men Pool Cash So One Can Have Date-Filled Trip," *Life 42*, 22 April 1957, 162–63.

37. "Spring + youth: A case with complications," *Life 42*, 10 June 1957, 30–31.

38. "Surprise for a rocket," *Life 42*, 6 May 1957, 61–62.

39. "Music to Drop Pins By," *Life 48*, 14 March 1960, 69–70.

40. "Big Campus Chess Game," *Life 48*, 2 May 1960, 49–50, 52.

41. "The Big Ten Look: In Custom as Well as Dress It Is Both Casual, Colorful," *Life 37*, 24 October 1954, 95–100.

42. "Of Dates & Drags," *Time 52*, 29 November 1948, 54.

43. "Under the Biltmore Clock: It Is Favorite Place for College Dating," *Life 32*, 21 April 1952, 158–62; and "Beer and Bikes from Yale to Vassar: Men From Eli Guzzle and Pedal 77 Miles to See Girl Friends," *Life 32*, 28 April 1952, 136–43.

44. "Campus Love Left Out in Cold: Outcry Over Indoor Kisses Leads Michigan Dorm to Bar Them in Lounge," *Life 42*, 11 March 1957, 49–50, 52.

45. "Campus Romance: Steve Ambrose and Judy Dorlester, of the University of Wisconsin, will take marriage vows with his bachelor's degrees" *Ladies' Home Journal 74*, May 1957, 109–12+.

46. C.W. Cole, "American Youth Goes Monogamous: Dating habits of the young have changed so radically that today's college students are bewildered by the customs of their parents' generation," *Reader's Digest 70*, May 1957, 57–60.

47. "Too much sex on campus," *ibid.*
48. Loren Pope, "Facts to Know in Picking a College," *Reader's Digest 101*, December 1972, 169–76.
49. "Nighty-night!: And sweet dreams . . .," *Time 115*, May 26, 1980, 96.
50. "Coed dorms," *ibid.*
51. P. Gottlieb, "The Reunion: Arm in arm, we three aging musketeers felt young again, and strong. Only later would we understand why," *Reader's Digest 124*, April 1984, 191–94.
52. D. C. Norman, "Passport to popularity," *Ladies' Home Journal 65*, September 1948, 216, 249.
53. D. J. Singal, "The Other Crisis in Our Schools: Our brightest students are getting a dumbed-down education," *Reader's Digest 140*, April 1992, 111–15.

Chapter 5: Populist Anti-Elitism and Higher Education

1. "Lots of Little Ones," *Time 51*, 1 March 1948, 60.
2. "Flunked Out," *Time 52*, 20 September 1948, 78–9.
3. James B. Conant, "Who Should Go to College?" *Ladies' Home Journal 65*, June 1948, 40+.
4. "This University Wants YOU! It is a buyer's market as colleges scramble to fill spaces," *Time 91*, 29 May 1968, 69.
5. "The Campus Scramble to Recruit: Colleges Chase Stars While a Lot of Good Students Go Begging," *Time 131*, 2 May 1988, 66.
6. Nicholas Lemann, "With College for All: More than the cost of Harvard, it is the rising tuition at state schools that subverts the democratic ideal," *Time 147*, 10 June 1996, 67–68.
7. L. Stowe, "What You Need Nowadays to Get into College," *Reader's Digest 71*, July 1957, 40–45.
8. "Freshman Class: 1960; Flood of grown-up babies finds colleges unready—and *Life* looks ahead with a guide for applicants," *Life 49*, 2 October 1960, 94–101.
9. "Brains v. Bluebloods," *Time 83*, 3 January 1964, 68.
10. S. Tiff, "Welcome to Madison Avenue U.," *Time 132*, 19 December 1988, 75–76.
11. "Gambling on Open Admissions," *Time 96*, 28 September 1970, 36–8.
12. "Open Admissions: American Dream of Disaster," *Time 96*, 19 October 1970, 63–66.
13. R. O'Brien, "How to Get Through College on Less Money," *Reader's Digest 92*, February 1968, 97–101.
14. "Now, $30,000 diplomas: College costs, up 77% in a decade, are still soaring," *Time 112*, 11 September 1978, 66.
15. J. T. Freeman, "Pink-House Bobos of Atlanta, Ga.," *Ladies' Home Journal 71*, November 1954, 345–49.
16. "Open Admissions," *ibid.*
17. "Courses to Turn You On," *Time 100*, 2 October 1972, 57–58.
18. "Charitable Conspiracy: A judge finds M.I.T. and the Ivy League guilty of price fixing," *Time 140*, 14 September 1992, 25.

19. "Ivy Harvest," *Time 75*, 23 May 1960, 44+.

20. J. P. Baxter, "Inflation Hits the Colleges," *Reader's Digest 52*, May 1948, 106–8.

21. "Set the Student Free," *Time 69*, 15 April 1957, 87.

22. "The No-Nonsense Kids," *Time 70*, 18 November 1957, 51–52+.

23. "College Girls' Migration for Studious Vacation," *Life 48*, 25 April 1960, 142–50.

24. "Homework on Big City Kicks: Student Guide to New York," *Life 49*, 7 November 1960, 137–39.

25. "Little Known—& Good," *Time 76*, 5 December 1960, 46–47.

26. Edward B. Fiske, "Are Private Colleges an Endangered Species?" *Reader's Digest 109*, November 1976, 91–96.

27. "Trojan horse at Southern Cal?" *Time 112*, 13 November 1978, 75.

28. "Fraternity Rushing," *ibid.*

29. "Freshman Class: 1960," *ibid.*

30. "A Welcome for Wu: An injury is healed by a new fraternity bid," *Life 42*, 25 February 1957, 52.

31. "An intimate revolution in campus life," *ibid.*

32. "Undoing Diversity: A bombshell court ruling curtails affirmative action," *Time 147*, 1 April 1996, 54.

33. "Here Come the War Babies! U.S. Colleges are Ill Prepared for Their Invasion," *Time 69*, 4 February 1957, 41–42.

34. Gilbert Highet, "Her Sons—'Alert and Grateful': Competitiveness and diversity stimulate students and challenge teachers," *Life 36*, 15 February 1954, 126–31.

35. "The No-Nonsense Kids," *ibid.*

36. A. C. Eurich and others, "Campus 1980: The Student is King," *Time 92*, 13 September 1968, 39–40.

37. Conant, "Who should go to college?" *ibid.*

38. S. I. Hayakawa, "Real Root of Student Disorder?" *Reader's Digest*, November 1970, 167–68.

39. "Illiterates," *Time 51*, 19 April 1948, 88.

40. "Religious Illiterates," *Time 56*, 25 September 1950, 56.

41. W. McWhirter, "A most uncommon scold," *Time 132*, 17 October 1988, 74–76.

42. Anonymous, "Why Students Turn to Drugs: A Recent College Graduate who Has 'Been There' Re-evaluates His Experience—and Sounds a Warning," *Reader's Digest 92*, April 1968, 173–74.

43. "Campus Concern: Who's afraid of the bomb?" *Time 124*, 29 October 1984, 78.

44. Isaiah Berlin, "Too Many Helpers," *Time 54*, 12 December 1949, 71–73.

45. "Harvard grads go blue collar," *Life 72*, 11 February 1972, 62–71.

46. Joan Didion, "A generation not for the barricades," *Life 68*, 5 June 1970, 26.

47. "Who's Cutting Up on Campus," *Life 54*, 22 May 1964, 4.

48. "An intimate revolution in campus life," *ibid.*

49. "Exceptionally Exceptional," *Time 67*, 2 April 1956, 63.

50. J. Estes, "Gifted Boy Finds His Way: Barry Wichmann's Escape from Mediocrity," *Life 79*, 4 December 1964, 79–85.

51. "Slim Pickings for the Class of '76," *Time 107*, 29 March 1976, 46–48; "Dear Candidates: Watch Out," *Time 108*, 11 October 1976, 70.

52. "What You Need Nowadays to Get into College," *Reader's Digest 70*, July 1957, 40–45.
53. "Ivy Harvest," *Time 75*, 23 May 1960, 44, 47.
54. "Poisoned Ivy," *Time 75*, 30 May 1960, 64.
55. "Something Has to Give," *Time 75*, 6 June 1960, 42.
56. "Luck & Pluck," *Time 76*, 21 November 1960, 53.
57. "The Search for Something Else," *Time 91*, 26 April 1968.
58. "New Ways into College," *Time 99*, 1 May 1972, 64.
59. "Freshman Class: 1960," *ibid.*
60. Nevitt Sanford, "Is College Education Wasted on Women?" *Ladies' Home Journal 74*, May 1957, 78–79.
61. "College, Who Needs It?" *Time 99*, 12 June 1972, 37.
62. "College—Who Needs It?" *Reader's Digest*, August 1976, 75–78, abbreviated from, "Who needs college?" *Newsweek*, 26 April 1976.
63. "Pulling Back from Permissiveness, Curriculum Reform," *Time 111*, 27 March 1978, 76.
64. "When in Doubt, 'Stop Out': More and more students are hitting the road instead of the books," *Time 111*, 22 May 1978, 73.
65. "Amid the rah-rah: reality; U.S. college mock political conventions," *Time 83*, 15 May 1964, 38–39.
66. "Intimations of Miami," *Time 99*, 22 May 1972, 23.
67. Anders Henriksson, "College Kids Say the Darnedest Things: Mrs. Malaprop is alive and well in today's halls of ivy," *Reader's Digest 124*, January 1984, 120–22.
68. "What You Need Nowadays to Get into College," *ibid.*
69. M. Smith, "Sad news from campus: Nobody loves the football hero now," *Life 43*, 11 November 1957, 149–50+.
70. "Slim Pickings for the Class of '76," *ibid.*
71. "College—Who Needs It?" *ibid.*
72. "Milk vs. Cream? Acute discovery from 1928," *Time 135*, 31 March 1980, 39.
73. Grayson Kirk, "College Shouldn't Take Four Years," *Reader's Digest 77*, July 1960, 76–79.
74. "Little Known—& Good," *ibid.*
75. "A Teacher Speaks," *Time 75*, 9 May 1960.
76. W. P. Pitt, "The Many Commencements of Callie Trent," *Reader's Digest 84*, June 1964, 49–53.
77. "A Way to Finish Earlier," *Time 84*, 31 July 1964, 41.
78. "Antidotes for Anguish," *Time 84*, 6 November 1964, 58.
79. "Cheers for Old Curmudgeon! A noted commentator conjures up the college of his choice," *Reader's Digest 97*, September 1970, 188–90.
80. "Gambling on Open Admissions," *ibid.*
81. "Expensive, Expansive Equality," *Time 92*, 20 December 1968, 47.
82. "Campus 1980," *ibid.*
83. "Courses to Turn You On," *ibid.*

Chapter 6: Unreflective Instrumentalism, Hedonism, Sexism, and Age Discrimination

1. Berlin, "Too Many Helpers," *ibid.*
2. "This Is College Youth Today," *Reader's Digest 52*, March 1948, 6–9.
3. "Campus Idealism," *Time 70*, 30 September 1957, 72.
4. "No-nonsense kids?," *ibid.*
5. "Extracurricular Tycoon," *Time 68*, 24 December 1956.
6. "The big year off: More and more students are spending time between high school and college to learn about themselves," *Life 72*, 16 June 1972, 72–78.
7. "Why Those Students Are Protesting," *Time*, 3 May 1968, 24–25.
8. "The Cynical Idealists of '68," *Time 91*, 7 June 1968, 78–83.
9. "'70 stages its last confrontation: After four tumultuous college years," *Life 68*, 19 June 1970, 20–29.
10. "New Campus Mood: From Rage to Reform," *Time 96*, 30 November 1970, 38+.
11. "Crusade of the Ballot Children," *Time 91*, 22 March 1968, 13.
12. "How Goes the Second Children's Crusade?," *Time 96*, 20 July 1970, 14–15.
13. "Two Perceptions," *Time 95*, 4 May 1970, 59–60.
14. "Protest Season on Campus," *Time 95*, May 11, 1970, 19–25.
15. *Ibid.*
16. "Youthful Volunteers," *Time 96*, 27 July 1970, 12; "Uneasy Return to Campus," *Time 96*, 21 September 1970, 65; "The Politics of the Cop-Out," *Time 96*, 2 November 1970, 10; "The Aggressive Moderates," *Time 95*, 1 June 1970, 81; C. Leinster, "A Student Campaign to Get Peace Started," *Life 68*, 5 June 1970, 45–46; and "Kent State: Another View," *Time 96*, 26 October 1970.
17. "Wake Up!," *Time 81*, 2 February 1963, 76.
18. "Slim Pickings for the Class of '76," *ibid.*
19. "Class of '48: Its members are going into a world eager to give them jobs," *Life 24*, 7 June 1948, 111–17.
20. "That College Look," *Time 52*, 5 July 1948, 37.
21. E. Havemann and P. West, "The Old Grad," *Time 59*, 7 April 1952, 78–80.
22. "Men of '36," *Time 60*, 8 September 1952, 65.
23. "Big Southern Campus," *Time 60*, 15 September 1952, 91–92.
24. Herrymonn Maurer, "Twenty minutes to a career," *Reader's Digest 68*, June 1956, 100–2; abbreviated from "Our Most Wanted Men—College Seniors," *Fortune 53*, March 1956, 116–19+.
25. D. Elton Trueblood, "Why I Chose a Small College," *Reader's Digest 69*, September 1956, 38–42.
26. "The Newsman Shortage," *Time 68*, 17 December 1956, 65.
27. N. Sanford, "Is College Education Wasted on Women?" *Ladies' Home Journal 74*, May 1957, 78–79+.
28. "The Power of Professors," *Time 91*, 24 May 1968, 53–54.
29. J. Jerome, "The System Really Isn't Working," *Life 65*, 1 November 1968.
30. "Student Moviemakers," *Time 91*, 2 February 1968, 78–79.
31. Pope, "Facts to Know in Picking a College," *ibid.*
32. "Harvard grads go blue collar," *ibid.*

33. Carl T. Rowan and David M. Mazie, "A College Education; Exciting New Ways to Get One: Some colleges now let you design your own exams, some have no campuses or classrooms at all. Whether they work out or not—and some may not—they're certainly not irrelevant or dull," *Reader's Digest 101*, August 1972, 64–68.

34. "Bear Market in Sheepskins," *Time 95*, 30 March 1970, 84.

35. "College, Who Needs It?," *ibid.*

36. "College—Who Needs It,?" *ibid.*

37. Ellie McGrath, "Taking a Course in Go-Getting: Students hustle as company recruiters return to campus," *Time 123*, 19 March 1984, 41; Gordon Bock, "In Demand: The Class of '88" (in the "Economy & Business" section), *Time 131*, 23 May 1988, 38.

38. "Hail and Beware, Freshmen: Some hard choices ahead for the class of '92," *Time 132*, 12 September 1988, 62–64.

39. J. Elson, "Campus of the Future," *Time 139*, 13 April 1992, 54–58.

40. W. Warren, "Missing: The Common Core," *Time 67*, 13 February 1956, 54+.

41. "Set the Student Free," *Time 69*, 15 April 1957, 87.

42. "Surging into the '60s," *Time 75*, 4 January 1960, 35.

43. Elson, "Campus of the Future," *ibid.*

44. Berlin, "Too Many Helpers," *ibid.*

45. "Fall Openings: 1944," *Time 44*, 25 September 1944, 64.

46. "The New Woman," *Time 69*, 29 April 1957, 46.

47. "Sound of Girlish Voices Strikes a New Note at Muhlenberg," *Life 43*, Oct. 21, 1957, 111–15.

48. "Is College Education Wasted on Women?," *ibid.*

49. "Freshman Class: 1960," *ibid.*

50. "Bryn Mawr, tough training ground for women's minds," *Life 41*, 24 December 1956, 102–7.

51. Berlin, "Too Many Helpers," *ibid.*

Chapter 7: Anti-Intellectualism, the Mass Media, and Society

1. Several times I have been asked my opinion about life in a hypothetical United States that is "too intellectual" rather that "too anti-intellectual." Such a possibility is so infinitely remote that none of us need to worry about it.

2. See Jack Fuller, *News values: Ideas for an information age* (Chicago: The University of Chicago Press, 1996); David J. Krajicek, *Scooped! Media miss real story on crime while chasing sex, sleaze, and celebrities* (New York: Columbia University Press, 1998); and Rem Rieder, "Playing to their strengths: Depth and context are newspapers' key advantages. They should exploit them, not try to be something they're not," *American Journalism Review*, April 1999, 6, to name just a few.

3. Fuller, *News values, ibid.*

4. Rieder, "Playing to their strengths," *ibid.*

5. Hanno Hardt, "Among the media: Journalism education in a commercial culture," remarks to the Qualitative Studies Division, Association for Education in Journalism

and Mass Communication Convention, Baltimore, Md., 1988.

Appendix: Sources of Evidence and Methods of Inquiry

1. See A.C.H. Smith, with Elizabeth Immirzi and Trevor Blackwell, *Paper Voices: The Popular Press and Social Change, 1935–1965* (London: Chatto and Windus, 1975), 12, 14, 15.
2. Smith, *Paper Voices*, 16, 17; O'Sullivan *et al.*, 317, 239.
3. Smith, *Paper Voices*, 20, 21, 23.
4. *Ibid*, 12, 13, 22.
5. Magazine groupings and their readerships (by leaders and other citizens) in Aberdeen and Huron, South Dakota, in Donald F. Scannell, Mass media use, information, and opinions concerning higher education (unpublished doctoral dissertation, University of Minnesota, 1966), 125, were: *Reader's Digest, Saturday Evening Post, Coronet, Redbook* and/or *Holiday*: 58.4% (Huron citizens) to 65% (Aberdeen leaders); *Time, Newsweek* and/or *U.S. News & World Report*: 24.8% (Huron citizens) to 67.5% (Aberdeen leaders); "Others (mainly business and professional)": 51% (Aberdeen citizens) to 75.6% (Huron leaders); *Life* and/or *Look*: 34.4% (Huron citizens) to 40% (Aberdeen leaders); "Ladies and Home magazines": 17.1% (Huron leaders) to 31.7% (Huron citizens); Sports magazines: 5% (Aberdeen leaders) to 14.6% (Huron leaders); *True* and/or *Glamour*: 4.7% (Aberdeen citizens) to 7.5% (Aberdeen leaders); *Harper's, Atlantic* and/or *New Yorker*: 0.7% (Aberdeen citizens) to 7.5% (Aberdeen leaders); *Parade* and/or *This Week*: 0% (Aberdeen citizens and Huron leaders) to 5% (Aberdeen leaders); *USA-1, Current, Reporter, Commonweal, America, Progressive* and/or *Saturday Review*: 0.4% (Huron citizens) to 4.9% (Huron leaders); *Esquire* and/or *Playboy*: 0% (Huron leaders, Aberdeen leaders) to 1.8% (Aberdeen citizens).
6. Fred Fedler and Phillip Taylor, "Broadcasting's impact on selection of news stories by readers," *Journalism Quarterly 55* (1978): 301–5; Genevieve Ginglinger, "Basic values in 'Reader's Digest,' 'Selection,' and 'Constellation,'" *Journalism Quarterly 32* (1955): 56–61; William H. Peters, "Two measures of print advertising's social responsibility level," *Journalism Quarterly 50* (1973): 702–7; Ron F. Smith and Linda Decker-Amos, "Of lasting interest? A study of change in the content of *Reader's Digest*," *Journalism Quarterly 62* (1985): 127–31; Patricia A. Stout and Young S. Moon, "Use of endorsers in magazine advertisements," *Journalism and Mass Communication Quarterly 67* (1990): 536–46; and Shawny Anderson, *Condensed hegemony: A cultural/ideological critique of* Reader's Digest (unpublished doctoral dissertation, Purdue University, 1994).
7. D. J. Caldwell, *Education, citizenship, and vocations in the* Ladies' Home Journal, *1883–1953*; Stout and Moon, "Use of Endorsers."
8. *Time's* position in the market and in journalism has been unusual enough to focus briefly here on its history. In short, *Time* took a circuitous route to the position that it holds today, that of being an institution in the U.S. media and an icon of sorts in U.S. culture. Founded in 1923 with the goal of providing impartial reporting, observers have admitted that *Time* was at least "reasonably impartial" until 1940 (see

Jon Tebbell, *The American magazine: A compact history* [New York: Hawthorn Books, 1969], 228). That year, however, the magazine's political coverage was "highly biased" toward Republican presidential nominee Wendell Willkie, and *Time* was to reflect obviously pro-Republican, anti-communist biases for at least the next thirty years. By the 1950s, one scholar on magazines complained that "facts are aligned, joined, related, explained, and built toward an opinion ready-made for the peruser of *Time*" (see James P. Wood, *Magazines in the United States* [New York: Ronald Press Co., 1956], 206). Wrote Louisiana Polytechnic Institute professor H.J. Sacks ("Henry Luce and I," *The Nation*, 4 July 1953, 13):

> ...Luce can order hundreds of persons to write what he wants them to write, and he can use only that part of their writing which he likes. I cast my little vote. He helps makes presidents...Hundreds of college teachers...are better educated, more intelligent, and more honest than Luce; yet Luce probably has more influence on public opinion in the United States than all the college teachers combined.

A late 1950s *New Yorker* cartoon shows three young people sitting at a coffee shop table; a woman is saying to one of two men, "But Lester, is it not enough just being against everything that *Time* magazine is for?" (Roland E. Wolseley, *The changing magazine: Trends in readership and management* [New York: Hastings House, Publishers, 1973], 82).

Another cultural impact of *Time* is the effects of its writing on both journalism and everyday language in the United States. For example, J. J. Firebaugh ("The vocabulary of *Time* magazine." *American Speech 16* [1940]: 232–42) commented that *Time* editors "are using the language so freely and boldly as to suggest conscious experiment." O. C. K. Chiang (*A study of journalistic writing as developed by* Time *magazine* [unpublished master's thesis, Pittsburg State University, 1961]) repeated Wolcott Gibbs' ("*Time...Fortune...Life...*Luce," in *A subtreasury of American humor*, eds. Elwyn B. White and Katharine S. White [New York: Coward-McCann, Inc., 1941]) claim that *Time* co-founder Briton Hadden hated abstractions in writing and Dwight MacDonald's observation that its other co-founder, Henry Luce, was a "hater of 'theories'" (see D. MacDonald, "*Time* and Henry Luce," *The Nation*, 1 May 1937, 500–3). Their pre-launch prospectus for the magazine also had asserted:

> There will be no editorial page in *Time*. No article will be written to prove any special case. But the editors recognize that complete neutrality on public questions and important news is probably as undesirable as it is impossible, and are therefore ready to acknowledge certain prejudices which may in varying measure predetermine their opinions on the news.

One of their "prejudices" was—significantly for this book:

> An interest in the new, particularly in ideas. But this magazine is not founded to promulgate prejudices, liberal or conservative. "To keep men

well-informed"—that, first and last, is the only axe this magazine has to grind...

If *Time*'s editorial policy seemed firm in tone but also vague, this also was true of *Time*'s writing style: P.I. Prentice, *Time*'s publisher in 1941–1945, flatly stated that "There is really no such thing as *Time* style," and managing editor Otto Fuerbringer in 1961 told Chiang that *Time* did not have its own stylebook, keep track of words that it coined nor even continue using them (because as "novelties," their continued use would destroy that status), or conduct its own "special or specific writing program for new writers" (Chiang, pp. 105–6). All of this, of course, makes what impact *Time*'s writing had more difficult to pinpoint but even more impressive because it came without consistent usage of certain words or structures. Firebaugh ("The Vocabulary," 232) attributed *Time*'s influence on American English primarily to its popularity. (On the other hand, *Time*'s frequently tortured sentence structures still prompted Gibbs ["*Time...Fortune...Life...*Luce," 586–87] to famously complain: "Backward ran sentences until reeled the mind.") Chiang (p. 91) speculated that *Time*'s writing style was indicative of its editors' worldview: a purely American form of democracy displaying "contempt for standard of all sorts, skepticism toward established conventions, and the refusal to take seriously the arbitrary pronouncements of self-constituted authority." He also concluded that *Time* "despises authority but admires power and success." For example, commenting on *Time*'s coverage of Harvard sociologist David Riesman after the release of *The Lonely Crowd* (1950), Steven Weiland wrote in his *Intellectual craftsmen:*

> Eager to claim discovery of the model American intellectual—few cultural critics have been so well received since—*Time* ignored Riesman's own cautions about the methodological limits of his books and essays...[F]or *Time*, Riesman's "upper-class" Eastern background and comfortable Chicago home (with servants and a wine cellar) were points in his favor, at least insofar as they may have comforted *Time*'s readers, given his otherwise discomforting message about the direction of American society.

9. Michel A. Barkocy, "Censorship against *Time* and *Life* international editions," *Journalism Quarterly 40* (1963): 517–24; Dorothy A. Bowles and Rebbeca V. Bromley, "Newsmagazine coverage of the Supreme Court during the Reagan administration," *Journalism Quarterly 69* (1992): 948–59; William G. Christ and Sammye Johnson, "Images through *Time*: Man-of-the-Year covers." *Journalism Quarterly 62* (1985): 891–93; Fred Fedler, Milan Meeske, and J. Hall, "*Time* magazine revisited: Presidential stereotypes persist," *Journalism Education 56* (1979): 353–59; Fred Fedler, R. Smith, and Milan Meeske, "*Time* and *Newsweek* favor John F. Kennedy, criticize Robert and Edward Kennedy," *Journalism Quarterly 60* (1983): 489–96; Gilbert L. Fowler Jr., "Readability of delayed and immediate reward content in *Time* and *Newsweek*," *Journalism Quarterly 59* (1982): 431–34; M. Griffin and J. Lee, "Picturing the Gulf War: Constructing an image of war in *Time*, *Newsweek*, and *U.S. News & World Report*," *Journalism Quarterly 72* (1995): 813–25; Anette Grube and Karin Boehme-Duerr, "AIDS in international news magazines," *Journalism Quar-*

terly 65 (1988): 686–89; Roderick P. Hart, Kathleen J. Turner and Ralph E. Knupp, "A rhetorical profile of religious news: *Time*, 1947–1976," *Journal of Communication 31*, 3 (1981): 58–68; Roderick P. Hart, Deborah Smith-Howell and John Llewellyn, "The mindscape of the presidency: *Time* Magazine, 1945–1985," *Journal of Communication 41* (1991): 6–25; Sammye Johnson and William G. Christ, "Women through *Time*: Who gets covered?" *Journalism Quarterly 65* (1988): 889–97; Kuo-Jen Tsang, "News photos in *Time* and *Newsweek*," *Journalism Quarterly 61* (1984): 578–84; Roy E. Larsen, "Our franchise to publish comes from the public..." *Journalism Quarterly 21* (1944): 297–303; Paul Lester and Ron Smith, "African-American photo coverage in *Life, Newsweek*, and *Time*, 1937–1988," *Journalism Quarterly 67* (1990): 128–36; Cheryl L. Marlin, "Space race propaganda: U.S. coverage of the Soviet Sputniks in 1957," *Journalism Quarterly 64* (1987): 544–49; John C. Merrill, "How *Time* stereotyped three U.S. presidents," *Journalism Quarterly 42* (1965): 563–70; Sandra E. Moriarty and Mark N. Popovich, "Newsmagazine visuals and the 1988 presidential election," *Journalism Quarterly 68* (1991): 371–80; David K. Perry, "Foreign industrial disputes in *Time* and *Newsweek*, 1966–1973," *Journalism Quarterly 58* (1981): 439–43; William H. Peters, "Two measures of print advertising's social responsibility level," *Journalism Quarterly 50* (1973): 702–7; Brian K. Simmons and David N. Lowry, "Terrorists in the news, as reflected in three news magazines, 1980–1988," *Journalism Quarterly 67* (1990): 692–96; Clement Y. K. So, "The summit as war: How journalists use metaphors," *Journalism Quarterly 64* (1987): 623–26; William S. Solomon, "News frames and media packages: Covering El Salvador," *Critical Studies in Mass Communication 9* (1992): 56–74; Glenn G. Sparks and Christine L. Fehlner, "Faces in the news: Gender comparisons of magazine photographs," *Journal of Communication 36* (1986): 70–79; Joseph Turow, "Hidden conflicts and journalistic norms: The case of self-coverage," *Journal of Communication 44* (1994): 29–46; John J. Watkins, "The demise of the public figure doctrine," *Journal of Communication 27* (1977): 47–53; Bruce H. Westley, Charles E. Higbie, Timothy Burke, David J. Lippert, Leonard Maurer, and Vernon A. Stone, "The news magazines and the 1960 Conventions," *Journalism Quarterly 40* (1963): 525–31; and Aileen Yagade and David M. Dozier, "The media agenda-setting affect of concrete versus abstract issues," *Journalism Quarterly 67* (1990): 3–10.

10. Dora J. Hamblin, *That was the Life* (New York: W.W. Norton & Co., 1994), 49.

11. Wendy Kozol, *Life's America: Family and nation in postwar photojournalism* (Philadelphia: Temple University Press, 1994), 39.

12. W. D. Anderson, *A study of the causes of failure of prominent periodicals, 1926–1956* (unpublished master's thesis, The University of Georgia, 1958), 8; Edward G. McGrath, *The political ideals of* Life *magazine* (unpublished doctoral dissertation, Syracuse University, 1961); Michael A. Barkocy, "Censorship against *Time* and *Life* international editions," *Journalism Quarterly 40* (1963): 517–24; Dave Berkman, "Advertising in *Ebony* and *Life*: Negro aspirations vs. reality," *Journalism Quarterly 40* (1963): 53–64; Sharon Bramlett-Solomon and Vanessa Wilson, "Images of the elderly in *Life* and *Ebony*," *Journalism Quarterly 66* (1989): 185–88; David E. Carter, "The changing face of *Life's* advertisements, 1950–66," *Journalism Quarterly 46* (1969): 87–93; Paul Lester and Ron Smith, "African-

American photo coverage in *Life, Newsweek,* and *Time,* 1937–1988," *Journalism Quarterly 67* (1990): 128–36; William H. Peters, "Two measures of print advertising's social responsibility level," *Journalism Quarterly 50* (1973): 702–7; Mary Alice Sentman, "Black and white: Disparity in coverage by *Life* magazine from 1937–1972," *Journalism Quarterly 60* (1983): 501–8; and C. Zoe Smith, "Germany's Kurt Korff: An emigre's influence on early *Life,*" *Journalism Quarterly 65* (1988): 412–19.

13. Howard Carswell, "Business news and reader interest," *Journalism Quarterly 15* (1938): 191–95; Thomas V. DiBacco, "The business press and Vietnam: Ecstasy or agony?" *Journalism Quarterly 45* (1968): 426–35; Julien Elfenbein, "Businesspapers: The place to start the magazine career?" *Journalism Quarterly 25* (1948): 233–38; Kathleen L. Endres, "Ownership and employment in specialized business press," *Journalism Quarterly 65* (1988): 996–98; James E. Grunig, "Washington reporter publics of corporate public affairs programs," *Journalism Quarterly 60* (1983): 603–14; Herbert H. Howard, E. Blick, and J. P. Quarles, "Media choices for specialized news," *Journalism Quarterly 64* (1987): 620–23; J. T. W. Hubbard, "The explosive new demand for business news," *Journalism Quarterly 43* (1966): 703–8; J. T. W. Hubbard, "Business news in post-Watergate era," *Journalism Quarterly 53* (1976): 488–93; Dominic L. Lasorsa and Stephen D. Rcese, "News source use in the Crash of 1987: A study of four national media," *Journalism Quarterly 67* (1990): 60–71; Steven L. McShane, "Occupational, gender, and geographic representation of information sources in U.S. and Canadian business magazines," *Journalism Quarterly 72* (1995): 190–204; Charles Mayo and Yorgo Pasadeos, "Changes in the international focus of U.S. business magazines, 1964–1988," *Journalism Quarterly 68* (1991): 509–14; C. E. Rogers, "The social justification of the business press," *Journalism Quarterly 11* (1934): 235–45.

14. Stories examined were indexed under the following headings and subheadings in the *Reader's Guide to Periodical Literature*: College, Choice of; College Education; College Education, Cost of; College Education, Value of; College Fraternities; College graduates; College students (all subsections, which includes but are not limited to: Adjustment, Aid, Elimination from college, Employment, Expenditures, Health and hygiene, Housing, Reading, and Recreation); College students, Mentally superior; College students, Women; the following subheadings under the general heading of Colleges and Universities: Attendance, Curriculum, Entrance Requirements, Religious Life, Standards, Student Recruiting, and United States); Student Activities (when they concerned college students); Student Life. By the 1970s, the *Reader's Guide* used the heading, "College Students, Mentally Superior," less and less until the index, curiously, apparently stopped using it altogether.

Bibliography

Adam, G. Stuart. 1997. "Introduction: James Carey's academy," in *James Carey: A critical reader*, eds. Eve S. Munson and Catherine A. Warren. Minneapolis, Minn.: The University of Minnesota Press.

Altbach, Phillip G. 1974. *University reform: Comparative perspectives for the seventies*. Cambridge, Mass.: Schenkman Publishing Company.

Anderson, Martin. 1992. *Imposters in the temple: American intellectuals are destroying our universities and cheating our students of their future*. New York: Simon & Schuster.

Anderson, Shawny. 1994. *Condensed hegemony: A cultural/ideological critique of Reader's Digest*. Unpublished doctoral dissertation, Purdue University.

Anderson, W. D. 1958. *A study of the causes of failure of prominent periodicals, 1926–1956*. Unpublished master's thesis, The University of Georgia, 1958.

Aronowitz, Stanley, and Henry A. Giroux. 1988. Review of The Closing of the American Mind, *Harvard Educational Review 58*, no. 2 (May): 172.

Bailey, Jeff. 1998. "Joy to the world; Despite everything, America still embraces a culture of optimism: Impeachment? Iraq tensions? Humbug! Markets soar, polls rise, masses spend; The good-feelings premium." *The Wall Street Journal* (22 December).

Baker, John R. 1986, "Fundamentalism as anti-intellectualism." *The Humanist* (March–April): 26–28.

Baker, Susan S. 1982. *Out of the engagement; Richard Hofstadter: The genesis of a historian*. Unpublished doctoral dissertation, Case Western Reserve University.
———. 1985. *Radical beginnings: Richard Hofstadter and the 1930s*. Westport, Conn.: Greenwood.

Baldesty, Gerald J. 1984. "The press and politics in the age of Jackson." *Journalism Monographs 89*.

Barber, Benjamin R. 2001. *The Truth of Power: Intellectual Affairs in the Clinton White House*. New York: W.W. Norton.

Barkocy, Michael A. 1963. "Censorship against *Time* and *Life* international editions." *Journalism Quarterly 40*: 517–24.

Baron, Steve. 1981. *Unpopular education: Schooling and social democracy in England since 1944*. London: Hutchinson/Centre for Contemporary Cultural Studies, University of Birmingham.

Barton, Len, and Stephen Walker, eds. *Race, class, and education*. London: Croom Helm, 1983.

Barzun, Jacques. 1959. *The house of the intellect*. New York: Harper Brothers.

Bell, Daniel. 1976/1996. *The cultural contradictions of capitalism, 20th anniversary edition*. New York: Basic Books.

Berger, Peter L. 1963. *Invitation to sociology: A humanistic perspective*. Garden City, N.Y.: Doubleday and Co., Inc.

Berkman, Dave. 1963. "Advertising in *Ebony* and *Life*: Negro aspirations vs. reality." *Journalism Quarterly 40*: 53–64.

Bernstein, C. S. 1982. *Coverage of education in two metropolitan-area dailies*. Unpublished master's thesis, University of Missouri–Columbia.

Best, Steven, and David Kellner. 1991. *Postmodern theory: Critical interrogations*. New York: The Guilford Press.

Binzen, P. H. 1962. "Less pap for the press." *College and University Journal 1*, 3: 17–18.

Birnbaum, Norman. 1988. *The radical renewal: The politics of ideas in modern America*. New York: Pantheon Books.

Bloom, Allan D. 1987. *The closing of the American mind: How higher education has failed democracy and impoverished the souls of today's students*. New York: Simon and Schuster.

Bluefarb, Sam. 1968. "Hippies: Another view." *Journal of Popular Culture 2*: 468–80.

Bonfiglio, Robert A. 1990. *The history of public relations in American higher education in the twentieth century: From self-interest to national interest*. Unpublished doctoral dissertation, Columbia University Teachers College.

Boothman, Derek, ed./trans. 1995. *Antonio Gramsci: Further selections from* The Prison Notebooks. London: Lawrence & Wishart.

Bowen, Howard R. 1980. *The costs of higher education*. San Francisco: Jossey-Bass Publishers.

Bowles, Dorothy A., and Rebecca V. Bromley. 1992. "Newsmagazine coverage of the Supreme Court during the Reagan administration." *Journalism Quarterly 69*: 948–59.

Bramlett-Solomon, Sharon, and Vanessa Wilson. 1989. "Images of the elderly in *Life* and *Ebony." Journalism Quarterly 66*: 185–88.

Brick, Howard. 1998. *Age of contradiction: American thought and culture in the 1960s*. New York: Twayne Publishers/Simon & Schuster Macmillan.

Brinton, Crane. 1950. *Ideas and men*. New York: Prentice Hall, Inc.

Bromwich, David. 1996. "Anti-intellectualism." *Raritan 16*: 18–27.

Brooks, David. 2000. *BOBOS in paradise: The new upper class and how they got there*. New York: Simon & Schuster.

Broudy, Harry S. 1955. "Thought and the educative process." *Philosophy Forum 13*: 54–77.

Brown, Richard D. 1996. *The strength of the people: The idea of an informed citizenry in America, 1650–1870*. Chapel Hill, N.C.: University of North Carolina Press.

Brown, William R. 1972. "Will Rogers: Ironist as persuader." *Speech Monographs 39*, no. 3: 183–92.

Buckley, William K., and James Seaton. 1992. *Beyond cheering and bashing: New perspectives on* The closing of the American mind. Bowling Green, Ohio: Bowling Green State University Press.

Cain, William E., ed. 1994. *Teaching the conflicts: Gerald Graff, curricular reform, and the culture wars*. New York: Garland Publishing Co.

Caldwell, D. J. 1954. *Education, citizenship, and vocations in the* Ladies' Home Journal, *1883–1953*. Unpublished master's thesis, The University of Missouri.

Campbell, Angus, and William C. Eckerman. 1964. *Public concepts of the values and costs of higher education*. Ann Arbor, Mich.: Survey Research Center, University of Michigan.

Carey, James W. 1992. "Political correctness and cultural studies." *Journal of Communication 42* (Spring): 56–72.

———. 1997. "Salvation by machines: Can technology save education?" In *James Carey: A Critical Reader*, eds. Eve Stryker Munson and Catherine A. Warren. Minneapolis: The University of Minnesota Press.

Cargill, Oscar. 1941. *Intellectual America: Ideas on the march*. New York: Macmillan.

Carstensen, Vernon. 1977. "The good old days or the bad old days? History and related muses in the Northwest in the 1930s." *Pacific Northwest Quarterly 68*, no. 3: 105–11.

Carswell, Howard. 1938. "Business news and reader interest." *Journalism Quarterly 15*: 191–95.

Carter, David E. 1969. "The changing face of *Life's* advertisements, 1950–66." *Journalism Quarterly 46*: 87–93.

Carter, Paul A. 1983. *Another part of the Fifties*. New York: Columbia University Press.

———. 1989. *Revolt against destiny: An intellectual history of the United States*. New York: Columbia University Press.

Caudill, Edward. 1989. *Darwinism in the press: The evolution of an idea*. Hillsdale, N.J.: Lawrence Erlbaum Associates.

Chance, William. 1993. *The press and California higher education*. San Jose, Calif.: The California Higher Education Policy Center.

Chang, Chin-Hwa F. 1988. *The notion of power in mass communication research:*

Foucault and critical communication studies. Unpublished doctoral dissertation, The University of Iowa.

Chiang, O. C. K. 1961. *A study of journalistic writing as developed by* Time *magazine*. Unpublished master's thesis, Pittsburg (Kan.) State University.

Chomsky, Noam. 1987. *On power and ideology: The Managua lectures*. Boston: South End Press.

————— (C.P. Otero, ed.). 1988. *Language and politics*. Montreal: Black Rose Books.

—————. 1989. *Necessary illusions: Thought control in democratic societies*. London: Pluto.

—————. 1989. Interview edited and published in *Bill Moyers: A World of Ideas*, ed. Bill Moyers. New York: Doubleday.

—————. 1992. Speech at Macalester College, St. Paul, Minn. (23 April).

Christ, Frank L., and Gerard E. Sherry, eds. *American Catholicism and the intellectual ideal*. New York: Appleton-Century-Crofts.

Christ, William G., and Sammye Johnson. 1985. "Images through *Time*: Man-of-the-Year covers." *Journalism Quarterly 62*: 891–93.

Clark, Burton R., and Martin Trow. 1966. "Determinants of the sub-cultures of college students—The organizational context." In *College peer groups*, eds. Theodore M. Newcomb and Everett K. Wilson. Chicago: Aldine.

Colangelo, Nicholas, and Gary A. Davis, eds. 1991. *Handbook of gifted education*. Boston: Allyn and Bacon.

Coles, Richard. 1983. "Instances of modernist anti-intellectualism." In *Modernism Reconsidered*, ed. R. Kiely. Cambridge, Mass.: Harvard University Press.

Collins, Robert M. 1989. "The originality trap: Richard Hofstadter on Populism." *Journal of American History 76*: 151–67.

Commager, Henry Steele. 1950. *The American mind: An interpretation of American thought and character since the 1880's*. New Haven, Conn.: Yale University Press.

Coser, Lewis A. 1965. *Men of ideas: A sociologist's view*. New York: Free Press Paperbacks/Simon & Schuster.

Cox, D. 1987. "The Gottschalk-Colvin case: A study in academic purpose and command." *Register of the Kentucky Historical Society 85*: 46–68.

Cox, R. L. 1969. *A variance and factor analysis of readers' preferences for three types of higher education news*. Unpublished master's thesis, Oklahoma State University.

Cremin, Lawrence A. 1972. *Richard Hofstadter (1916–1970)*. N.c.: National Academy of Education.

Cronin, Thomas E. 1999. "The presidents' man: Henry Steele Commager." *The New York Times Magazine* (3 January): 43.

Cross, Robert D. 1990. "The historical development of anti-intellectualism in American society: Implications for the schooling of African Americans." *The Journal of Negro Education 59*: 19–28.

Culliton, Barbara J. 1978. "Science's restive public." *Daedalus 107*: 147–56.

Curran, James, David Morley and Valerie Walkerdine, eds. 1996. *Cultural studies and communication*. London: Arnold.

Curti, Merle. 1964/1943. *The growth of American thought*, 3d ed. New York: Harper

& Row, Publishers.

Cutlip, Scott M. 1970. "'Advertising' higher education: The early years of college public relations." *College and University Journal 9* (Fall): 21–28.

———. 1971. "'Advertising' higher education: The early years of college public relations—part II." *College and University Journal 9* (July): 25–33.

Cutlip, Scott M., and Allen H. Center. 1964. *Effective public relations,* 3d ed. Englewood Cliffs, N.J.: Prentice Hall Inc.

DeFazio, Frank A. 1987. *The role of public relations as perceived by presidents and public relations officers at private comprehensive universities and colleges.* Unpublished doctoral dissertation, Drake University.

Dennis, Everette E., and Ellen Wartella, eds. 1996. *American communication research: The remembered history.* Mahweh, N.J.: Lawrence Erlbaum Associates.

Detweiler, R. 1973. "Ben Franklin's 'Dirty Pettifoggers.'" *American Bar Association Journal 59*: 1165–67.

DiBacco, Thomas V. 1968. "The business press and Vietnam: Ecstasy or agony?" *Journalism Quarterly 45*: 426–35.

Diggins, John P. 1994. *The promise of pragmatism: Modernism and the crisis of knowledge and authority.* Chicago: The University of Chicago Press.

Douglas, Susan J. 1994. *Where the girls are: Growing up female with the mass media.* New York: Random House.

Dreger, Alice. 1998. "When medicine goes too far in pursuit of normality." *The New York Times* (28 July): B10.

D'Souza, Dinesh. 1991. *Illiberal education: The politics of race and sex on campus.* New York: The Free Press.

Du Gay, Paul, Stuart Hall, Linda Janes, Hugh Mackay, and Keith Negus. 1997. *Doing cultural studies: The story of the Sony Walkman.* London: Sage Publications, in association with The Open University.

Dzimian, A.D. 1953. *A survey to determine the proportional allotment of education in Life magazine from 1937 to 1951.* Unpublished master's thesis, Canisius College.

Easton, John. 1997. "Bloom in review." *University of Chicago Magazine* (August): 22–24.

Edelstein, Alex S., Youichi Ito, and Hans M. Kepplinger. 1989. *Communication & culture: A comparative approach.* New York: Longman.

Edwards, Scott. 1972. "Reich, Roszak and the New Jerusalem." *Midwest Quarterly 13*: 185–98.

Elfenbein, Julien. 1948. "Businesspapers: The place to start the magazine career?" *Journalism Quarterly 25*: 233–38.

Elkins. Stanley, and Eric L. McKittrick, eds. 1974. *The Hofstadter aegis: A memorial.* New York: Alfred A. Knopf, Inc.

Endres, Kathleen L. 1988. "Ownership and employment in specialized business press." *Journalism Quarterly 65*: 996–98.

Epstein, Barbara. 1985. "The culture of direct action: Livermore Action Group and the peace movement." *Socialist Review 15*, nos. 4–5: 31–61.

Eschholz, Paul A., and Alfred F. Rosa. 1970. "Course names: Another aspect of college slang." *American Speech 45*, nos. 1–2: 85–90.

Evans, Robert. 1966. "Hemingway and the pale cast of thought." *American Literature* *38*, no. 2: 161–76.

Ewell, Peter T. 1994. "A matter of integrity: Accountability and the future of self-regulation," *Change 26*, no. 6 (November–December): 24–29.

Eyerman, Ron, Lennart G. Svensson, and Thomas Soderqvist. 1987. *Intellectuals, universities, and the state in western modern societies.* Berkeley, Calif.: University of California Press.

Fedler, Fred, Milan Meeske, and J. Hall. 1979. *"Time* magazine revisited: Presidential stereotypes persist." *Journalism Education 56*: 353–59.

Fedler, Fred, Ron F. Smith, and Milan Meeske. 1983. *"Time* and *Newsweek* favor John F. Kennedy, criticize Robert and Edward Kennedy." *Journalism Quarterly 60*: 489–96.

Fedler, Fred, and Phillip Taylor. 1978. "Broadcasting's impact on selection of news stories by readers." *Journalism Quarterly 55*: 301–5.

Feuer, Lewis S. 1972. "Student unrest in the United States." *Annals of the American Academy of Political and Social Science 404*: 170–82.

Fink, Leon. 1997. *Progressive intellectuals and the dilemmas of democratic commitment.* Cambridge, Mass.: Harvard University Press.

Fink, Leon, Stephen T. Leonard, and Donald M. Reid, eds. 1996. *Intellectuals and public life: Between radicalism and reform.* Ithaca, N.Y.: Cornell University Press.

Firebaugh, Joseph J. 1940. "The vocabulary of *Time* magazine." *American Speech 16* (October): 232–42.

Flynn, Charles E. 1966. "The unprofessional professional." *College and University Journal 5*, no. 2: 13.

Forgacs, David, and Geoffrey Nowell-Smith, eds. 1985. *Antonio Gramsci: Selections from cultural writings.* Cambridge, Mass.: Harvard University Press.

Fowler, Gilbert L., Jr. 1982. "Readability of delayed and immediate reward content in *Time* and *Newsweek." Journalism Quarterly 59*: 431–34.

Freeland, Richard M. 1992. *Academia's golden age: Universities in Massachusetts, 1945–1970.* New York: Oxford University Press.

Freidin, Seymour, and George Bailey. 1968. *The experts.* New York: The Macmillan Company.

Friedman, Jeffrey. 1994. "On libertarian anti-intellectualism: Rejoinder to Shaw and Anderson & Leal." *Critical Review 8*: 483–92.

Froome, R.D. 1965. *The anti-intellectual case of articulate McCarthyism.* Unpublished master's thesis, University of Wyoming.

Fuller, Jack. 1996. *News values: Ideas for an information age.* Chicago: The University of Chicago Press.

Garnham, Nicholas. 1995. "The media and narratives of the intellectual." *Media, Culture & Society 17*: 359–84.

———. 1997. "Political economy and the practice of cultural studies." In *Cultural studies in question,* eds. Marjorie Ferguson and Peter Golding. London: Sage Publications.

Gibbs, Wolcott. 1941. *"Time...Fortune...Life...Luce."* In *A subtreasury of American humor,* eds. Elwyn B. White and Katharine S. White. New York: Coward-

McCann, Inc.

Gibson, Harold E. 1945. *Public relations practices in institutions of higher education for women.* Unpublished doctoral dissertation, University of Missouri.

Gillam, Richard. 1977–78. "Richard Hofstadter, C. Wright Mills, and the 'critical ideal.'" *American Scholar 47*: 69–85.

Ginglinger, Genevieve. 1955. "Basic values in *Reader's Digest, Selection,* and *Constellation.*" *Journalism Quarterly 32*: 56–61.

Giroux, Henry A. 1988. *Teachers as intellectuals: Toward a critical pedagogy of learning.* Granby, Mass.: Bergin & Garvey.

Goar, Heidi K. 1992. *Anti-intellectualism as a social control: Reflexivity and con formity.* Unpublished master's thesis, Mankato State University.

Goldfarb, Jeffrey C. 1998. *Civility and subversion: The intellectual in democratic society.* Cambridge, UK, and New York: Cambridge University Press.

Goldin, Daniel. 2001. "Help Wanted: The Head of NASA Forecasts a Bleak Future for American Science." *The Atlantic Monthly* (September), 28.

Gouldner, Alvin W. 1979. *The future of intellectuals and the rise of the new class.* New York: Seabury Press.

Gramsci, Antonio (R. Bellamy, ed.). 1994. *Pre-prison writings.* Cambridge, U.K.: Cambridge University Press.

Greenberg, B. "How smart is too smart to be a police officer?" The *Athens* (Ga.) *Daily News* (6 June): 1A.

Greenburg, David. 1998. "Richard Hofstadter's tradition: Fifty years ago, amid trying personal circumstances, an audacious young historian wrote a book of lasting merit about American Presidents and their politics." *The Atlantic Monthly 282,* no. 5 (November): 132–37.

Griffin, Michael, and Jongsoo Lee. 1995. "Picturing the Gulf War: Constructing an image of war in *Time, Newsweek,* and *U.S. News & World Report.*" *Journalism Quarterly 72*: 813–25.

Griffin, Paul R. 1983. *Black founders of Reconstruction Era Methodist colleges: Daniel A. Payne, Joseph C. Price, and Isaac Lane, 1863–1890.* Unpublished doctoral dissertation, Emory University.

Grube, Anette, and Karin Boehme-Duerr. 1988. "AIDS in international news magazines." *Journalism Quarterly 65*: 686–89.

Grunig, James E. 1983. "Washington reporter publics of corporate public affairs programs." *Journalism Quarterly 60*: 603–14.

Gunn, Giles. 1992. *Thinking across the American grain: Ideology, intellect, and the new pragmatism.* Chicago: The University of Chicago Press.

Habermas, Jürgen. 1975. *Legitimation crisis.* Boston: Beacon Press.

———. 1970. *Toward a rational society.* Boston: Beacon Press.

———. 1976. *Communication and the evolution of society.* Boston: Beacon Press.

———. 1989. *The public sphere.* Cambridge, Mass.: MIT Press.

Hage, George S. 1956. *Anti-intellectualism in newspaper comment of the elections of 1828 and 1952.* Unpublished doctoral dissertation, University of Minnesota.

Hamblin, Dora J. 1994. *That was the* Life. New York: W. W. Norton & Co.

Handlin, Oscar, and Mary F. Handlin. 1970. *The American college and American culture; socialization as a function of higher education.* New York: McGraw-Hill.

Hardt, Hanno. 1998. "Among the media: Journalism education in a commercial culture," remarks to the Qualitative Studies Division, Association for Education in Journalism and Mass Communication Convention, Baltimore, Md., August.

———. 1992. *Critical communication studies: Communication, history and the theory in America.* London: Routledge.

Hardt, Hanno, and Bonnie Brennen, eds. 1995. *Newsworkers: Toward a history of the rank and file.* Minneapolis, Minn.: The University of Minnesota Press.

Hart, Roderick P., Deborah Smith-Howell, and John Llewellyn. 1991. "The mindscape of the presidency: *Time* Magazine, 1945–1985." *Journal of Communication 41*: 6–25.

Hart, Roderick P., Kathleen J. Turner, and Ralph E. Knupp. 1981. "A rhetorical profile of religious news: *Time,* 1947–1976." *Journal of Communication 31*, no. 3: 58–68.

Hauptman, Arthur M. 1990. *The college tuition spiral.* Washington, D.C.: American Council on Education.

Havemann, Ernest, and Patricia S. West. 1952. *They went to college.* New York: Harcourt, Brace.

Hazard, W.R. 1963. *A study of attitudes and opinions held by 465 Iowans concerning higher education and the State University of Iowa.* Ames, Iowa: SUI Alumnae Research Committee.

Held, David. 1980. *Introduction to critical theory: Horkheimer to Habermas.* Berkeley, Calif.: The University of California Press.

Henry, David D. 1961. *What priority for education?* Urbana-Champaign, Ill.: University of Illinois Press.

Henry, Jules. 1963. *Culture against man.* New York: Alfred A. Knopf, Inc.

Henry, William A. III. 1994. *In defense of elitism.* New York: Anchor/Doubleday.

Herman, Edward, and Noam Chomsky. 1988. *Manufacturing consent: The political economy of the mass media.* New York: Pantheon.

Hernandez, D. 1971. "Anti-intellectualism: Tumor in American education." *American Foreign Language Teacher 1*, no. 3: 17–21.

"Higher education." 1949. Supplement to *Fortune 40*, no. 3 (September).

Hoare, Quintin, and Geoffrey N. Smith, eds./trans. 1971. *Selections from the prison notebooks of Antonio Gramsci.* London: Lawrence and Wishart.

Hoeveler, David J. Jr. 1996. *The postmodernist turn: American thought and culture in the 1970s.* New York: Twayne Publishers/Simon & Schuster Macmillan.

Hofstadter, Richard. 1948. *The American political tradition and the men who made it.* New York: Alfred A. Knopf.

———. 1953. "Democracy and anti-intellectualism in America." *Michigan Alumnus Quarterly Review 59* (8 August 1953), 281–95.

———. 1963. *Anti-intellectualism in American life.* New York: Alfred A. Knopf, Inc.

Hofstader, Richard, and Walter P. Metzger. 1955. *The development of academic freedom in the United States.* New York: Columbia University Press.

Hollinger, David A. 1996. *Science, Jews, and secular culture: Studies in mid-twentieth-century American intellectual history.* Princeton, N.J.: Princeton University Press.

Horowitz, Helen Lefkowitz. 1987. *Campus life: Undergraduate cultures from the end of the eighteenth century to the present*. New York: Alfred A. Knopf.

Hossler, Don. 1998. "Everybody Wants to Be Number One: The Effects of the Media's College Rankings," in Gene I. Maeroff (ed.), *Imaging education: The media and schools in America* (New York: Teachers College Press.)

Howard, Herbert H., Edward Blick, and Jan P. Quarles. 1987. "Media choices for specialized news." *Journalism Quarterly 64*: 620–23.

Howe, Daniel W., and Peter E. Finn. 1974. "Richard Hofstadter: The ironies of an American historian." *Pacific Historical Review 43*: 1–23.

Howley, Aimee, Edwina D. Pendarvis, and Craig B. Howley. 1990. *Anti-intellectualism in U.S. schools*. Huntington, W.V.: Marshall University.

———. 1987. "Anti-intellectualism in programs for able students (beware of gifts): an application." *Social Epistemology 1*: 175–81.

Howley, Craig B., Aimee Howley, and Edwina D. Pendarvis. 1995. *Out of our minds: Anti-intellectualism and talent development in American schooling*. New York: Columbia University Teachers College.

Hoy, David C., ed. 1986. *Foucault: A critical reader*. Oxford: B. Blackwell.

Hubbard, J. T. W. 1966. "The explosive new demand for business news." *Journalism Quarterly 43*: 703–8.

———. 1976. "Business news in post-Watergate era." *Journalism Quarterly 53*: 488–93.

Hughes, Henry S. 1975. *The sea change: The migration of social thought, 1930–1965*. New York: Harper & Row, Publishers.

Hynds, Ernest C. 1989. "Survey finds large daily newspapers have improved coverage of education." *Journalism Quarterly 66*: 692–96, 780.

Irwin, William, Mark T. Conard, and Aeon J. Skoble. 2001. *The Simpsons and Philosophy: The D'Oh! of Homer*. Chicago: Open Court, 2001.

Isaacson, David. 1982. "Anti-intellectualism in American libraries." *Library Journal* 107 (February): 227–32.

Jackson, Sandra, and Jose Solis, eds. 1995. *Beyond comfort zones in multiculturalism: Confronting the politics of privilege*. Westport, Conn.: Bergin & Garvey.

Jacoby, Russell. 1987. *The last intellectuals: American culture in the age of academe*. New York: Noonday.

Jamison, Andrew, and Ron Eyerman. 1994. *Seeds of the Sixties*. Berkeley, Calif.: University of California Press.

Johnson, Sammye, and William G. Christ. 1988. "Women through *Time*: Who gets covered?" *Journalism Quarterly 65*: 889–97.

Jovanovich, William. 1972. "A tumult of talk." *American Scholar 41*: 40–49.

Kadushin, Charles. 1974. *The American intellectual elite*. Boston: Little, Brown & Co.

Katchadourian, Herant A., and John Boli. 1985. *Careerism and intellectualism among college students*. San Francisco: Jossey-Bass Publishers.

Kazin, Alfred. 1971. "Richard Hofstadter, 1916–1970." *American Scholar 40*: 397.

Keniston, Kenneth. 1966. "The faces in the lecture room." In *The contemporary university: U.S.A.*, ed. Robert S. Morison. Boston: Houghton Mifflin.

Kennedy, J. Gerald. 1976. "Cooper's anti-intellectualism: The comic man of learning." *Studies in American Humor 3*, no. 2: 69–75.

Kerr, Clark. 1963. *The uses of the university*. Cambridge, Mass.: Harvard University Press.

Kimball, Roger. 1990/1998. *Tenured radicals: How politics has corrupted our higher education*. Chicago: Elephant Paperbacks.

Klobuchar, Myrna N. 1991. *H.L. Mencken and "the fabulous foul of the pedagogical aviary."* Unpublished doctoral dissertation, University of Minnesota.

Kozol, Wendy. 1994. Life's *America: Family and nation in postwar photojournalism*. Philadelphia: Temple University Press.

Krajicek, David J. 1998. *Scooped! Media miss real story on crime while chasing sex, sleaze, and celebrities*. New York: Columbia University Press.

Laakaniemi, Ray E. 1966. *A content analysis of higher education news related to four Michigan universities*. Unpublished master's thesis, Ohio University.

Lace, William W. 1987. *Opinions of news media members toward public higher education in Texas and predictions of those opinions by college and university public relations directors*. Unpublished doctoral dissertation, University of North Texas.

Ladd, Everett C., and Seymour M. Lipset. 1975. *The divided academy: Professors and politics*. New York: W.W. Norton and Co., Inc.

Larsen, Roy E. 1944. "Our franchise to publish comes from the public..." *Journalism Quarterly 21*: 297–303.

Lasch, Christopher. 1978. *The culture of narcissism: American life in an age of diminishing expectations*. New York: W.W. Norton and Company.

———. 1991. *The true and only heaven: Progress and its critics*. New York: W.W. Norton and Company.

Lasorsa, Dominic L., and Stephen D. Reese. 1990. "News source use in the Crash of 1987: A study of four national media." *Journalism Quarterly 67*: 60–71.

Leonard, Thomas C. 1995. *News for all*. New York: Oxford University Press.

Lester, Elizabeth P. 1995. "Discursive strategies of exclusion: The ideological construction of newsworkers." In *Newsworkers: Towards a history of the rank and file*, eds. Hanno Hardt and Bonnie Brennen. Minneapolis, Minn.: The University of Minnesota Press.

Lester, Paul, and Ron Smith. 1990. "African-American photo coverage in *Life, Newsweek*, and *Time*, 1937–1988." *Journalism Quarterly 67*: 128–36.

Levine, David O. 1986. *The American college and the culture of aspiration, 1915–1940*. Ithaca, N.Y.: Cornell University Press.

Levine, Lawrence W. 1996. *The opening of the American mind: Canons, culture, and history*. Boston: Beacon Press.

Levy, Bernard-Henri. 2000. *What good are intellectuals? 44 writers share their thoughts*. New York: Algora Publishing.

Liesz, Thomas J. 1989. *An interpretive analysis of factors influencing higher education appropriation and allocation levels in the Pacific Northwest*. Unpublished doctoral dissertation, University of Idaho.

Lilla, Mark. 2001. *The reckless mind: Intellectuals in politics*. New York: New York Review Books.

Loeb, Paul R. 1994. *Generation at the crossroads: Apathy and action on the American campus*. New Brunswick, N.J.: Rutgers University Press.

Lyotard, Jean-Francois. 1984. *The postmodern condition: A report on knowledge.* Minneapolis: University of Minnesota Press.

MacDonald, D. 1937. "*Time* and Henry Luce." *The Nation 144* (1 May): 500–3.

Maeroff, Gene I., ed. 1998. *Imaging education: The media and schools in America* New York: Teachers College Press.

McCain, J.M. 1995. *Anti-intellectual fideism: A case study of evangelical Southern Baptist attitudes toward homosexuality.* Unpublished master's thesis, Georgia State University.

McGowan, John. 2002. *Democracy's children: Intellectuals and the rise of cultural politics.* Ithaca and London: Cornell University Press.

McGrath, Edward G. 1961. *The political ideals of* Life *magazine.* Unpublished doctoral dissertation, Syracuse University.

McLaren, Peter L., and James M. Giarelli. 1995. *Critical theory and educational research.* Albany, N.Y.: State University of New York Press.

McShane, Steven L. 1995. "Occupational, gender, and geographic representation of information sources in U.S. and Canadian business magazines." *Journalism Quarterly 72*: 190–204.

McWhorter, John. 2000. *Losing the race: Self-sabotage in Black America.* New York: The Free Press.

Marcuse, Herbert (1964). *One-dimensional man.* Boston: Beacon Press.

Marlin, Cheryl L. 1987. "Space race propaganda: U.S. coverage of the Soviet Sputniks in 1957." *Journalism Quarterly 64*: 544–49.

Marshall, James D. 1996. *Michel Foucault: Personal autonomy and education.* Boston: Kluwer Academic Publishers.

Marx, Karl. 1967. *Capital: A critique of political economy, volume 1.* New York: International Publishers.

Massy, William F., and Andrea K. Wilger. 1992. "Productivity in postsecondary education: A new approach." *Educational Evaluation and Policy Analysis 14*: 361–76.

Mayhew, Lewis B. 1969. "Faculty demands and faculty militance." *Journal of Higher Education 40*: 337–50.

Mayo, Charles, and Yorgo Pasadeos. 1991. "Changes in the international focus of U.S. business magazines, 1964–1988." *Journalism Quarterly 68*: 509–14.

Merrill, John C. 1965. "How *Time* stereotyped three U.S. presidents." *Journalism Quarterly 42*: 563–70.

Merton, Robert K. 1968. *Social theory and social structure.* New York: Free Press.

Mezirow, Jack, and Associates. 1990. *Fostering critical reflection in adulthood: A guide to transformative and emancipatory learning.* San Francisco: Jossey-Bass Publishers.

Michael, John. 2000. *Anxious intellects: Academic professionals, public intellectuals, and Enlightenment values.* Durham and London: Duke University Press.

Millett, John D. 1952. *Financing higher education in the United States.* New York: Columbia University Press.

Mills, C. Wright. 1956. *The power elite.* New York: Oxford University Press.

———. 1959. *The sociological imagination.* New York: Oxford University Press.

———. (ed. I.L. Horowitz). 1963. *Power, politics, and people: The collected essays of C. Wright Mills.* New York: Ballantine.

Mishel, Lawrence, and Jared Bernstein. 1993. *The state of working America, 1992–93.* Armonk, N.Y.: M.E. Sharp.

Moll, Richard W., and B. Ann Wright. 1998. "What College Selectivity Looks Like to the Public," in Gene I. Maeroff (ed.), *Imaging education: The media and schools in America* (New York: Teachers College Press).

Moriarty, Sandra E., and Mark N. Popovich. 1991. "Newsmagazine visuals and the 1988 presidential election." *Journalism Quarterly 68*: 371–80.

Morris, Meaghan, and Paul Patton, eds. 1979. *Michel Foucault: Power, truth, strategy.* Sidney, Australia: Feral Publications.

Mott, Frank Luther. 1952. *The news in America.* Cambridge, Mass.: Harvard University Press.

Mourad, Roger P. Jr. 1997. *Postmodern philosophical critique and the pursuit of knowledge in higher education.* Westport, Conn.: Bergin & Garvey.

Moyers, Bill. 1988. *A world of ideas: Conversations with thoughtful men and women about American life today and the ideas shaping our future.* New York: Doubleday.

Munson, Eve S., and Catherine A. Warren, eds. 1997. *James Carey: A critical reader.* Minneapolis, Minn.: The University of Minnesota Press.

Murray, Gaylon E. "Gene." 1991. *Texas education reporters' and university public relations directors' perceptions of public relations, occupations, and news values.* Unpublished doctoral dissertation, Texas A&M University.

Neeley, S.M. 1994. *News periodical coverage of American student activism, 1961–1987.* Unpublished master's thesis, The University of Tennessee.

Newman, S.A. 1973. "Where Southern Baptists stand on anti-intellectualism." *Search 1*: 22–27.

———. 1993. "Where Southern Baptists stand on anti-intellectualism: 1973–1989." *Perspectives in Religious Studies 20*: 417–30.

O'Brien, George Dennis. 1998. *All the essential half-truths about higher education.* Chicago and London: The University of Chicago Press.

Outhwaite, William. 1996. *The Habermas reader.* Cambridge, U.K.: Polity Press.

Padilla, Raymond V., and Miguel Montiel. 1998. *Debatable diversity: Critical dialogues on change in American universities.* Lanham, Md.: Rowman and Littlefield Publishers.

Payne, Lynn W. 1998. *Black business students' post-baccalaureate employment expectations: What are they and from where do they originate?* Unpublished doctoral dissertation, The University of Oklahoma.

Pemberton, Wilfred A. 1963. *Ability, values, and college achievement (University of Delaware studies in higher education, no. 1).* Newark, Del.: University of Delaware.

Perry, David K. 1981. "Foreign industrial disputes in *Time* and *Newsweek*, 1966–1973." *Journalism Quarterly 58*: 439–43.

Peters, John D. 1993. "Distrust of representation: Habermas on the public sphere." *Media, Culture and Society 15*: 541–71.

Peters, William H. 1973. "Two measures of print advertising's social responsibility level." *Journalism Quarterly 50*: 702–7.

Posner, M.A. 1994. "Read all about it." *Currents 20*, no. 1: 8–11.

Posner, Richard A. 2001. *Public intellectuals: A study of decline.* Cambridge: Harvard University Press.

Postman, Neil. 1985. *Amusing ourselves to death: Public discourse in the age of show business.* New York: Viking Penguin.

Quinnan, Timothy W. 1997. *Adult students "at-risk": Cultural bias in higher education.* Westport, Conn.: Bergin & Garvey.

Racevskis, Karlis. 1983. *Michel Foucault and the subversion of the intellect.* Ithaca, N.Y.: Cornell University Press.

Rai, Milan. 1995. *Chomsky's politics.* London: Verso.

Ratcliff, Gary R. 1996. *Ivorytowers, watchdogs, and boosters: A comparative case study of how metropolitan newspapers cover public research universities.* Unpublished doctoral dissertation, The Pennsylvania State University.

Ratcliff, Gary R., and Roger L. Williams. 1994. What the numbers tell us: Higher education coverage at seven newspapers. *Currents 20* no. 1: 13–14.

Ravitch, Diane. 1983. *The troubled crusade: American education, 1945–1980.* New York: Basic Books, Inc., Publishers.

Reck, Waldo E. 1976. *The changing world of college relations: History and philosophy, 1917–1974.* Washington, D.C.: Council for the Advancement and Support of Higher Education.

Renden, Laura I., Richard O. Hope, and Associates. 1996. *Educating a new majority: Transforming America's educational system for diversity.* San Francisco: Jossey-Bass Publishers.

Rhoads, Robert A., and James R. Valadez. 1996. *Democracy, multiculturalism, and the community college: A critical perspective.* New York: Garland Publishing.

Rieder, Rem. 1999. "Playing to their strengths: Depth and context are newspapers' key advantages. They should exploit them, not try to be something they're not." *American Journalism Review 21* (April): 6.

Riesman, David, and Nathan Glazer. 1955. "The intellectuals and the discontented classes." In *The New American Right,* ed. Daniel Bell. New York: Criterion Books.

Rigney, Daniel. 1991. "Three kinds of anti-intellectualism: Rethinking Hofstadter." *Sociological Inquiry 61*: 434–51.

Rigney, Daniel, and Thomas J. Hoffman. 1993. "Is American Catholicism anti-intellectual?" *Journal for the Scientific Study of Religion 32*: 211–22.

Rogers, C. E. 1934. "The social justification of the business press." *Journalism Quarterly 11*: 235–45.

Ross, Bonnie L. 1983. "Education reporting in *The Los Angeles Times." Journalism Quarterly 60*: 348–52.

Rowland, Albert W. 1955. *A study of three selected factors in the public relations programs of colleges and universities in the United States.* Unpublished doctoral dissertation, Michigan State University.

Rozwenc, Edwin C., and Thomas Bender. 1978. *The making of American society, Volume II since 1865,* 2d ed. New York: Alfred A. Knopf.

Rudolph, Frederick. 1962/1990. *The American college & university: A history.* Athens, Ga.: The University of Georgia Press.

Sacks, H.J. 1953. "Henry Luce and I." *The Nation 177* (4 July): 13.

Said, Edward W. 1994. *Representations of the intellectuals (The 1993 Reith Lectures)*. New York: Pantheon Books.

Scannell, Donald F. 1966. *Mass media use, information, and opinions concerning higher education*. Unpublished doctoral dissertation, University of Minnesota.

Schiff, Martin. 1973. "Neo-transcendentalism in the New Left Counter-culture: A vision of the future looking back." *Comparative Studies in Society and History* *15*: 130–42.

Schlag, Pierre. 1995. "Anti-intellectualism." *Cardozo Law Review 16*: 1111–20.

Schlesinger, Arthur M. Jr. 1969. "Richard Hofstadter." Pp. 278–315 in *Pastmasters: Some essays on American historians*, eds. Marcus Cunliffe and Robin W. Winks. New York: Harper & Row.

Schramm, Wilbur L. (Stephen H. Chaffee & Everett M. Rogers, eds.). 1997. *The beginnings of communication study in America: A personal memoir*. Thousand Oaks, Calif.: Sage Publications.

Schratz, Paul R. 1984. "The hundred year growing pain: Opposition and opportunity." *Naval War College Review 37*, no. 5: 71–85.

Schubert, J. Daniel, Joan V. Vecchia, and Richard H. Brown. 1995. *Higher education in a postmodern era: Ethics, politics, and practices*. Thousand Oaks, Calif.: Sage Periodicals Press.

Schudson, Michael. 1978. *Discovering the news*. New York: Basic Books.

Scott, Joan W. 1992a. "The campaign against political correctness: What's really at stake." *Radical History Review 54*: 59–79.

———. 1992b. "The new university: Beyond political correctness." *Perspectives: Newsletter of the American Historical Association 30*, no. 7: 14–18.

Sentman, Mary Alice. 1983. "Black and white: Disparity in coverage by *Life* magazine from 1937–1972." *Journalism Quarterly 60*: 501–8.

Shaw, Donald L. 1967. "News bias and the telegraph: A study of historical change." *Journalism Quarterly 44*, no. 1: 3–12, 21.

Shaw, Peter. 1989. *The war against the intellect: Episodes in the decline of discourse*. Iowa City: University of Iowa Press.

Sherman, Malcolm J. 1976. "Anti-intellectualism and civil rights." *Change 8*, no. 11: 34–40.

Shils, Edward A. 1972. *The intellectuals and the powers and other essays*. Chicago: The University of Chicago Press.

Sholle, David J. 1988. "Critical studies: From the theory of ideology to power/knowledge." *Critical Studies in Mass Communication 5*: 16–41.

Simmons, Brian K., and David N. Lowry. 1990. "Terrorists in the news, as reflected in three news magazines, 1980–1988." *Journalism Quarterly 67*: 692–96.

Singal, Daniel J. 1984. "Beyond consensus: Richard Hofstadter and American historiography." *American Historical Review 89*: 976–1004.

Singer, Barnett. 1977. "The new anti-intellectualism in America." *Colorado Quarterly 26*, no. 2: 4–18.

Skoble, Aeon J. 2001. "Lisa and American Anti-intellectualism." In *The Simpsons and Philosophy: The D'Oh! of Homer*, eds. William Irwin, Mark T. Conard, and Aeon J. Skoble. Chicago: Open Court, 2001.

Smith, A.C.H., with Elizabeth Immirzi and Trevor Blackwell. 1975. *Paper voices:*

The popular press and social change, 1936–1965. London: Chatto and Windus.

Smith, C. Zoe. 1988. "Germany's Kurt Korff: An emigre's influence on early *Life*." *Journalism Quarterly 65*: 412–19.

Smith, Ron F., and Linda Decker-Amos. 1985. "Of lasting interest? A study of change in the content of *Reader's Digest*." *Journalism Quarterly 62*: 127–31.

So, Clement Y. K. 1987. "The summit as war: How journalists use metaphors." *Journalism Quarterly 64*: 623–26.

Solmon, Lewis C., and Paul J. Taubman. 1973. *Does college matter? Some evidence on the impacts of higher education.* New York: Academic Press.

Solomon, William S. 1992. "News frames and media packages: Covering El Salvador." *Critical Studies in Mass Communication 9*: 56–74.

Sparks, Glenn G., and Christine L. Fehlner. 1986. "Faces in the news: Gender comparisons of magazine photographs." *Journal of Communication 36*: 70–79.

Stanfield, Rochelle E. 1998. "The Media and Public Perceptions of Tuition Costs," in Gene I. Maeroff (ed.), *Imaging education: The media and schools in America* (New York: Teachers College Press).

Stegall, Sandra Kruger. 1985. *A Q-methodological coorientation study of college and university public relations directors and newspaper reporters in Missouri.* Unpublished master's thesis, University of Missouri–Columbia.

Stepp, Carl Sessions. 2003. "Higher Examination: Once treated with reverence, universities and colleges are now receiving more skeptical and probing coverage. But the economic downturn has prompted some news organizations to scale back their commitment to the beat." *American Journalism Review 25* (January–February): 18–25.

Stern, Fritz. 1971. "Reflections on the international student movement." *American Scholar 40*: 123–37.

Stone, Robert L., ed. 1989. *Essays on* The closing of the American mind. Chicago: Chicago Review Press.

Stout, Patricia A., and Young S. Moon. 1990. "Use of endorsers in magazine advertisements." *Journalism and Mass Communication Quarterly 67*: 536–46.

Sullivan, Randall. 1998. "A boy's life: Kip Kinkel and the Springfield, Oregon, shooting, Part 1." *Rolling Stone 795* (17 September): 76–85, 106–7.

Suskind, Ron. 2003. "Why Are These Men Laughing?" *Esquire* (January).

Susman, Warren I. 1973. *Culture as history: The transformation of American society in the Twentieth century.* New York: Pantheon Books.

Sykes, Charles J. 1988. *ProfScam: Professors and the demise of higher education.* New York: St. Martin's Press.

Tallack, Douglas. 1991. *Twentieth-century America: The intellectual and cultural context.* London, U.K.: Longman.

Taussig, Harold E. 1966. *Anti-intellectualism in the public schools: A study of the cultural values underlying Twentieth Century educational practices.* Unpublished doctoral dissertation, University of Pennsylvania.

Tebbell, Jon. 1969. *The American magazine: A compact history.* New York: Hawthorn Books.

Terrien, Frederic W. 1953. "Who thinks what about educators." *American Journal of Sociology 59* (September): 151–58.

Tierney, William G., ed. 1991. *Culture and ideology in higher education: Advancing a critical agenda*. New York: Praeger.

———. 1993. *Building communities of difference: Higher education in the Twenty-First Century*. Westport, Conn.: Bergin & Garvey.

Torres, Carlos A., and Theodore R. Mitchell. 1998. *Sociology of education: Emerging perspectives*. Albany, N.Y.: State University of New York Press.

Tsang, Kuo-Jen. 1984. "News photos in *Time* and *Newsweek*." *Journalism Quarterly* 61: 578–84.

Tully, Alan. 1972. "Literacy levels and educational development in rural Pennsylvania 1729–1775." *Pennsylvania History 39*: 301–12.

Turow, Joseph. 1994. "Hidden conflicts and journalistic norms: The case of self-coverage." *Journal of Communication 44*: 29–46.

University of Michigan Survey Research Center. 1964. *The public image of state and private universities*. Ann Arbor, Mich.: Author.

Ursenbach, Maureen. 1975. "Three women and the life of the mind." *Utah Historical Quarterly 43*, no. 1: 26–40.

van Broekhoven, Deborah B. 1984. "Crisis in the life of a literary patriot: Brockden Brown's shift from cosmopolitan to chronicler." *Psychohistory Review 12*, nos. 3–4: 34–44.

Veblen, Thorstein. 1922. *The higher learning in America*. New York: Sagamore Press.

Walzer, P. 1995. "Selling higher education stories to your editor." *The IRE Journal 18* (January–February): 3–6.

Warehime, Nancy. 1993. *To be one of us: Cultural conflict, creative democracy, and education*. Albany, N.Y.: State University of New York Press.

Warren, Jonathan R. 1966. *Patterns of college experiences*. U.S. Department of Health, Education, and Welfare Cooperative Research Project S-327. Claremont, Calif.: College Graduate School and University Center.

———. 1968. "Student perceptions of college subcultures." *American Educational Research Journal 5*: 213–32.

Watkins, John J. 1977. "The demise of the public figure doctrine." *Journal of Communication 27*: 47–53.

Weiland, Steven. 1988. "The academic attitude: Richard Hofstadter and the anti-intellectuals." *Antioch Review 46*: 462–72.

———. 1991. *Intellectual craftsmen: Ways and works in American scholarship, 1935–1990*. New Brunswick, N.J.: Transaction Publishers.

Welch, Betty Jo H. 1980. *A study of perceived academic ability, ability to finance education, encouragement, and anti-intellectualism as they relate to postsecondary education decisions*. Unpublished doctoral dissertation, Vanderbilt University.

Wells, A.S. 1986. *A study of education reporting in American newspapers*. Unpublished master's thesis, Boston University.

Westley, Bruce H., Charles E. Higbie, Timothy Burke, David J. Lippert, Leonard Maurer, & Vernon A. Stone. 1963. "The news magazines and the 1960 Conventions." *Journalism Quarterly 40*: 525–31.

White, Krista E. 1996. *How the girls really are? Images of college women in* Life *magazine during the 1960s.* Unpublished master's thesis, University of Colorado–Boulder.

Williams, Raymond. 1985. *Keywords: A Vocabulary of Culture and Society.* New York: Oxford University Press.

Willis, Paul E. 1977. *Learning to labour: How working class kids get working class jobs.* London: Saxon House.

Winthrop, H. 1971. "The anti-intellectualism of student radicals." *Colorado Quarterly* 20 no. 2: 191–204.

Wolf, Alison. 2002. *Does education matter? Myths about education and economic growth.* London: Penguin Books.

Wolseley, Roland E. 1973. *The changing magazine: Trends in readership and management.* New York: Hastings House, Publishers.

Wood, Donald N. 1996. *Post-intellectualism and the decline of democracy: The failure of reason and responsibility in the Twentieth Century.* Westport, Conn.: Praeger.

Wood, James P. 1956. *Magazines in the United States.* New York: Ronald Press Co.

Woodworth, George F. 1995. *An analysis of the concept "anti-intellectualism": Implications for the education of gifted and talented students.* Unpublished doctoral dissertation, The University of Connecticut.

Wulfemeyer, K. Tim. 1985. "How and why anonymous attribution is used by *Time* and *Newsweek.*" *Journalism Quarterly* 62: 81–86.

Yagade, Aileen, and David M. Dozier. 1990. "The media agenda-setting affect of concrete versus abstract issues." *Journalism Quarterly* 67: 3–10.

Yarrington, Roger. 1984. "Meet the education press." *Currents* (February): 35–40.

———. 1985. "J-Schools should encourage higher education writers." *Journalism Educator 39,* no. 4: 11–12.

Yoder, Sharon L. 1987. *Organizational politics as news: University dissent and the community press.* Unpublished doctoral dissertation, The University of Missouri–Columbia.

Young, Fred D. 1995. *Richard M. Weaver, 1910–1963: A life of the mind.* Columbia, Mo.: University of Missouri Press.

Young, Robert E. 1990. *A critical theory of education: Habermas and our children's future.* New York: Teachers College Press, Columbia University.

For Further Reading

Arendt, Hannah. 1971. *The life of the mind.* San Diego: Harcourt Brace Jovanovich.

Ball, Stephen J., ed. 1990. *Foucault and education: Disciplines and knowledge.* London: Routledge.

Barber, Bernard. 1955. "Sociological aspects of anti-intellectualism." *Journal of Social Issues* 11, no. 3: 25–30.

Barrow, Clyde W. 1987. "Intellectuals in contemporary social theory: A radical critique." *Sociological Inquiry 57*: 415–30.

Beaud, Paul, and Francisco Panese. 1995. "From one galaxy to another: The trajectories of French intellectuals." *Media, Culture & Society 17*: 385–412.

Becker, Howard S., Blanche Geer, and Everett C. Hughes. 1995. *Making the grade:*

The academic side of college life. New Brunswick, N.J.: Transaction Publishers.

Bender, Thomas. 1993. *Intellect and public life: Essays on the social history of academic intellectuals in the United States.* Baltimore: Johns Hopkins University Press.

Bernier, Normand R. 1973. *Beyond beliefs: Ideological formations of American education.* Englewood Cliffs, N.J.: Prentice-Hall.

Carson, Mina J. 1980. "Anti-intellectualism" [letter to the editor]. *The New Republic 183*, nos. 1–2 (5–12 July).

Coates, J.F. 1973. "Anti-intellectualism and other plagues on managing the future." *Technological Forecasting and Social Change 4*: 243.

Curti, Merle. 1955. Intellectuals and other people. *The American Historical Review 60*: 272–73.

———. 1956. *American paradox: The conflict of thought and action.* New Brunswick, N.J.: Rutgers University Press.

Dewey, John. 1916. *Democracy and education.* New York: Macmillan.

———. 1916. *The school and society.* Chicago: The University of Chicago Press.

Earnest, Ernest P. 1970. *The single vision: The alienation of American intellectuals.* New York: New York University Press.

Elliott, P. 1982. "Intellectuals, the 'information society' and the disappearance of the public sphere." *Media, Culture and Society 4*: 243–53.

Eyerman, Ron, and Andrew Jamison. 1995. "Social movements and cultural transformation: Popular music in the 1960s." *Media, Culture & Society 17*: 449–68.

Foucault, Michel. 1971. *The order of things: An archaeology of the human sciences.* New York: Pantheon Books.

———. 1972. *The archaeology of knowledge.* New York: Pantheon Books.

———. (Colin Gordon, ed.). 1980. *Power/knowledge: Selected interviews and other writings, 1972–1977.* New York: Pantheon Books.

———. 1984. "What is enlightenment?" In *The Foucault Reader*, ed. P. Rabinow. New York: Pantheon.

Gabriel, Ralph H. 1986. *The course of American democratic thought: An intellectual history since 1815.* New York: Greenwood Press.

Gagnon, Alain G., ed. 1987. *Intellectuals in liberal democracies: Political influence and social involvement.* New York: Praeger.

Gorman, Paul R. 1996. *Left intellectuals & popular culture in twentieth-century America.* Chapel Hill, N.C.: University of North Carolina Press.

Greeley, Andrew M. 1977. *The American Catholic.* New York: Basic Books.

Heyer, Paul. 1988. *Communications and history: Theories of media, knowledge, and civilization.* Westport, Conn.: Greenwood Press.

Hilton, Keith O. 1996. *How higher education is portrayed in the African-American newspaper press: An agenda setting press.* Unpublished doctoral dissertation, The Claremont Graduate School.

Jacobson, Harvey. 1964. "Newsweekly education reporting." *College and University Journal 3*, no. 2 (Spring): 44–48.

Jacoby, Russell. 1994. *Dogmatic wisdom: How the culture wars divert education and distract America.* New York: Doubleday.

Kadushin, Charles. 1982. "Intellectuals and cultural power." *Media, Culture and Soci-*

ety 4: 255–62.

Kellner, Douglas. 1995. "Intellectuals and new technologies." *Media, Culture and Society* 17: 427–448.

Kostecki, M.J., and K. Mrela. 1982. "Workers and intelligentsia in Poland: During the hot days and in between." *Media, Culture and Society* 4: 225–41.

Kramer, L. 1996. Habermas, Foucault, and Enlightenment intellectuals. In *Intellectuals and public life: Between radicalism and reform*, eds. Leon Fink, Stephen T. Leonard, and Donald M. Reid. Ithaca: Cornell University Press.

Luik, John C. 1991. "Democracy, elitism, and the academy: Thoughts after Bloom." *Interchange* 22, nos. 1–2: 5–14.

Mattelart, Armand, and Michele Mattelart. 1992. *Rethinking media theory: Signposts and new directions*. Minneapolis, Minn.: University of Minnesota Press.

Park, J. Charles. 1979. "Anti-intellectualism, democracy, and teacher education: A look at selected problems associated with critics and the schools." *High School Journal* 62, no. 8: 339–45.

Pasquinelli, Carla. 1995. "From organic to neo-corporatist intellectuals: The changing relations between Italian intellectuals and political power." *Media, Culture & Society* 17: 413–25.

Popkewitz, Thomas S., and Marie Brennan, eds. 1998. *Foucault's challenge: Discourse, knowledge, and power in education*. New York: Teachers College Press, Columbia University.

Punke, Harold H. 1972. "Anti-intellectualism and the university." *Improving College and University Teaching* 20, no. 3: 112–14.

Rakower, B. 1960. *The implications of anti-intellectual thought on democracy*. Unpublished master's thesis, Queens College.

Reader, K.A. 1982. "The intellectuals: notes towards a comparative study of their position in the social formations of France and Britain." *Media, Culture and Society* 4: 263–73.

Rieff, Phillip, ed. 1970. *On intellectuals*. Garden City, N.Y.: Doubleday and Company.

Robbins, Bruce. 1990. *Intellectuals: Aesthetics, politics, academics*. Minneapolis: University of Minnesota Press.

Ross, Andrew. 1989. *No respect: Intellectuals and popular culture*. New York: Routledge.

Said, Edward W. 1997. *Covering Islam: How the media and the experts determine how we see the rest of the world (Revised ed.)* New York: Vintage Books/Random House Inc.

Sanchez, Raul Jr. 1994. David Bleich and the politics of anti-intellectualism: A response. *Journal of Advanced Composition* 14: 579–81.

Schlesinger, Arthur M. Jr., and Morton G. White, eds. 1963. *Paths of American thought*. Boston: Houghton Mifflin.

Schlesinger, P. 1982. "In search of the intellectuals: Some comments on recent theory." *Media, Culture and Society* 4: 203–23.

Shaffer, Leigh S. 1977. "The Golden Fleece: Anti-intellectualism and social science." *American Psychologist* 32: 814–23.

Smith, Wilson, ed. 1975. *Essays in American intellectual history*. Hinsdale, Ill.:

Dryden Press.

Spaulding, Cheryl L. 1988. Addressing the charges of anti-intellectualism and irrelevancy in teacher education. *Teacher Educator 24*, no. 1: 2–9.

Tierney, William G., ed. 1990. *Assessing academic climates and cultures (New Directions for Institutional Research No. 68)*. San Francisco: Jossey-Bass Inc., Publishers.

de Tocqueville, Alexis. 1838. *Democracy in America (Second American Ed.)*. New York: G. Adlard.

Wainright, Loudon. 1986. *The great American magazine: An inside history of* Life. New York: Alfred A. Knopf, Inc.

Washburn, Katherine, and John F. Thornton, eds. 1996. *Dumbing down: Essays on the strip mining of American culture*. New York: W.W. Norton Co.

Wilson, F.G. 1954. "Public opinion and the intellectuals." *American Political Science Review 48*: 321–39.

Index

Questions about the Purpose(s) of Colleges and Universities

Norm Denzin,

Josef Progler,

Joe L. Kincheloe,

Shirley R. Steinberg

General Editors

What are the purposes of higher education? When undergraduates "declare their majors," they agree to enter into a world defined by the parameters of a particular academic discourse—a discipline. But who decides those parameters? How do they come about? What are the discussions and proposed outcomes of disciplined inquiry? What should an undergraduate know to be considered educated in a discipline? How does the disciplinary knowledge base inform its pedagogy? Why are there different disciplines? When has a discipline "run its course"? Where do new disciplines come from? Where do old ones go? How does a discipline produce its knowledge? What are the meanings and purposes of disciplinary research and teaching? What are the key questions of disciplined inquiry? What questions are taboo within a discipline? What can the disciplines learn from one another? What might they not want to learn and why?

Once we begin asking these kinds of questions, positionality becomes a key issue. One reason why there aren't many books on the meaning and purpose of higher education is that once such questions are opened for discussion, one's subjectivity becomes an issue with respect to the presumed objective stances of Western higher education. Academics don't have positions because positions are "biased," "subjective," "slanted," and therefore somehow invalid. So the first thing to do is to provide a sense—however broad and general—of what kinds of positionalities will inform the books and chapters on the above questions. Certainly the questions themselves, and any others we might ask, are already suggesting a particular "bent," but as the series takes shape, the authors we engage will no doubt have positions on these questions.

From the stance of interdisciplinary, multidisciplinary, or transdisciplinary practitioners, will the chapters and books we solicit solidify disciplinary discourses, or liquefy them? Depending on who is asked, interdisciplinary inquiry is either a polite collaboration among scholars firmly situated in their own particular discourses, or it is a blurring of the restrictive parameters that define the very notion of disciplinary discourse. So will the series have a stance on the meaning and purpose of interdisciplinary inquiry and teaching? This can possibly be finessed by attracting thinkers from disciplines that are already multidisciplinary, for example, the various kinds of "studies" programs (women's, Islamic, American, cultural, etc.), or the hybrid disciplines like ethnomusicology (musicology, folklore, anthropology). But by including people from these fields (areas? disciplines?) in our series, we are already taking a stand on disciplined inquiry. A question on the comprehensive exam for the Columbia University Ethnomusicology Program was to defend ethnomusicology as a "field" or a "discipline." One's answer determined one's future, at least to the extent that the gatekeepers had a say in such matters. So, in the end, what we are proposing will no doubt involve political struggles.

For additional information about this series or for the submission of manuscripts, please contact Joe L. Kincheloe, 128 Chestnut Street, Lakewood, NJ 08701-5804. To order other books in this series, please contact our Customer Service Department at: (800) 770-LANG (within the U.S.), (212) 647-7706 (outside the U.S.), (212) 647-7707 FAX, or browse online by series at: www.peterlangusa.com.